Japan and East Asia

Japan and East Asia

The New International Order

DONALD C. HELLMANN

PRAEGER PUBLISHERS
New York · Washington · London

PRAEGER PUBLISHERS
111 Fourth Avenue, New York, N.Y. 10003, U.S.A.
5, Cromwell Place, London SW7 2JL, England
Published in the United States of America in 1972
by Praeger Publishers, Inc.
© 1972 by Praeger Publishers, Inc.
All rights reserved
Library of Congress Catalog Card Number: 78-101663

Printed in the United States of America

To
Margery

Contents

List of Tables

Foreword

International events have given to this study a relevance that was not fully expected when it was launched in the mid-1960's. At that time, Japan's relations with East Asia were still seen as a minor entry in the ledger of international politics, and the project was undertaken primarily because it naturally complemented my previous research on Japanese politics and international relations. After devoting a number of years to examining the impact of domestic politics on Japan's foreign policy, it had become clear that a full understanding of the nation's role in Asia and the world required special emphasis on the influence of the external environment. This was my original incentive for initiating research for this book. However, by self-consciously stressing the dynamics of the international system at a time when global bipolarity was giving way to multipolarity, the whole cast of the endeavor gradually changed. What started as a straightforward look at Japan's diplomacy in Asia was transformed into a much broader interpretive effort touching on many of the major issues of contemporary international politics: nuclear proliferation, regionalism, the political-military imperatives of foreign trade, aid and investment, and the risks and promises of America's new strategic policy in East Asia. All of these issues took on new and often unfamiliar dimensions when examined from the perspective of Tokyo against the backdrop of Japan's postwar diplomatic history and the tangle of domestic politics. Because of this study's broader and more interpretive cast, it may well raise more questions than it answers, but now that Japan has been thrust into the center of regional and global politics, the time has come to provide an analysis of postwar Japanese foreign policy in terms of the same general categories that have been employed regarding the international relations of all of the other major powers.

This book is particularly pertinent to American foreign policy in Asia. The vision of the international system underlying the argument presented here is fully congruent with the fundamental premises of the Nixon Doctrine. In particular, peace in Asia is seen as ultimately a function of a "power balance" in which the two superpowers and China and Japan must all participate. By emphasizing the inevitability of national conflicts and the need for *Realpolitik*, the approach is in accord with that of the orthodox, European school of international affairs of which the most conspicuous current proponent and practitioner is Henry Kissinger. At the same time, this is not an apologia for the Nixon Doctrine. Indeed, because of certain shared assumptions, critical differences between the conclusions of this study and the details of America's new Asian strategy stand out. This is perhaps most notable in the serious doubts I have regarding the capacities of Japan for flexible response in a competitive and fluid international milieu. If the Kissinger vision is fulfilled and East Asia becomes an arena for a complex game of multipolar power politics, Japan is not at all likely to be a skilled player. This would be a troublesome development for all concerned and underscores once again the need for basic and systematic research in what can hardly continue to be considered an exotic area.

For many Americans, the sudden improvement in relations with China and the reduction of U.S. involvement in Vietnam have raised expectations for peace in Asia to a degree that has obscured persistent problems conducive to international conflict. During the first half of the 1970's, America's relations with East Asia are in certain basic respects similar to those during the years immediately following World War II, when its long-term priorities were still unformed and the elemental shape of the international landscape in the region was unclear. Once more, it is a matter of dispute as to whether and how the United States will again be militarily engaged and which nation, China or Japan, will hold the key to regional stability. To suggest that, in the context of this uncertain and fluid situation and in the wake of

America's greatest foreign-policy misadventure, the great powers will be able to achieve an appropriate power balance through management of international conflict implies a strategic adroitness notably absent during the last twenty-five years in Asia. Indeed, the game of power politics in East Asia in a multipolar world order presents a fresh and particularly formidable challenge to American diplomacy. Despite the enormity of U.S. political-military commitments and the obsessive grip the Vietnam war has held on the domestic foreign-policy debate, there have been remarkably few efforts to provide the basic understanding of politics throughout the entire region that a long-term strategic reappraisal now requires. Regarding the broad nature of Japanese foreign policy, there have been even fewer efforts at understanding. Thus, the effort to delineate Japan's role in East Asia can be seen as a necessary step to suggest appropriate new directions for U.S. policy in a region that has been a cockpit for international politics.

Since the potential for Japanese rearmament and militarism has recently been accorded such serious concern, remarks on the "realistic" approach I have taken here are in order. Japan has closely hewn to the spirit of the 1947 "peace constitution," narrowly limiting security aims to the defense of the home islands and keeping its armed forces at a very low level. Moreover, there is no truly significant domestic political force pressing to reverse this policy at the present time. Furthermore, Tokyo's foreign policy continues to have a peculiarly unidimensional economic quality pulling Japan into the global group of non-Communist industrial countries—a tendency that will continue to draw the country away from nation-centered political rivalries into transnational and global spheres of activity. Nevertheless, it is doubtful that an international power of the magnitude of Japan can remain wholly aloof from *Realpolitik* while progressively more engaged in East Asia. Unless peace breaks out in the region, once Japan is fully engaged in competitive power politics in Asia, some form of nuclear as well as augmented conventional armament seems inevitable. Particularly in light of my dim view of the capacities of the Japanese Government for effective and responsible policy leadership, I am singularly apprehensive about the prospects that Japan will develop nuclear weapons. However, whether the United States or any power can ultimately affect this development depends first of all on seeing the issue in clear perspective, not as in the past through a moral fog or in terms of a simplistic strategic calculus.

This study represents my own intellectual odyssey of five or six years' duration, which *ipso facto* prevents a complete acknowledgment of all of the various associates and colleagues who contributed in some way to its completion. It is possible, however, to identify the sources of funds for the voyage. An International Affairs Fellowship from the Council on Foreign Relations allowed me to spend a year (1970–71) in Tokyo, where much of the final research and writing was finished. The Far Eastern and Russian Institute of the University of Washington has given generous support to my research since 1967, including a grant to spend the summer of 1968 in Tokyo. Portions of the study were initially prepared for a consultant's report for the Research Analysis Corporation, and Fulbright-Hayes contributed to my longer stay in Japan.

My intellectual debts are scattered throughout the United States and Japan. Several of the chapters were presented as papers to professional meetings, and one was published in modified form in *The International Studies Quarterly*. Needless to say, I benefited from the commentaries and editorial assistance that were provided in all instances. Much of the manuscript survived and profited from the searching criticisms offered by members of the Modern Japan Seminar at the University of Washington. Of the many Japanese who extended help to me, I wish to acknowledge my debt to two scholars in particular. Professor Junnosuke Masumi, who has served as my tutor for more than a decade, continued to provide wisdom and insight into the murky world of contemporary Japanese politics. During my year in Tokyo, Professor Jun Tsunoda offered invaluable comments on all aspects of the manuscript and at the same time undertook to provide me with a basic education on Japanese defense policy. The book appears in its final form thanks to the careful editing of Mervyn Adams. Finally, the patience, encouragement, and demanding editorial assistance of my wife, Margery, contributed more than any single factor to the completion of this study. I, of course, am fully responsible for all views expressed.

Japan and East Asia

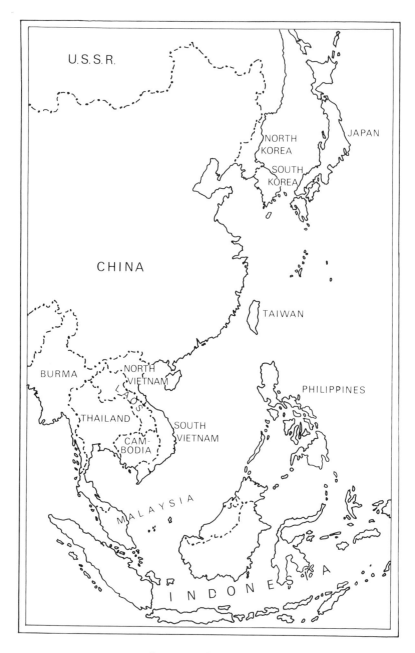

Japan and East Asia

1 Japan: Phoenix Arisen

Japan must play a central and vastly expanded role in East Asia.*
This is one of the few matters on which the United States, the
Soviet Union, and the People's Republic of China are agreed.
Nevertheless, the nature of this role remains remarkably unde-
fined. International politics throughout East Asia is in an extreme
state of flux. The chronic conflicts in and among the underdeveloped nations persist, while the frustrations and uncertainties of
the Vietnam war and the defiant independence of China have
now called into question the capabilities and future commitments
in the region of the superpowers. Japan today is in the eye of the
Asian hurricane—a precarious position, however temporary it may
prove to be. In the face of this fluid external environment, the
Japanese have pursued cautious and flexible policies; but there is
an unmistakable trend toward more positive engagement in Asia,
and a turning point has been reached regarding security dependence on the United States. With the end of the prolonged "postwar era" finally at hand, Japan must now confront the dilemmas
of international politics so fortuitously avoided since 1945.
Japan's return to the *Realpolitik* of East Asian international
order will grow out of the policies and the pattern of external
relations developed during the past years of *sotto voce* diplomacy.
That is the subject of this book.

Internationally, Japan continues to live in the shadow of its

* East Asia in the following discussion includes China, Japan, Korea, Taiwan,
and the Southeast Asian nations—Burma, Thailand, Cambodia, Laos, Vietnam,
Malaysia, Singapore, the Philippines, and Indonesia. See Chapter 2.

defeat in World War II. Surrender brought revolutionary domestic reform and completely shattered Japanese foreign relations. The country was reduced to the size it had at the time of Commodore Perry's visit, and the loss of the overseas empire not only obliterated the conquests of the Pacific War but eradicated the achievements of Japanese foreign policy in the modern era. The past was repudiated. Extraordinary measures were taken by the Occupation authorities to insure that the Japanese would remain on the sidelines of international politics. All remnants of military power were destroyed, and in the American-drafted constitution Japan formally renounced the right to use force in the conduct of foreign affairs. With the economy almost completely destroyed and the prewar political order utterly discredited and disestablished, the punitive and idealistic policies during the first years of the Occupation transformed Japan internationally into a kind of modern-day Carthage. Even with rapid economic recovery, it is understandable that the Japanese have moved slowly toward an active and independent international role.

In the years following the Occupation, the international environment provided few opportunities for independent foreign policy initiatives, even if the Japanese had had the capacity and desire to act. International politics during the 1950's was dominated by the global confrontation between the United States and the Soviet Union. Japan regained independence as an American ally and from the outset was closely tied to the Western bloc, politically, economically, and strategically. This severely inhibited any Japanese initiatives, since U.S. cold-war diplomacy extended deeply into the region—most notably in major military operations in Korea and in the wide-ranging efforts to contain and isolate China. Moreover, few incentives were provided for Japanese action in those aspects of East Asian politics not directly touched by the cold war, for an inherently unstable and uncertain situation was created by the rapid collapse of Western colonial empires and the proliferation of new, economically poor, and politically weak states on the periphery of China. Postwar Japanese foreign policy was thus launched in an extremely unsettled Asian international setting, one almost constantly beset by war and sharply divided by cold-war tensions. The basic direction of this policy—withdrawal behind the American alliance from all concerns of *Realpolitik*, while strengthening global and regional trade and political relations—was the inevitable result of the circumstances of the times.

The ten-year extension of the Mutual Security Treaty in 1960 laid the basis for continued Japanese disengagement from the *Sturm und Drang* of international politics, and this isolation was greatly encouraged by the extraordinary increase of America's involvement in Vietnam. In many ways, this second phase of Japan's "peace and prosperity" foreign policy was even more successful than the first. Economic relations with the West developed at an accelerated rate, trade with both China and Russia sharply expanded, and an accepted place among the leading nations of the global international order followed as a matter of course. As in the case of Korea, the Japanese again profited heavily from American involvement in a war in Asia and, even more important, the intensification of the Vietnam war led to greatly increased political and economic ties between Japan and the non-Communist countries in the region. Indeed, by the end of the decade, many of the economic aims that would have ensued from the Greater East Asian Co-prosperity Sphere of the Pacific War were reached without any of the costs of imperial conquest. By 1970, Japan had achieved both unprecedented prosperity and an international standing beyond all past expectations, while enjoying peace in a world of turbulence. The government could rightly note with satisfaction "the wisdom of the national choice regarding the course of our [past] external policy."[1]

Yet, during the 1960's, the storm clouds that had lingered so long over the rest of Asia moved closer to Tokyo. In the same communiqué that extolled past achievements, the government was constrained to note that future Japanese policy must change in accordance with "a correct appraisal of hard realities and the evolution of the times."[2] Three of the "hard realities" presenting the most immediate demands for a new diplomatic posture remain: (1) a reduction of American military involvement in East Asia, touched off by the frustrations in Vietnam; (2) a nuclear-armed China pursuing an independent foreign policy in a fluid and unstable international milieu; and (3) the broader implications of the growing web of Japanese economic and political involvement in Asia. All raise pressure for Japan to pursue a more independent and activist role in the world at a time when it has reached a new level of material capacity to act and renascent nationalism has become evident in politically significant proportions.

What gives these developments special significance is the extremely reactive character of Japan's international role. To an unusual degree, the vital interests of Japan have been largely defined by the outside environment, and any move toward greatly expanded political involvement or military engagement in Asia will almost certainly result from external pressures, not from an internally generated strategy for an international place in the sun. The pattern of past relations and the place of war and conflict in Asian international politics, which Japan of necessity accords special priority, will continue to give basic direction to Japanese foreign policy. This emphasis on the derivative nature of Japan's international actions underlies the approach taken in this book. Inevitably, it downplays the importance of policy and politics in Tokyo, but it places in bold relief the mounting forces for change that the Japanese now confront.

DOMESTIC POLITICS AND FOREIGN POLICY

Domestic politics remains, of course, the filter through which all Japanese foreign policy must flow, and one key to the past reactive pattern of actions lies in the decision-making process having prevented bold leadership. This has been in large part due to the cleavages in and among the political parties and the lack of consensus on certain basic foreign-policy goals. The vehement and unqualified opposition of the Japanese left to any move toward a more activist position beyond "disarmed neutralism" has discouraged government initiatives by increasing the domestic political risks. In addition, persistent conflict among the factions of the Liberal-Democratic Party (the conservatives), which has held power since the end of the Occupation in 1952, has impeded innovation by successive prime ministers and deterred decisive moves by projecting intraparty politics deeply into all issues of foreign affairs. The result has been a kind of policy immobilism.[3] Barring an unexpected reversal of past trends altering the relative strength and *modus operandi* of the parties or the sudden emergence of a nationalist consensus, this style of policy formulation will continue to restrain leadership no matter what the personalities or issues of the moment. This restraint will tend to prolong the passivity of Japan on the international stage and virtually preclude a Gaullist-style move away from the American alliance. An expanded political and military role may well be undertaken, but the timing and substance of any actions will be closely related to changes in the international milieu rather than initiated independently by Japanese policy-makers.

Japan has avoided the concerns of *Realpolitik* to a degree without precedent for a country of comparable stature in the modern world. As in the nations of Western Europe, the destruction and debilitation of World War II, the loss of an overseas empire, and the configuration of the cold war resulted in a determined concentration on economic progress and social change, with a drastic downplay of international power interests. What is remarkable about the Japanese case is the extent and prolonged duration of this disengagement, owing to the peculiar nature of the American alliance and American commitments in Asia. But also involved are the unique place of pacifism in postwar Japan and the integral ties between the dominant forces in the internal political system and the extraordinary achievements of Tokyo's economically skewed policies.

Japanese abdication of any independent concern for the "high" politics of power and prestige finds its roots in the shattered self-confidence of total defeat, in the demilitarization policy of the early Occupation, and especially in the legacies of the "no war" clause (Article IX) of the constitution. Once incorporated into the basic law of the country, pacifism was quickly reified by the Japanese left as a kind of "inalienable right" and has served as a moral cudgel to attack all efforts to strengthen the Self-Defense Forces and the American alliance. Additionally, the consistently high level of support for pacifism among the Japanese people as seen in numerous public-opinion polls, has limited the discretion of the government. At the same time, the conservatives have been able to use these pacifist sentiments expressed by the public and the opposition and embodied in the constitution to counter successfully U.S. pressure to expand Japanese military capabilities more rapidly. The persistence and intensity of the controversy over the legitimacy of force as an instrument of foreign policy, involving for differing reasons all politically articulate groups, have created a formidable obstacle to any decision for large-scale rearmament or the extension of the Japanese security sphere beyond the homeland, no matter how serious an international crisis may be.

Japan has pursued almost exclusively only those foreign-policy goals that are susceptible to the kind of rational calculation of rewards commonly associated with economic problems. Even on issues such as recognition of China, where the Japanese could have exercised political initiatives without seriously jeopardizing their basic alliance with the West, nothing was done. Yet, Japan is not just conducting a calculated pursuit of limited goals. Having abandoned the military dimension of diplomacy, whenever possible, it has made a further effort to separate politics from economics. By restricting activities and defining aims in narrowly economic terms, the Japanese have not only minimized the risks inherent in international political actions, they have also developed a foreign policy more like that of a trading company than a nation. Undeniable benefits have resulted from this highly prudential, essentially nonpolitical posture, but this very success will hinder the realistic acceptance of Japan's inevitably expanding role. Perhaps the most damaging legacy is the persistent illusion that the economic, political, and military dimensions of foreign policy are not interdependent and can be dealt with in discrete fashion. The weak and reactive style of policy leadership provided by the fragmented Liberal-Democratic Party and the internal bases of support for this policy stand as additional liabilities. Neither the economic interests in Japan that have profited most nor the politicians who have for so long avoided considerations of *Realpolitik* are likely to respond quickly or effectively to a change in the external environment requiring a basic shift in policy direction. The aims and skills of statesmen and those of international entrepreneurs are far from identical.

Nevertheless, since the first successful Chinese nuclear tests in 1964 and the subsequent uncertainties wrought by the escalation of American involvement in Vietnam, there has been a significant shift in Japanese attitudes toward foreign affairs. A more "realistic" approach to security matters has been evident in the continuing debate on the expansion of conventional military capacities and in the mounting concern over the need for an independent nuclear force. A similar change has taken place in the mood of the Japanese public, evident in the now overwhelming acceptance of the military value of the Self-Defense Forces, the conspicuous efforts to revise attitudes toward the once discredited presurrender past, and the self-conscious delight in the achievements of the country in the postwar era. In sum, with the return of national self-confidence, there has been a modest revival of nationalism. These changes are only partially reflected in present policies; but no longer is there the easy, almost automatic identification of American and Japanese interests, and there is surprisingly wide support for a more self-sufficient defense capacity. Thus, however much domestic politics may constrain the formulation of specific foreign policies, the door is now ajar for acceptance of a fresh orientation to global and regional international relations involving much broader Japanese engagement.

CONTEMPORARY INTERNATIONAL MILIEU

The United States

America's entire Asian policy is now in the midst of the first fundamental revision since the Korean war, and this more than any other single factor will ultimately determine the future destiny of Japan. Both the timing and substance of the revision are in direct response to bitter domestic political divisions and spiraling material and international costs growing out of the Vietnam war. Beyond a commitment to reduce the American military presence and to avoid future large-scale conventional involvement in Asia, the implications of gradual U.S. disengagement from the region remain unclear. These uncertainties regarding the American role are likely to persist, sustained by the fluidity of

events in East Asia and the growing consensus in the United
States supporting a substantial reduction of all overseas military
commitments developed since the cold war.[4] American formal and
informal assurances notwithstanding, the Japanese security position has radically changed, and, for the first time since 1945,
Japan must directly confront the broader issues of war and peace
throughout East Asia. As President Nixon has implied, any serious effort to have Asians assume primary responsibility for Asian
security depends ultimately on the active participation of Japan.[5]
In evaluating Japanese-American relations, emphasis is usually
given to bilateral ties. But the indirect effects of U.S. security
commitments throughout East Asia, which are currently linked
to the ultimate form of a Vietnam settlement, are of increasing
significance as Japan becomes more and more enmeshed in the
web of international relations of the region. Only by juxtaposing
the roles of Japan and the United States in this broader regional
context can we see the changing nature of the alliance in proper
perspective.

Bilateral relations have, in fact, reflected the change in the
international setting from the bipolar, cold-war conditions that
shaped the basic contours of the Japanese-American alliance to a
more complex and intractable situation in Asia and global multipolarity. In these new circumstances, the United States has prod-
ded the Japanese to assume a more active international role
without clearly specifying what its dimensions should be or fundamentally altering the patron-client security relationship that has
grown up during the past two decades. The Japanese reaction
has been to avoid any broader, concrete security commitments
and thus to keep all policy options open. Following its automatic
extension in 1970, the Mutual Security Treaty can now be terminated by either party with one year's notice, and Prime Minister
Sato has candidly stated that extension of the pact beyond the
next two or three years will depend upon "the future development of science and technology" and "changes in the international military and political situation."[6] Similarly, when Japan
signed the Treaty on the Non-Proliferation of Nuclear Weapons
in early 1970, Tokyo released a strongly worded official statement setting forth reservations that make its early ratification by

the Diet most improbable.* Relations have also been unsettled by growing economic conflicts as Japan becomes a formidable and aggressive competitor of the United States in world trade. The dramatic moves by President Nixon in August, 1971, to rectify the U.S. balance of payments and force an international monetary reform had Japan as the main target. Even more shocking were the American initiatives for accommodation with Peking, which were taken with minimal concern for the short-term impact on Japan. Weakening of the Japanese-American entente has been brought about not by a breakdown of understanding or maladroit diplomacy but by the adoption by both nations of new priorities in their relations with each other as a result of basic changes in global as well as regional international politics.

The People's Republic of China

China is today, as it has been during the greater part of this century, the major diplomatic problem facing Japan. Although Japan's policy toward China has remained essentially the same since the end of the Occupation, nevertheless relations between the two countries have undergone a significant transformation during the past decade. The Japanese, who still formally recognize only the Nationalist Government on Taiwan, generally followed the hard-line policy taken by the United States until mid-1971. Although Japan may encounter frustrations in establishing satisfactory formal diplomatic relations with Peking, its unofficial contacts with the mainland have been so substantial in both number and variety that it has replaced the Soviet Union as China's leading trading partner. As a result of the Chinese dispute with the Russians and their maneuvering regarding the war in Vietnam, Peking's interests in Asia and especially in the various Asian national Communist movements have been accented. This development is of profound importance for international politics in the region, especially to the Japanese, who have enormously expanded economic and political relations with the non-Communist states in Asia during recent years and are thus more vulnerable to a collision with Chinese interests.

Chinese development of nuclear weapons and the Sino-Soviet

* See Appendix C.

split have greatly complicated the whole question of Japanese security. Disintegration of the Communist bloc destroyed a basic assumption of the Mutual Security Treaty regarding the direction and nature of the military threat to Japan and cast doubts on past defense strategy. Whatever constraints were provided by the global engagement during the era of rigid bipolarity have been removed as Peking has struck out on its own, encouraging a global trend toward multipolarity and confounding both the United States and the Soviet Union in their policies toward Asia. China has now moved to alter its role as an international pariah free from all external restraints beyond confrontation with power.

Short-term changes notwithstanding, it remains very much an open question how rapidly the world's leading revolutionary power will be transformed into a moderate international force. Doubts about lasting internal restraints on Chinese foreign policy have been raised both by the revolutionary rhetoric and aims that continue to characterize Peking's pronouncements on foreign affairs and by the political confusion and erratic policies that accompanied the Cultural Revolution from 1966 to 1968. These developments, together with China's rapid progress toward becoming a major nuclear power, have had a sobering effect on the Japanese Government and have given impetus to Tokyo's steady drive for increased defense capabilities. The military threat from China takes on meaning not in terms of a possible military conquest of Japan proper but in terms of the effect on the American alliance and the capacities of the Japanese to participate in East Asian politics. When, during the coming decade, Peking acquires nuclear strike capabilities to threaten the American homeland, the credibility of the U.S. "nuclear umbrella" as a haven for Japan—and for the other non-Communist allies of the United States in Asia—will be severely tested. Furthermore, without nuclear weapons, Japan cannot be fully engaged as a rival with China in regional international politics. Whether Japan embarks on the path toward nuclear armament, with the Chinese threat as a catalyst, will depend not so much on the designs of political leaders in Tokyo as on the ways in which the two dominant regional powers are caught up in the maelstrom of international politics in East Asia and whether, after Vietnam, the United States and the Soviet Union choose to extend their involvement in East Asia, where the costs of past policies have proved so exorbitant.

Non-Communist Asia

To a degree not generally appreciated, Japan is already deeply involved in East Asia. During the past decade, the Japanese jumped into a clearly dominant position in international trade throughout the region, and this position is steadily improving. Reparations for World War II and the overwhelming proportion of Japanese foreign aid have been concentrated in East Asia, and aid and trade will sharply increase in the immediate future.

Japan is a leading member of the many multilateral economic and political organizations that have proliferated among the non-Communist Asian states during recent years, such as the Asian and Pacific Council (ASPAC) and the Asian Bank, and has taken the initiative in establishing institutions for promoting regional economic prosperity. In addition, there remains within Japan a vague but strong psychological attraction to Asia as the area in which the country has a special role and where its international destiny will be defined. These sentiments, which are especially strong among the ruling conservative elite, give added meaning to the patterns of interaction that have emerged and could lead to a broadened concept of Japanese security interests. In any event, both the scope and intensity of this engagement in Asia have added another dimension to Japanese foreign policy, one that is closely related to the security dilemmas posed by the changes in American policy and in the regional role of a nuclear China.

A New Economic Superpower

The awesome expansion of Japan's material power during the past ten years, and the added capabilities this provides, greatly enhance the country's present and potential international role. By 1960, the largest annual economic output of the prewar period had been substantially surpassed in gross terms, but in level of technology and in size Japan remained a rather poor, second-rate power. By 1970, the gross national product (GNP) had more than quadrupled to an astonishing $200 billion, and, even with reevaluation of the yen in late 1971, most projections foresee no substantial reduction in this rate of growth during the next five years. The Japanese economy is now exceeded only by the two superpowers in size; a condition of "chronic surplus" has developed in the balance of payments; and, except in a very few selected industries (e.g., computers and supersonic aircraft), technological parity and independence commensurate with the scale of the economy have been achieved. With remarkable rapidity and with little fanfare, Japan has become a true economic superpower.

When and how this newly acquired strength will be more fully translated into specific meaning in terms of foreign policy remain open questions. Two constraints on a more politically assertive policy have been created by the pattern of economic development. First, even more than in other "postindustrial" societies, affluence and rapid economic growth have brought into being problems of environmental pollution and social disruption. Policies to cope with internal dislocation were prominent in the six-year Social-Economic Development Plan announced by the government in early 1970, and domestic needs will vie with international affairs for policy priority in the next decade. Secondly, there are powerful incentives for Japan to concentrate on further integration into the global industrial economy by maintaining priority on economic matters and turning away from traditional political concerns defined in terms of "national interest." The Japanese do have an indispensable stake in strengthening their position in the world economy and cannot undertake policies that will imperil their growing share of world trade. Nevertheless, neither the domestic problems of a postindustrial society nor the aggressive expansion of economic intercourse with developed countries precludes the unfettered pursuit of political objectives, especially if the policies center on East Asia and do not provide direct strategic challenge to the superpowers. More basically, however, what is important is not what the Japanese choose to do but what they are obliged or led to do by external pressures. Such pressures are directly linked with Japan's sharply increased international weight and involvement, which in turn are largely derivative from the nation's economic power.

THE ASIAN SETTING

Although deeply involved in the world economy and closely allied with the United States, Japanese international aims and actions have come to be peculiarly centered in East Asia. In the wake of the Vietnam war and China's nuclear progress, the Japanese increasingly view the region as the primary source of security problems as well. Partly this is the result of global changes in international politics, and partly it is because of the greatly augmented interests of Japan in Asia. Basic changes in the global system, such as nuclear proliferation, the loosening of bloc alliances, and the now unfolding reduction of American military men and commitments in Asia have had the effect of bringing into being for Japan new, regionally centered security and political relations, that is, of creating an area of international interaction where the superpowers play a decreasing role. Vietnam seems destined to be the last drama in East Asia played according to the cold-war scenario, and the legacies of this prolonged conflict for regional politics are already substantial. Cleavages between Asian Communist and non-Communist governments and movements have widened; there has been an intensified pattern of economic and political interaction among those states allied with America; and, with growing doubts about future U.S. policies, both international cooperation and competition are increasingly cast in regional terms. In spite of the greater complexity and continuing fluidity in international relations in the area, a regional subsystem with Japan and China as the main actors can be identified. It is in the context of an East Asian subsystem that the enlarged place of Japan in the region and the reciprocal influence of this development on Japanese foreign policy can be best elucidated.

In elaborating the structure and dynamics of the East Asian regional subsystem, three fundamental assumptions are made about the nature of international politics that are sufficiently "old-fashioned" or at odds with past Japanese actions and policies to warrant some prefatory comment. First, it is assumed that nation-states of the region will be the main actors in the subsystem, despite the questionable viability of several Asian countries in their current form, the bloc-oriented intervention of the super-powers, and the universalist claims of revolutionary Maoism. Secondly, conflict and war are seen as inevitable features of in-ternational relations in the region, given the multitude of revo-lutionary, destabilizing forces and almost total absence of com-pensating counterforces. Those factors insuring conflict are the highly uncertain implications for international behavior of the profound economic and social changes occurring in nations other than Japan; the clashes of interest linked with past and current national competition, which are aggravated by the sharp ideo-logical cleavages between Communist and non-Communist polit-ical groups; the virtual impossibility of a "power balance," given the permeability of many states to "people's wars" and China's stubborn opposition to any attempt to freeze the *status quo;* and, finally, the failure of both superpowers to articulate clearly their short-term objectives in Asia, let alone to build effective alliance systems. Harold Isaacs' prescient prophecy at the end of World War II seems even more appropriate today—there will be "no peace for Asia" in the years ahead.[7] Accordingly, the third as-sumption is that Japan cannot participate fully or for long in regional politics with a military role narrowly restricted to the home islands.

Japan, now at the threshold of a new diplomatic era, stands in a singularly anomalous position regarding Asia and the world. From one perspective, the Japanese are riding on a crest of eco-nomic strength and political prestige. From another, gaps and inadequacies latent in past policies are now surfacing under changing external pressures, especially a reduced American mili-tary role in Asia. Japan cannot expand engagement in a region that has been almost continuously at war since 1945 and keep an aloof and pacifist position. Similarly, the extraordinary im-balance between its material capabilities and its international performance will increasingly strain relations with its allies and neighbors. How the transition from the past is made without rad-ically disrupting the domestic political system, or whether it precipitates a headlong plunge into the vortex of Asian politics, will have a decisive impact on the future of the region. Having risen as a phoenix from the ashes of 1945, the Japanese once again tower over Asia, with the capacity to shape fundamentally the international order that has emerged from an earlier generation's attempt to create an "Asia for the Asiatics" under the hegemony of Tokyo.

2 The Emergence of an East Asian International Subsystem

East Asia, two decades ago a war ravaged and largely postcolonial backwater, has moved to the forefront of the contemporary international scene. For almost ten years, the Vietnam quagmire has made the complex and, until recently, remote world of Asian politics the daily fare of Western statesmen and poets alike. The seeming intractability of the immediate conflict, and the inherently fragile and unstable conditions prevalent in the region neighboring China, have revived long-dormant apprehensions about the insoluble problems of the East. Especially in the United States, widespread sentiments of isolationism have been aroused; indeed, the current American defense policy has ironically adopted, in effect, the same slogan used by Japanese nationalists during World War II—"Asia for the Asiatics." Other legacies of the Vietnam experience are a more general awareness that the principal locus of persistent international conflict and tension has shifted from Europe to Asia[1] and a recognition that international politics in Asia has increasingly gained a momentum distinct from that of the still dominantly bipolar global system.[2] Despite these developments, the contours of Asian politics remain largely unexplored. Surprisingly few works beyond those specifically concerned with Vietnam strategy have dealt comprehensively with the international relations of the region. The subject demands a frontal assault, and the most direct method is to treat East Asia as a regional subsystem.

REGIONALISM AND EAST ASIA

The concepts of "regionalism" and "regional subsystem" have become increasingly popular in analyses of international relations,[3] but the varied and often ambiguous ways in which they have been used have had uneven and frequently dubious results. Proliferation of regionally based multilateral and supranational organizations, and the need to deal with extensive international interaction not directly integral to the global system, have provided the basic incentives for concentration on regionalism. Further stimulus has come from the application of systems analysis to international affairs—an approach particularly useful in analyzing subordinate and coordinate regional subsystems. Regions have, in fact, been established for various purposes with differing and overlapping boundaries. Similarly, for analytical purposes, they can be defined in any way that advances an understanding of international relations.[4] Here, the boundaries of the East Asian subsystem have been established by multiple criteria and, although the region is in one sense an analytical construct, it is essentially a real and important arena of international politics.

Underlying our discussion is a somewhat loose and general definition of a regional subsystem—"a pattern of relations among basic units in world politics which exhibits a particular degree of intensity," plus an awareness of this pattern among the participating units.[5] It is important to emphasize that the units involved are nations in geographical propinquity and that the subsystem includes forms of interaction as diverse as bilateral trade and military confrontation, as well as explicit institutional and legal relations among the regional states. A systemic framework of this sort departs from the orthodox approach of systems theory, falling more in the tradition of "historical sociology" that is usually identified with the writings of Stanley Hoffmann and Raymond Aron.[6] It is an approach particularly well suited to the analysis of the concrete circumstances of East Asian international politics during the past decade.

Four distinct but interrelated variables are basic to the development of the East Asian subsystem: (1) the shift in the structure of the global international order from bipolarity toward multipolarity; (2) changes in the Asian policies of the superpowers brought on by the vastly altered and more complex international situation; (3) new patterns of interaction among the national units in East Asia; and (4) the capabilities and policies in the region of the world's "middle-range powers," China and Japan. Further delineation of the subsystem thus envisaged requires consideration of the connections between the global and regional systems and the elaboration of the relations among the East Asian states in terms of political, socio-economic, and military levels of action. It should be noted at the outset that both the scope of the region and the unusual stress given to the role of Japan depart from previous analysis of Asian international politics.

The East Asian region includes China, Japan, Korea, and Taiwan, together with what is normally considered to be Southeast Asia—Malaysia, Singapore, Thailand, Cambodia, Laos, North and South Vietnam, Burma, Indonesia, and the Philippines. Burma, which has, in effect, withdrawn from almost all aspects of international relations, is the most marginal member of the subsystem. It is nevertheless included because the Chinese political-military threat to Burma and Japanese reparations and aid are distinctive features of Burma's limited role in foreign affairs. Previously, the boundaries of the Asian region have been variously defined in terms of the policy pronouncements of national political leaders, membership in programs and organizations devoted to political and economic cooperation, immediate participation in regional power politics, the common socio-economic condition of underdevelopment, and other factors.[7] Insufficient attention has been paid to patterns of trade, aid, and direct investment, which are curiously called "politically insignificant involvement" by Cantori and Spiegel,[8] and to the nature of perceived security threats from neighboring states.

The underdeveloped countries of Southeast Asia are often regarded as a regional unit if not as a subsystem. Although there are good empirical as well as analytical reasons for dealing with them in discrete fashion, the basic dimensions of international politics are thereby distorted because the two major Asian actors, China and Japan, are excluded. Only by including the roles of the Japanese and the Chinese can the regional patterns of interaction be fully identified. Similarly, the full meaning for East Asian politics of the shift from a bipolar toward a multipolar system can be understood only by elaborating on the new and enlarged roles of China and Japan in the region.

Before turning to the structure and dynamics of the subsystem, an explanation why certain countries are excluded from the region would seem in order. India, Pakistan, and Ceylon are commonly considered Asian states and are members of numerous international organizations, such as the Economic Commission for Asia and the Far East (ECAFE) and the Asian Development Bank, which involve other nations in the area. Furthermore, India, whose civilization has left a strong imprint on Southeast Asia, held a leading place among countries throughout the region during the heyday of neutralism in the 1950's. During the past decade, however, these countries have moved more and more to the periphery of East Asia, militarily, economically, and politically. All are currently burdened with internal problems and lack the capacities and commitment for broad and significant engagement beyond the South Asian area. The continuing confrontation between India and China represents an issue of substantial importance for East Asian international relations, especially if it should lead to the Indian development of nuclear weapons. But India tends to view the conflict with China in bilateral terms, or as directly involving relations with the superpowers, and not in the context of East Asian politics. The lingering effects of the India-Pakistan confrontation will therefore continue to deflect the attention of both states from East Asian affairs.

New Zealand and especially Australia are increasingly involved both in defense matters and trade relations with the region. This trend should continue, and their participation in multilateral defense arrangements may well take on considerable importance.[9] Nevertheless, the limited capabilities of these two countries to act alone and their obvious non-Asian identity place them in a special but clearly external position regarding the subsystem.

EAST ASIA AND THE GLOBAL INTERNATIONAL SYSTEM

The breakdown of global bipolarity and the formation of regional foci of international interaction have been brought about by a variety of factors—the proliferation of nuclear weapons, changes in the distribution of economic power, self-limitations by the superpowers on the use of force (especially nuclear force) as an instrument of policy,[10] and the many efforts to foster economic and political collaboration in various parts of the world.[11] Both the blocs and the supporting alliances have already been extensively altered, and the process of change is continuing. In this period of transition, it is particularly difficult to perceive the full meaning of these changes. This is especially so in Asia, where the war in Vietnam has led to an exaggerated emphasis on the ultimate strategic dependence of Asian countries on the superpowers—seemingly a reaffirmation of the global style of international politics of the 1950's, when the world was more rigidly bipolar. Because multipolarity and polycentrism are defined largely in a military and strategic sense, the East Asian subsystem must first be elaborated in terms of the relationship between the region and global *Realpolitik*.

Bipolarity: Strategic Limitations

Strategically, the world remains bipolar. Only two states possess the military and material capabilities to play a significant role in all parts of the globe, and their policies accordingly involve them in the international affairs of virtually all nations. The so-called depolarization process signifies, therefore, not so much a challenge to the global hegemony of the superpowers —which would imply a kind of resurrected Great Powers system— as an increased capacity on the part of certain nations to act decisively in the narrower regional systems of which they are members.[12] At present, the United States is the pre-eminent power, capable of dominating any political-military problem in Asia.*

---

*The dispute over the Sino-Soviet border is here treated as a bilateral extraregional issue. Obviously, relations with the Soviet Union are of highest priority to the Chinese, but direct, full-scale conflict with Russia not only seems unlikely but would bring into play fundamental strategic considerations that would involve the global system and the other superpower.

The scale and nature of Russian support for North Vietnam is indicative of their capabilities and commitment when a major issue is at stake in Asia. American and Soviet capacities, together with their current policies of deep engagement, have led many to conclude that "it is difficult to conceive of any viable procedures for balancing the Asian subsystem in the absence of prominent participation of the superpowers."[13] Such assertions should not be accepted without qualification, however, for the extreme extent to which the superpowers have been committed in Asia has also contributed to the growth of polycentrism in the world and has forced reconsideration of their policies in the region.

On the one hand, Vietnam illustrates the persistence of bipolarity. On the other hand, the prolonged military stalemate there has demonstrated the limited capabilities of the superpowers to control international affairs in Asia. Despite enormous expenditures of political as well as military capital, neither the United States nor the Soviet Union has yet fully achieved its objectives. This is owing partly to the basic intractability of events in a remote, underdeveloped country racked by internal war, and partly to the Sino-Soviet split and the simultaneous loosening of the Western bloc. Chinese defiance of Russia, on the one hand, and the qualified support of, or opposition to, the United States on the part of its major Western allies, on the other, have served to inhibit the transformation of an Asian regional issue into a cold-war problem or into a question involving global alliances. Even with the superpowers' preponderant military and economic strength, it is now clear that *Realpolitik* in East Asia requires that they scrupulously assign priorities to security objectives in the region. Despite common interests in maintaining a stable balance of power in the area and in dealing with the threat of China, the now obvious costs and complexities of engagement in the region make likely *less*, not more, direct military involvement of the United States and Russia—no matter what form the Vietnam settlement may assume. Thus, one of the most frequently cited causes of global depolarization—the limitations on the use of coercive force by the superpowers (limits linked to the apocalyptic nature of the nuclear balance of terror as well as to the debilitating demands of a global dispersion of military forces)[14]—has accelerated the development of the East Asian regional subsystem.

Peking's challenge to both superpowers, its ambitious weapons program, and the revolutionary cast of its foreign policy have made the problem of nuclear proliferation essentially an Asian question.* To be sure, China's development of nuclear weapons will not be translated into a global capacity to act in the immediate future. The strategic importance of such weapons, however, is immediately manifest on the regional level, where China can act against equal or lesser powers. The threat has been felt most strongly in Japan and India, where the pressures for nuclear parity have steadily grown and ratification of the Treaty on the Non-Proliferation of Nuclear Weapons has been postponed. Future acquisition of an effective delivery system by the Chinese will not immediately present a direct threat to Soviet or American security, but it will further inhibit military action by the superpowers in the Asian region.

Primarily because of the frustrations and dilemmas of Vietnam and China, both the United States and the Soviet Union have been forced to revise fundamentally their policies toward East Asia. *Prima facie,* the so-called Nixon Doctrine commits the United States to gradual military disengagement from the region, renders most improbable the future dispatch of American ground forces, and assigns to Asians responsibility for their own conventional defenses.[15] The doctrine represents a major departure from the policy operative since the Korean war, which involved full and direct U.S. military participation in the containment of Communism. What new Asia-centered, non-Communist security arrangement will be established, and how the United States will honor past treaty commitments that demand a major deployment of our troops, are highly uncertain and will doubtless remain so. Confronted with ambiguities regarding future tactics, all non-Communist nations in Asia are profoundly concerned over ultimate American goals and intentions in East Asia. This concern is understandable. A general security com-

---

* Many other nations may have occasion to go nuclear, but China, because of its head start and political ambitions, and Japan, because of its material capabilities, make the issue special.

mitment of the sort underlying the North Atlantic Treaty Organization (NATO) is missing. The American alliance system is a patchwork affair, consisting of a series of bilateral treaties (with Japan, the Republic of China, South Korea, and the Philippines) and the limited and somewhat ambiguous obligations of the Southeast Asia Treaty Organization[16]—leaving latitude for American response on a case-by-case basis. Even more disturbing to these countries is the change in tone of American policy; for, in the past, the United States has moved in direct reaction to the exigencies of the moment, not in fulfillment of formal treaty obligations. Here, a comparison with American intentions regarding Europe is instructive. It is inconceivable that any administration would urge that Europe be defended by Europeans while at the same time reducing our general troop deployment and giving currency to the idea that U.S. forces would not participate in a future land war on the continent. For the United States, Asia does not now hold an equivalent place in policy priority, official statements notwithstanding. Thus, the attenuation of the American military presence and the accompanying climate of insecurity will hasten regionalization of security matters and accent the short-term fluidity of the international situation in East Asia. In this way, American policy is contributing both directly and indirectly to the creation of an East Asian regional subsystem.

In the decade since the Sino-Soviet split, the Chinese have complicated Russian policies toward the United States and the Communist world and have carved out a special sphere of influence in East Asia. The confrontation between the two Communist countries, marked by increasing virulence, has vitiated their bilateral alliance of 1950 and resulted in regional, as well as global, competition for control of national Communist movements. For instance, Peking, despite the disruptive and debilitating effects of the Cultural Revolution, has succeeded, in North Korea and North Vietnam, in cultivating a position of influence comparable to that of the Soviet Union. To balance the weight of extensive Soviet aid, the Chinese have made the most of ideological affinity, geographical proximity, selective aid, and skillful policy maneuvers. All insurrectionary Communist movements in

East Asia, except the Japanese, are dominated by groups aligned with China, now the indisputable leader of the "revolutionary, anti-imperialist" forces in the region.[17]

The rift with the Soviet Union has not only induced a kind of Peking-centered regionalism within the Communist world but has also led the Chinese and the Russians to distinct and conflicting diplomatic and strategic policies vis-à-vis non-Communist East Asian nations. Both China and Russia are relatively isolated politically and economically from the rest of Asia, but China, by virtue of its size, proximity, national ambitions, and place at the vanguard of revolutionary forces is viewed by most nations of the region as the major threat to external security and internal stability. With the exigencies of the Vietnam war greatly strengthening relations between non-Communist countries and the United States and muting intraregional conflict, the Soviet Union has had little room for policy initiatives regarding these nations. Whatever opportunities may develop after Vietnam, China is now such a serious rival that the major incentive for increased Soviet involvement in the political and military quicksands of the underdeveloped countries of East Asia may well be to check the expansion of Chinese influence. In any event, Soviet short-term tactics and long-term goals regarding the region are even more obscure and uncertain than those of the United States. This can be seen both as a symptom and a cause of the emergence of an East Asian subsystem.

Bipolarity: Economic Limitations

Bipolarity has also been modified by the rapid growth of economic power in Western Europe and Japan and by the increased capacities for independent international action that such growth provides. The case of Japan is certainly the most remarkable; for, in less than twenty-five years, the country has moved from the position of an impoverished international outcaste to that of the third most economically powerful nation in the world. Following the abnormally high rate of development connected with postwar reconstruction, the Japanese economy has grown for fifteen years at the astonishing annual rate of roughly 10.5 per cent in real terms, by far the highest in the world. Much has been said about this "economic miracle," but only in the latter half of the 1960's did it become of general international significance and concern as the GNP soared beyond that in all other countries except the superpowers and Japan became a truly major factor in world trade. Some understanding of the enormity of this development is provided by noting how fully the positions of the Chinese and Japanese economies have been reversed.

TABLE 1

GROSS NATIONAL PRODUCTS OF LEADING GLOBAL AND
EAST ASIAN NATIONS

(In billions of U.S. dollars)

	1957	1969	1975, projected in 1969 dollars[a]
United States	443	932	1,145
Soviet Union[b]	215 (1958)	380	485
Japan	28	167	325
West Germany	50	142	185
China[c]	46	56	71

[a] The projected annual growth rate of Japan is 13 per cent for 1970 and 10.6 per cent for 1971–75—figures used by the Japanese Economic Council in its Economic-Social Development Plan for 1970–75. The annual growth rates assumed for the United States, the Soviet Union, and West Germany were 3.5 per cent, 4.5 per cent, and 4.5 per cent, respectively—figures on which there is general consensus among economists. For China, a liberal 4 per cent rate has been assumed.

[b] In view of the varied ways of computing the Soviet GNP, the data cited have been derived from a single source—Stanley H. Cohn, "Soviet Growth Retardation: Trends in Resource Availability and Efficiency," *New Directions in the Soviet Economy* (1966), a collection of studies prepared for the Subcommittee on Foreign Economic Policy of the Joint Economic Committee of the Congress of the United States, pp. 99–132. The figure for 1969 is a projection from the 1964 figure given in the report, assuming an average growth rate of 5.3 per cent, which was the average actual rate of growth for the Soviet economy from 1958 to 1964.

[c] Estimates of China's GNP are extremely hazardous, and the figures quoted are only rough approximations. The 1969 figure is a projection using a generous 4 per cent growth rate from a figure for the year 1966 cited by Dwight Perkins, "The Chinese Economy and Its International Impact," *SAIS Review* (Winter, 1968), p. 38.
Other Sources: Bruce M. Russett *et al., World Handbook of Political and Social Indicators* (New Haven: Yale University Press, 1964), pp. 149–57; *International Financial Statistics* (March, 1970); and *The Japan Times Weekly* (April 18, 1970).

In 1957, the Chinese economy was more than one and a half times the size of that of Japan, but, by 1969, Japan's economy had grown to be approximately *three times* as great as China's (Table 1). Similarly, dramatic changes regarding the leading global economic powers have followed from the sixfold expansion of the Japanese economy during this twelve-year period.

The already significant changes in the structure of the global and Asian international systems induced by this pattern of development will become even more pronounced in the immediate future. If past patterns of growth continue, by the mid-1970's Japan will have become the world's third economic superpower. As seen in Table 1, if the economies of the major world powers expand at their expected rates, the absolute size of the Japanese economy at the end of 1975 will have grown to two-thirds that of the Soviet Union—a figure roughly equal to that of the Common Market today. Most importantly, the gap between Japan and West Germany will have become so large ($140 billion) that Japan will be classified more appropriately with the superpowers. Thus, a world *à trois,* heretofore linked almost exclusively with the potential of a united Europe, will come into being in an economic sense, marking a fundamental change in the structure of the post-1945 world order. The question of when and how this shift from economic bipolarity to tripolarity will bring changes in Japan's political and military foreign policies is related to the evolution of the American alliance and the pressures felt by Japan from inevitably greater involvement in the East Asian region.

Economic tripolarity will become even more conclusive if the projected rates of economic growth continue throughout the next decade; but the vastly superior military capabilities and concomitant global political commitments of the United States and the Soviet Union will render even a nuclear Japan a second-level power in international politics, except in East Asia. Japan will be able to afford the costs, both materially and technically, for superpower military status, but its late start, together with the limited incentives for such a role, makes most improbable any effort beyond a concern for problems in the Asian region. But even in Asia, where Japan is likely to be fully engaged in international politics, China will assure that the configuration is quadripolar rather than tripolar. Whatever the ultimate implications, Japan's sharply increased importance will hasten the trend away from bipolarity and can therefore be viewed potentially as significant for global and regional politics as the rise of a revolutionary and nuclear China has been during the past two decades.

Regional Identity

In addition to these fundamental changes in the structure and dynamics of the global system, there is a psychological-historical factor conducive to an East Asian subsystem: a sense of regional identity among nations in the area that is persistently manifested in their foreign policies and rooted in attitudes nurtured throughout the last century. East Asia, far from having the kind of common cultural heritage found in Western Europe, is distinguished by extreme ethnic, cultural, and political diversity. Indeed, one of the most striking features of the modern era has been the collapse of the once pre-eminent cultural and political force of imperial China and the serious disruption of the more narrowly traditional Asian societies by Westernization, war, and economic change. In the post–World War II period, the decolonization process heightened the distinction between Western and Asian international politics, but this was blurred by the deep intrusion of global politics and the overlay of cold-war issues on nationalist movements and national rivalries. Inevitably, continuing war and upheaval have obviated any possibility for consensus among the new political elites on which to build a stable regional international order. Yet, precisely this shared experience of turbulence and change, brought on primarily by the political, cultural, and economic impact first of Western colonialism and then of the cold war, has encouraged the nations of East Asia to view themselves as a distinct group.[18] That is, a degree of regional consciousness has been fostered largely by international pressures from outside the region and through a common experience of disruption rather than cooperation. In the most general sense, the nations of East Asia have come to "experience [a common] destiny and observe a difference between what is happening inside and what is happening outside their geographic-historical zone," thereby fulfilling a broad criterion suggested by Aron for identifying an international subsystem.[19]

The complex history of the slogan "Asia for the Asiatics" suggests how a common sense of destiny has developed among the political elites of these nations. In various forms, this phrase is found in conspicuous use in the three basic phases of international politics in East Asia during the last century: the era of Western imperialism, the decades of Japanese expansion, and, since 1945, the struggle for national independence in the wake of the decline of colonialism, the rise of China, and the inexorable drift away from a bipolar world structure. Initially an expression signifying rejection of Western values as well as of the Western presence, the notion of "Asia for the Asiatics" came to be used by Japanese nationalists in the latter part of the nineteenth century to justify their country's expansion onto the mainland. In this form, it carried a strongly anti-imperialist, anti-Western, and pan-Asian tone, which proved extremely attractive to Sun Yat-sen and was incorporated with only slight modification into his concept of Chinese nationalism.[20] Ultimately, the notion of Asian brotherhood under Japanese leadership was a basic assumption on which the vision of the Greater East Asian Co-prosperity Sphere rested. In turn, following the Japanese occupation of Southeast Asia, the theme of pan-Asianism was taken up by many of the successful independence movements in the early postwar years.[21] Similar pan-Asian sentiments often have been found in the bitterly anti-Western indictments by outspoken nationalist leaders, such as Mao, Sukarno, and Sihanouk, and, in less strident terms, in the speeches of many non-Communist Asian statesmen. More recently, the pronouncements of the many regional organizations of non-Communist nations and the overt and implicit policies of Japan have incorporated this concept. Thus, for more than a century, the notion that Asia has a discrete and independent international identity has been a constant if not central theme in the politics of the region.

It should be emphasized, however, that pan-Asianism is currently a minor element in the region's international politics. Vague and unstructured in content, and lacking a vociferous and powerful local proponent, there is little possibility that it can alone exert a significant impact. Yet, in view of the trend toward regionalism that has accompanied the shift from bipolarity, in view of the fact that one of the superpowers is positively promoting "Asianism" (albeit with a peculiarly cold-war twist), and in view of the likelihood that the Japanese will seek legitimacy for their expanding national role in terms of apt revisions of past slogans, pan-Asianism is a significant addendum to an East Asian subsystem.

STRUCTURE AND DYNAMICS OF THE EAST ASIAN REGIONAL SUBSYSTEM

In addition to the global trends toward multipolarity and the impetus they provide for distinguishing Asian from world politics, changing relations among the East Asian states themselves have aided in the development of a regional subsystem. A profile of the subsystem, encompassing the economic, political, and military levels of interaction, provides an ideal backdrop on which the international role of Japan can be projected and analyzed in greater detail.

At the outset, it is important to underscore the point that the vicissitudes of intraregional politics have also led these nations to view themselves as a distinct group. East Asian states have shared common and almost continuous threats to their security for many years. The expansionist nationalism of Japan, culminating in the Greater East Asian Co-prosperity Sphere, left a profound impact. Virtually all the national governments—including, especially, the Chinese Communist—can trace their origins directly to the effects of the Japanese conquests. These more remote legacies have been supplemented by postwar experiences. As noted previously, despite a basically bipolar world order and massive American and Soviet intervention in the area, all Asian nations—neutral, Communist, and non-Communist—have been concerned with the threat posed by the growing power and ambitions of China.

Perhaps the most significant feature of contemporary regional politics is the importance of Japan and China. Both countries have the capacity to act throughout the region, and both give special priority to relations within this area even in the face of pressures from the global system. Neither nation, however, acts with equal effectiveness in all sectors of the subsystem—China being currently dominant in military terms and Japan in economic terms—but both retain a general commitment to, and a prominent place in, the international politics of the region. The trend during the past decade toward a more diffuse global international system has resulted in two power centers in Asia; the actions and policies of these two powers have been the most important influences on the structure and dynamics of intraregional politics.

STRUCTURE OF THE SUBSYSTEM

A clear view of the fundamental structure of the regional international order is provided by comparing the most recent estimates of the Gross National Products of Asian countries. GNP is generally accepted as the best single index of national power, for the total value of goods produced roughly combines in a single figure both a nation's size and its level of economic development.[22] Although it does not take into account factors such as the tightness of political control, the proportion of the economy in industrial production, and the over-all level of technical capacity, GNP is probably the most widely used index.[23] When this index is applied to the countries of East Asia, the results are rather startling (see Table 2).

In comparison with countries other than China, Japan, in absolute terms, is seventeen times as "powerful" as the third-ranking state (Indonesia), almost forty-five times the average size of small Asian powers, and three-and-one-half times their combined GNP. In fact, the Japanese economy is more than one-and-a-half times that of the rest of the region, including China. China's GNP, only one third the size of Japan's, is still greater than that of all the other countries in the region put together. Qualitative features accent the lopsided nature of this picture even more.

TABLE 2

GROSS NATIONAL PRODUCTS OF EAST ASIAN COUNTRIES, 1969

(In billions of U.S. dollars)

Country	GNP[a]
Japan	167.4
China	56.2
Indonesia	11.2
Philippines	8.0
South Korea	7.0
Thailand	6.0
Nationalist China	4.8
Malaysia	3.6
South Vietnam	3.0
Burma	2.0
North Vietnam	1.4
Cambodia	1.0
North Korea	1.0
Singapore	1.0
Laos	0.2

[a] The figures for South Vietnam, Burma, North Vietnam, Cambodia, North Korea, Singapore, and Laos are estimates. China's GNP has been estimated by projecting a generous 4 per cent growth rate from a figure for the year 1966 cited by Dwight Perkins in "The Chinese Economy and Its International Impact," *SAIS Review* (Winter, 1968), p. 38.

SOURCES: International Monetary Fund, *International Financial Statistics*, October, 1969, June, 1970; Agency for International Development, *Selected Economic Data for the Less-Developed Countries*, June, 1969; Agency for International Development, *Gross National Product: Growth Rates and Trend Data*, February, 1971; and Bureau of International Commerce, *Foreign Economic Trends and Their Implications for the U.S.*, 1969, 1970.

Not only are the smaller countries of the region economically underdeveloped and politically fragile, they are divided in ways that have thus far prevented prolonged international collaboration, except in cases of extreme crisis. It is true that South Korea, Taiwan, Thailand, and Malaysia have sustained impressive rates of economic growth over the last ten years, and that Indonesia, by far the largest and potentially the most powerful after China and Japan, finally seems to be placing its internal economic and political house in order. Nevertheless, the dominance, in the immediate future, of the two largest states in this index cannot be challenged, even with the most favorable possible growth among the other states. Japan and China are, and will be, the superpow-

ers of East Asia, the only nations capable of acting independently and effectively on a region-wide basis on several levels of international politics.

In terms of the GNP index, the structure of the East Asian subsystem is bipolar in much the same manner as the global system has been bipolar during the postwar period.[24] If anything, the quantitative and qualitative gap between China and Indonesia makes bipolarity in the region comparatively more extreme. Moreover, at a time when the differences and antagonisms between Communist and non-Communist nations seem to be lessening in Europe, they are becoming more intense in East Asia. The region-wide ramifications of the war in Indochina, the excesses of the Cultural Revolution, Chinese implication in the abortive Communist coup in Indonesia and in the insurgency in northern Thailand, and Peking's development of nuclear weapons have made other Asian states regard China and "Communism," variously defined, as the most immediate major regional threat. Furthermore, a semipermanent state of confrontation along Communist–non-Communist lines is assured by the continued division of both China and Korea and the potential partition of Vietnam, Cambodia, and Laos. Japan has been drawn into a quasi-bloc type of relationship with non-Communist Asian states as a result of intensified patterns of economic and political interaction and various multilateral and bilateral efforts to promote further collaboration in all but the military field. At the same time, China has remained virtually isolated from most of its East Asian neighbors, except North Vietnam, North Korea, and the various "liberation fronts." (It will take years to establish broad-based relations, even if the policy of accommodation initiated in 1970 continues.) Nevertheless, there is no indication that the East Asian subsystem will develop blocs led by hegemonic "superpowers," nor is any nonaligned "third force" grouping of states likely to endure. Rather, a region-wide competition between China and Japan may well develop, following a reduced level of military engagement by the United States and the Soviet Union.

A comparison of the power potential of China with that of Japan, in terms of the GNP index, is difficult, partly because the statistics regarding China are necessarily speculative, partly because the totalitarian form of China's government makes any direct comparison with Japan in these terms extremely misleading. China not only possesses nuclear weapons but in the past has been willing and able to control allocation of resources to maximize effectiveness in pursuing highly developed foreign-policy goals. Whether this advantage will continue depends on internal political stability and, even more, on international conditions, but it remains a critical feature of Chinese foreign policy. Economically, the advantages lie with Japan. The country is fully industrialized, has a superior balance as well as level of technical skills, and will in all probability continue to maintain one of the highest rates of economic growth in the world. Japan's enormous lead over Peking in terms of GNP will widen, further enhancing its already established place as the economic queen of Asia. This *de facto* economic pre-eminence, and the potential it affords for political leadership, constitute the most important new variable in the subsystem.

In addition to the dominance of China and Japan, another distinctive feature of the regional subsystem is the extreme weakness of the other countries. It is a system of two elephants and many squirrels. To appreciate the relative international power of small states, it is necessary to go beyond comparison simply in terms of economic strength, as seen in Table 2. During the postwar period, the ability of small states to utilize their positions within alliances and in international organizations has proved to be a central factor in preserving their independence and security.[25] However, because the existing alliance systems in East Asia are in the midst of change, and because international organizations have, without massive superpower participation, shown utter incapacity to cope with those crises involving force that predominate in the region, the capabilities of East Asian small states to maneuver in terms of "nonpower" factors are severely limited. Short of an effective great-power agreement to "neutralize" the region from international conflict, the crude, traditional calculus of power seems the appropriate measure of relative strength. In these terms, it is noteworthy that the small states of East Asia, because of their size, underdeveloped economies, and political instability, lack the capacity for effective international action, except in immediately contiguous areas. Even then, however, the support of a powerful ally is usually essential.

The comparative size and strength of the standing armies, as well as general military capabilities, of countries such as North and South Vietnam, North and South Korea, and Nationalist China, is the result of great-power subsidy, not independent capacities. Up to now, the general weakness of the East Asian squirrels and the commitments by the global superpowers have led to military intervention that has diluted the independence of the subsystem and its component states. Still, the extremely limited international capabilities of these small states are also major influences for regionalism, although the narrowed focus of their foreign policies may aggravate intraregional differences once the linkages with the global system have diminished.

REGIONAL PATTERNS OF INTERACTION

The magnitude and direction of East Asian trade development offer another perspective on Japan's place in the regional subsystem. Again the statistical picture is rather startling (see Table 3). Despite conditions of extreme political fluidity and economic uncertainty in most nations, despite almost continuous international disruption and war, and despite vestigial anti-Japanese feelings caused by World War II, Japan has moved into a commanding trade position in the region. Former European colonial powers have been displaced; China has been completely overshadowed; and the United States has been widely surpassed. Although, from 1958 through 1968 (the last year for which data for the whole region are available), all the major trading countries save Great Britain increased their trade sharply, in absolute terms, with East Asia,* Japan increased its trade by far the most —350 per cent to $4,665 million. More significant is the shift that occurred during this period in the proportions of the total trade

---

* In computing the total trade of the region and the proportion taken by the main trading nations, the total trade of Japan was excluded because of its disproportionate size.

TABLE 3

PERCENTAGE SHARES OF MAJOR TRADING COUNTRIES IN THE TOTAL
TRADE OF THE EAST ASIAN REGION,[a] 1958–68

(In millions of U.S. dollars)

	Japan	United States	United Kingdom	West Germany	France	Netherlands	Australia	China
1958								
Total Trade	1,046.1	1,495.9	690.4	553.7	270.0	236.9	233.7	231.2
Per cent	9.0	12.9	6.0	4.8	2.3	2.0	2.0	1.0
1959								
Total Trade	1,171.1	1,587.7	664.3	558.6	247.6	237.0	236.5	249.9
Per cent	9.5	12.8	5.4	4.5	1.0	1.9	1.9	2.0
1960								
Total Trade	1,486.4	1,634.2	785.9	645.0	316.3	218.1	234.2	233.0
Per cent	11.3	12.4	6.0	4.9	2.4	1.7	1.8	1.8
1961								
Total Trade	1,604.4	1,727.3	772.3	557.5	267.3	311.0	361.2	210.3
Per cent	13.2	14.2	6.3	4.6	2.2	2.6	3.0	1.7
1962								
Total Trade	1,667.8	1,793.2	711.1	513.2	277.9	179.8	260.7	141.1
Per cent	13.8	14.8	5.9	4.2	2.3	1.5	2.2	1.2
1963								
Total Trade	1,982.1	2,219.4	696.7	528.4	289.6	302.9	467.0	47.8
Per cent	16.1	18.0	5.7	4.3	2.4	2.5	3.8	0.4
1964								
Total Trade	2,381.0	2,112.9	750.7	584.9	382.3	399.9	454.7	63.1
Per cent	17.5	15.5	5.5	4.3	2.8	2.9	3.3	0.5
1965								
Total Trade	2,971.1	2,252.9	784.4	721.9	400.3	440.0	503.7	177.6
Per cent	20.0	15.6	5.4	5.0	2.8	3.0	3.5	1.2
1966								
Total Trade	3,623.2	2,611.6	814.6	867.0	412.1	328.1	445.3	135.2
Per cent	23.1	16.7	5.2	5.5	2.6	2.1	2.8	0.9
1967								
Total Trade	4,228.4	3,000.4	786.4	934.7	375.8	338.7	613.2	282.2
Per cent	25.6	18.2	4.8	5.7	2.3	2.0	3.7	1.7
1968								
Total Trade	4,665.7	3,569.1	775.2	992.6	383.3	332.3	559.0	n.a.
Per cent	27.9	21.4	4.6	5.9	2.3	2.0	3.3	n.a.

[a] Includes Burma, Cambodia, Communist China, Nationalist China, Indonesia, North Korea, South Korea, Laos, Malaysia (Malaya, Malaysia-Singapore), the Philippines, Singapore, Thailand, North Vietnam, and South Vietnam.

SOURCES: International Monetary Fund and International Bank for Reconstruction and Development, *Direction of Trade Annual,* 1958–62, 1963–67; May, 1968; March, 1969; June, 1969; and *Far Eastern Economic Review,* 1968 Yearbook; 1969 Yearbook.

of the region taken by these nations. None of the traders, except Japan and the United States, improved its position more than marginally. The Japanese share rose from 9 to 27.9 per cent—an increase of 210 per cent. The American share also rose markedly from 12.9 to 21.4 per cent, but the major portion of this growth came in the years 1965–68 and reflected largely the substantial, though temporary, expenditures related to the Vietnam war. The development of Japan's trade ascendancy during the past decade has served as a major argument for economic regionalism, and, according to estimates of the Japanese Ministry of International Trade and Industry, this trade will continue to grow at its present rate through 1975.[26]

TABLE 4

TRADE OF EAST ASIAN COUNTRIES WITH JAPAN AS A PERCENTAGE
OF THEIR TOTAL TRADE, 1968

(In millions of U.S. dollars)

Country[a]	Exports[b]		Imports[b]		Total		Rank (total trade)
	Amount	%	Amount	%	Amount	%	
Burma	12.4	15.2	39.3	24.2	51.7	21.3	1
Cambodia	6.6	21.5	20.3	28.0	26.9	26.1	2
China	224.2	16.9	325.5	29.5	549.7	22.6	1
Nationalist China	150.7	19.1	471.7	52.7	622.4	36.9	2[c]
Indonesia	251.9	34.7	146.6	22.1	398.5	28.7	1
South Korea	101.6	22.1	602.7	46.1	704.3	36.5	1[d]
Malaysia	343.4	30.6	104.5	15.9	447.9	25.2	1
Philippines	398.0	48.3	411.1	32.1	809.1	38.5	2[c]
Singapore	61.8	20.6	209.3	21.2	271.1	21.1	1
Thailand	147.0	34.4	365.5	35.8	512.5	35.4	1
South Vietnam	2.7	15.4	199.0	28.1	201.7	27.7	2

[a] North Vietnam and North Korea have been omitted because trade data with Communist nations are incomplete. Laos has been omitted because it is not statistically significant.

[b] As reported by Japan.

[c] Preliminary reports indicate that in 1970 Japan became the leading trading partner of both the Philippines and Nationalist China.

[d] Identical with that of the United States.

SOURCES: International Monetary Fund and International Bank for Reconstruction and Development, *Direction of Trade Annual*, 1963–67; *Direction of Trade*, June, 1968; August, 1968; February, 1969; March, 1969; April, 1969; May, 1969; June, 1969; July, 1969; September, 1969; November, 1969; February, 1970; and *Far Eastern Economic Review Yearbook*, 1969.

Just how fully the Japanese dominate intraregional trade is even more evident in the bilateral trade patterns between East Asian countries and Japan. As seen in Table 4, Japan is now the first or second leading trading partner of every country in the region, a degree of regional dominance comparable to that of the United States in Latin America. Clearly, there is a growing trade dependence among the nations in the region on Japan, for Japanese trade is now involved in such a large proportion of the international transactions of most East Asian countries that any sharp alteration of these relationships would result in severe economic dislocation. Indeed, such trading pre-eminence provides Japan with the opportunity for international influence beyond the economic sphere—an opportunity enhanced by the fact that the Japanese are not compelled by economic necessity to deal with East Asian nations.

Japan's trade with the leading non-Communist nations, notably Indonesia, the Philippines, Thailand, Malaysia, South Korea, and Nationalist China, is large, both absolutely and in terms of the proportion of each respective country's total trade. The trade with these countries will probably see the most rapid future expansion if the various schemes to promote economic growth in East Asia bear fruit. Not only does Japan have a strengthened position vis-à-vis other nations in the region, but its markedly increased economic stake makes involvement in the politics of the region more probable.

China's trade relations with non-Communist East Asian nations other than Japan have been extremely modest, especially when compared with Tokyo's. Its rupture with Indonesia has resulted in a loss of trade with that country, so that Peking now has significant commercial ties only with Malaysia, Singapore, Cambodia, Burma, and Hong Kong.* The Chinese are thus largely isolated economically as well as politically from most of the non-Communist countries in the region. In 1968, China had only $281 million of trade with the East Asian small powers. The

---

* Hong Kong was excluded from the regional trade figures because it is not a nation and because, despite sizable entrepôt trade, its heavy dependence on the mainland for basic needs skews the trading figures with China.

Trade with Cambodia has, of course, been disrupted by the outbreak of civil war in that country.

comparable figure for Japan was $4,116 million—roughly fifteen
times as great. Beyond Singapore and Malaysia, China's trade
was only token and left little opportunity for political pressures.
Moreover, Chinese exports in the past have been primarily light
industrial products and foodstuffs, areas in which the development programs in Southeast Asian countries are currently centered. This, of course, leaves limited potential for future expansion.

Beyond the network of trade ties created largely by the forces
of the economic market, the international climate has been particularly salutary for the modest moves undertaken by Japan
toward a somewhat expanded role in East Asia. As a result of the
Vietnam war, a rash of largely economically oriented multilateral organizations has sprouted among the non-Communist
nations. Participation in these organizations has cost the Japanese
very little and has not only yielded substantial good will but
promoted conditions of economic stability from which Japan
stands to profit handsomely. On the bilateral level, the normalization of relations with the Republic of Korea in 1965, and the
subsequent rapid expansion of trade, aid, investment, and political contracts, have forged a close link to the conflict-oriented
international situation on the Asian mainland—a link extended to
involve a "special" Japanese security interest in the communiqué
issued by Prime Minister Sato and President Nixon in November,
1969. The initiative taken in providing economic aid and promoting political relations with the Suharto government in Indonesia
has involved the Japanese to an unprecedented degree in a country
integrally caught in the morass of Southeast Asian international
politics. All of Japan's wartime reparations and the overwhelming proportion of its foreign aid are concentrated in the region
and constitute another growing level of contact. The combined
effects of these individually modest commitments is greatly to
increase Japan's contacts with and obligations toward non-Communist Asian states.

The power balance in East Asia and the patterns of security
arrangements are in the midst of upheaval. In the heady, anticolonial revolutionary politics of the early postindependence period in Southeast Asia, China seemed to be riding the wave of

the future. But the failure of the Great Leap Forward, repeated international setbacks (particularly in Indonesia), the widening rift with the Soviet Union, and the Cultural Revolution tarnished China's image and sharply altered the regional international milieu. The acceptance by most East Asian nations of Peking's efforts since 1970 to establish a more orthodox place in the international system should be seen essentially as recognition of the imperatives of the new realities of regional politics —not as an unqualified endorsement of the most recent cycle of "smiling diplomacy" by the People's Republic of China. Radical nationalism of the early postcolonial period has given way to a new emphasis on economic development and internal consolidation, for which Japan, not China, best serves as a model for the future. Internationally, the shift among the developing nations of Southeast Asia from global posturing to a heightened concern for national defense has increased awareness of the "China problem" and is a major influence for regionalism. In this regard, the most tangible evidence seen is the support, both direct and indirect, that most East Asian governments have given to the United States in Vietnam. South Korea's remarkable economic growth, military participation in Vietnam, and greatly broadened contacts with non-Communist nations have provided an additional dimension to regional politics. These developments, especially the intense concern over China and Communism, will strongly color, in the short run, future security alliances in the area, but they will not remove local conflicts (e.g., North Borneo), and the future, perceived threat from China will inevitably vary from state to state.

Despite their emphasis on national consolidation and defense, the small states of Asia still remain highly vulnerable to insurgency and "people's wars." The fluidity of politics within these countries, the link between Communism and nationalism in many societies,[27] and the proximity of China create conditions extremely conducive to this kind of conflict. Traditional defense calculations are peripherally relevant, and the promotion of security under these circumstances involves not simply maintaining order between states but developing within states economic and political conditions conducive to peace.[28] Since the costs of this sort of policy have proved exorbitant to the United States, it is likely that any intraregional alliance would have more restricted purposes or limited obligations and would depend at least partly on material aid from America. Nevertheless, it is important to emphasize that the intractability of the security problem for many small states, which has led a superpower to abandon a *full* effort to control power, will not lead to the abandonment of *all* efforts to control power, as suggested by some American critics.[29] International power politics will persist in East Asia.

For the Japanese, the recent dramatic changes in the military power balance in East Asia have brought them face to face with the problems of Asian security and altered the direction of the primary security threat from Moscow to Peking—from the global system to the regional subsystem. China's development of nuclear weapons has raised a credible and direct threat to Japanese security, which is certain to grow as Japan becomes more involved, and which has understandably provoked serious consideration of the heretofore unthinkable option—nuclear armament. Uncertainty about the future American security role in Asia, and the deeper involvement of Japan in regional nonmilitary affairs, have raised further questions about participation in conventional security issues beyond Japan. A new era is dawning, in which Japan's foreign policy must deal more realistically with the whole range of strategic considerations just at the moment when Tokyo's ties to the global system are being questioned and its security problems defined more narrowly in regional terms.

For China, the security situation is even more transitional and fluid. While aspiring to become a major actor in the global system, Peking's relations within the Communist world are undergoing fundamental change. Both superpowers, especially the Soviet Union, see China as a direct security threat, but they are also seeking to develop an Asian "balance" to the Chinese—thereby encouraging the trend toward regionalism and enhancing the importance of Japan.[30] China's limited capacity for military action reinforces its traditional Asia-oriented policy aims (which are reflected in the current Sinophobia of almost all nations in East Asia) and makes it likely that Peking will continue to give priority to political and military conditions within the region. Finally, with the intensification of a regional focus of international politics, the specter of Japan, so prominent in the troubled modern history of China, looms once again as a major potential rival.

The basic features of the East Asian subsystem are now visible in the accelerated trends toward regionalism in the military, as well as on the economic and political levels of international interaction. Japan and China will continue to play crucial, though widely differing, roles in this subsystem that, even more than the regional configuration in Western Europe, will add a new and distinct dimension to global international politics in the area of nuclear multipolarity. This is perhaps the most important international reality now confronting Japanese policy-makers.

3 Domestic Politics and Policy Toward East Asia

"Will you walk a little faster?" said a whiting to a snail,
"There's a porpoise close behind us, and he's treading on my tail.
See how eagerly the lobsters and the turtles all advance!
They are waiting on the shingle—will you come and join the dance?
Will you, won't you, will you, won't you, will you join the dance?
Will you, won't you, will you, won't you, won't you join the dance?"
"The Lobster's Quadrille"—Alice in Wonderland

Both the substance and the style of Japanese foreign policy have an *Alice in Wonderland* quality about them. The government has made major political decisions regarding foreign affairs only when it was no longer possible to avoid them, and then matters of factional and intraparty politics have intruded to blur international reality and stifle Japanese initiative. Public debate of the individual issues of the moment, not to mention matters of long-term planning or "national purpose," has normally been cast in vague, abstract terms or smothered in indiscriminate details. Discussions among Liberal-Democratic Party leaders, who are the real decision-makers, have taken place mainly in private. To be sure, the opposition left and the intellectuals have been obsessed with international affairs since the outbreak of the Korean war in 1950, but they have made little impression, because of political impotence and because their monologue has droned on in stereotyped terms within a very limited range—an undiscriminating moral commitment to peace, anti-Americanism, and disarmed neutralism. To consider an autonomous role

44

for Japan in international power politics is for them to think about the unthinkable. Those scholars and publicists who have participated in the "realistic" security debate since the mid-1960's have touched on the major foreign-policy dilemmas confronting Japan but then have assumed a quixotic position on the creation of international harmony without resort to force.

As in all democratic polities, the public has been only sporadically interested in, and largely shut out of, direct influence on foreign policy. The Japanese have moved from one concrete issue to another, absorbed in short-term international goals and internal political tactics, avoiding to an extreme degree matters of *Realpolitik* beyond the American alliance. Consequently, the foreign-policy debate within Japan and actual developments in international politics in Asia have progressed on generally parallel planes. In view of the internal political scene, the central question facing Japan today is not whether to select and execute a new strategic posture but, more basically, whether or not to join the international dance, and how to control its own movements once it has begun the dance.

One cannot fully comprehend Japan's role in Asia without delineating the fundamental features of its at once complex and bland style of foreign-policy formulation. Because Japan has been so fully allied with the United States, and because it has stayed on the sidelines of major international events, internal political considerations have assumed exaggerated importance in the foreign-policy-making process. Indeed, describing this process leads to discussion of the major features of domestic politics, particularly the party system, the nature of the conservatives' decision-making, and the resulting styles of policy leadership, as well as the roles of both business and public opinion.

THE PARTY SYSTEM

In Japan, international, not domestic, policies have been the main source of conflict between the ruling Liberal-Democratic Party and the splintered, largely left-wing, opposition parties. Since Prime Minister Shigeru Yoshida negotiated the Peace Treaty of 1952 and the accompanying security agreement with the United States, the conservatives have steadfastly maintained a pro-American and anti-Communist posture. The Communists, the various socialist parties,[1] and, more recently, the *Kōmeitō* (the political organ of *Sōka Gakkai,* a large, aggressive Buddhist sect that has sprung up since the end of World War II) have consistently, and often militantly, opposed the government and 'voiced support for various forms of anti-American, pro-Asian neutralism. Unrelieved partisan conflict on all major international issues has further deepened divisions among the politically articulate groups, has virtually precluded a constructive policy dialogue, and, by creating an atmosphere of confrontation, has inhibited policy initiatives by the government. Defeat of the Liberal-Democratic Party by the socialists or a left-of-center coalition would lead to a sharp break with past foreign policies, particularly regarding the United States and East Asia. Consequently, basic to all other questions about decision-making in Japan are the threat of a conservative electoral defeat and the specific import of the continuing confrontation by the opposition on matters of foreign policy.

During the past two decades, no nation has experienced more far-reaching and revolutionary socio-economic changes than Japan, and, conversely, no open political system (far less one with radically new institutions) has displayed greater continuity in politics. Until very recently, it was widely believed that this was a temporary phenomenon and that changes in the socio-economic substructure would ultimately alter the political superstructure in favor of a more "centrist" political group.[2] Continued urbanization was seen as strengthening the "modern" and progressive forces and undermining the tradition-dominated rural base and the older right-wing elements within the Liberal-Democratic Party. By placing the sociological cart before the political horse, the ability of the Liberal-Democratic Party to adapt successfully to politics in a mass society and to maintain party cohesion was underestimated.[3] Similarly, the ability of the left to adjust to the political realities of contemporary Japan and keep its own house in order was overestimated.

A look at the results of general elections since 1955 reveals how well the conservatives have utilized their political resources,

TABLE 5: VOTES IN GENERAL ELECTIONS AND PARTY AFFILIATIONS OF REPRESENTATIVES (In per cent)

Party	February, 1955		May, 1958		November, 1960		November, 1963		January, 1967		December, 1969	
	Vote	Seats	Vote	Seats	Vote	Seats	Vote	Seats	Vote	Seats	Vote	Seats
Conservatives												
Democratic	36.6	39.4	—	—	—	—	—	—	—	—	—	—
Liberal	26.6	24.0	—	—	—	—	—	—	—	—	—	—
Liberal-Democratic	—	—	57.8	61.5	57.6	63.6	54.7	60.6	48.8	54.0	47.6	59.3
Independent and miscellaneous	3.6	1.7	6.7	1.3	3.2	1.3	4.9	2.4	5.6	1.8	5.5	3.1
Total, Conservative and Independent[a]	66.8	65.1	64.5	62.8	60.8	64.9	59.6	63.0	54.4	58.8	53.1	62.4
Kōmeitō[b]	—	—	—	—	—	—	—	—	5.4	5.3	10.9	9.7
Reformists												
Left Socialist	15.3	19.1	—	—	—	—	—	—	—	—	—	—
Right Socialist	13.9	14.3	—	—	—	—	—	—	—	—	—	—
Communist and Farmer-Labor	2.9	1.3	—	—	—	—	—	—	—	—	—	—
Socialist	—	—	32.9	35.5	—	—	—	—	—	—	—	—
Communist	—	—	2.6	0.2	2.9	0.6	4.0	1.1	4.8	1.0	6.8	2.9
Social-Democrats	—	—	—	—	27.6	31.0	29.0	31.0	27.9	29.0	21.4	18.5
Democratic-Socialists	—	—	—	—	8.8	3.7	7.4	4.9	7.4	6.2	7.7	6.8
Total, Reformist	32.1	34.7	35.5	35.7	39.3	35.3	40.4	37.0	40.1	36.2	35.9	28.2

[a] It is not accurate in the strictest sense to combine the votes and the representatives of the independents and minor parties with the conservatives. However, virtually all elected independent representatives in all the elections become immediately affiliated with the Liberal-Democratic Party. Consequently, the combined figures do give a more realistic statistical picture of the effective structure of political power. In the 1967 and 1969 elections, one of the independents joined the Social-Democratic Party, and this is reflected in the table in the respective percentage of seats but not in the vote.

[b] The Kōmeitō first ran candidates in a general election in 1967 and because it is religiously based and purportedly "nonpartisan," it cannot be easily placed in either the reformist or conservative camp.

SOURCES: Asahi Nenkan, 1964, p. 264; Robert A. Scalapino and Junnosuke Masumi, Parties and Politics in Contemporary Japan (Berkeley: University of California Press, 1962), Appendix, Charts 2 and 3; and The Japan Times Weekly (International Edition), February 4, 1967; January 3, 1970.

while the over-all electoral effectiveness of the opposition has diminished. As can be seen in Table 5, the proportion of representatives held by the government has remained remarkably stable, despite a rather substantial growth in the popular vote for the opposition parties. In contrast, the decline of the Social-Democrats and the inability of the opposition to present a united front have led to a general failure of the latter to capitalize on its rise in popular support to augment its membership in the Diet. With but one exception, the Liberal-Democrats have controlled more than 62 per cent of the seats in the House of Representatives.[4] There is no comparably successful party record among any of the Western democracies over such an extended period.

Barring a party split or a truly unprecedented political or economic calamity, a variety of circumstances combine virtually to ensure continued rule by the Liberal-Democrats. The socialists are bad politicians. In contrast with the shrewd pragmatism of the conservatives, the socialists have combined ideological rigidity with the most distinguished record of tactical ineptitude among the major parties in industrialized nations.* Both of the socialist parties are internally fragmented, and these divisions have been aggravated by their prolonged absence from power and their scant hopes of ever participating in government. Especially among the Social-Democrats, this prolonged stay in the political wilderness has nurtured a kind of self-contained subculture that inhibits changes in policy and tactics despite repeated election defeats. The only way the opposition can hope to challenge the conservatives is by forming a coalition. But the prospects for a viable merger of these groups, even excluding the Communists, are not good. To bring together the essentially Marxist Social-Democrats, the non-Marxist Democratic-Socialists, and the religiously based Kōmeitō would involve an ideological sleight of hand of truly formidable proportions. Further, the

---

* An example *par excellence* of this ineptitude is found in the January, 1967, general election. The election was forced by the opposition as a result of scandals involving conservative cabinet ministers, but, in the campaign, the socialists doggedly emphasized their sympathies with the Cultural Revolution in China at the height of its excesses—which were being lucidly reported by Japanese correspondents in Peking. Not surprisingly, the party did not fare well at the polls.

long history of competition and enmity among the parties and the related rivalries within the labor movement make very improbable a coalition for anything but short-term tactics of opposition.

Even if gradual attrition of conservative strength in the Diet and a successful amalgamation of the more moderate opposition forces do bring an end to Liberal-Democratic Party dominance sometime in the next decade, it is not at all clear that this would precipitate a radical break with past policy. Decision-making within a motley left-of-center coalition, or one including the conservatives, would closely resemble the faction-dominated bargaining procedures of the last fifteen years and suffer the inherent inhibitions on policy initiatives imposed by this process. In sum, electoral change is not likely to bring about a fundamental alteration in Japanese foreign policy.

Despite the remoteness of a nonconservative government, the opposition, especially the socialists, will continue to have considerable influence on foreign affairs. Together, the opposition parties now command the support of 45 per cent of the national vote and have direct access to the formal policy-making process in the Diet. They thus occupy a strategic position from which to articulate and press their views. In the past, their influence has been exercised largely for negative ends—to obstruct governmental action and to turn the inevitably ambiguous results of all foreign policies to their own domestic political advantage through dramatic criticism of the government. Their effectiveness in these endeavors has been buttressed by the traditional Japanese notion of decision-making by consensus, not majority vote, in which there must be at least a formal display of unanimity on all major decisions. In practice, this makes overt dissent *per se* an effective means of opposition, because continuing open disagreement over any issue raises doubts about the legitimacy of the policy. This belief in consensus—that the government in power has a special obligation to respect and seek accommodation with the views of those out of power—has led the socialists to adopt rigid policy positions[5] and gives special import to the huge gap between the conservatives and the opposition over the goals of international action. Not only has this gap obviated suprapartisan cooperation, it has forced the Liberal-Democrats (despite their majority in the Diet) to consider scrupulously the socialist position on major issues or risk a serious political crisis that might, as in the 1960 Security Treaty incident, raise doubts about the stability of the entire political system.

The socialists affect Japan's international actions in another way. Their almost complete preoccupation with foreign-policy matters tends to force a similar emphasis in Diet debate in the election campaigns and in the mass media. In support of their causes, they have frequently adopted tactics of extralegal direct action—disruptive public demonstrations (*demos*) and physical obstruction of Diet proceedings—which offer dramatic embellishment to the otherwise drab political scene and are ideal grist for the journalists' mill. Such incessant and open criticism exacerbates conflict over all international issues and correspondingly magnifies the importance of domestic political considerations in foreign-policy decisions. It also assures that a vehemently anti-American position is continuously and conspicuously before the Japanese public. This capacity to shape both the intensity and the substance of the political debate remains one of the most effective means of foreign-policy influence for the Japanese opposition generally and the left in particular.

CONSERVATIVE DECISION-MAKING

The most important domestic determinant of Japanese foreign policy is the intraparty decision-making process of the Liberal-Democrats. All other components of the political system—the opposition, public opinion, pressure groups, and the bureaucracy —reach the major foreign-policy decisions primarily through access to this process. Formally, the Prime Minister (the president of the majority party in the lower house of the Diet) is vested with the responsibility for policy leadership, and he presides over both the governmental and the party institutions that are involved. In practice, however, his powers have been limited, primarily by the fragmented composition of the party and the close relationship between the formulation of policy on critical international issues and intraparty politics. Thus, the master-keys to conservative foreign-policy-making are the structure and dynamics of factional politics.

Factions (*habatsu*) are in a basic sense autonomous parties, having their own independent sources of finance, running their own candidates under the Liberal-Democratic Party label, and regularly caucusing for discussion of political strategy and, more recently, of policy matters.[6] The causes of factions are many and varied. In part, they reflect traditional social mores, for similar factional groupings appear in all Japanese organizations. The leader-follower relationship in the party *habatsu*—the leader providing funds, political positions, and services extending beyond economic assistance in exchange for personal loyalty—is a particular manifestation of general behavioral norms common in Japanese society. *Habatsu* have also developed in response to the peculiar conditions of the postwar political system. Perhaps their primary practical *raison d'être* is to provide the funds necessary for securing and holding office that usually neither the individual nor the party can fully supply. No person can long remain a successful faction leader without business connections or substantial personal wealth. Factions are most directly concerned with the distribution of power and positions in the party and in the executive offices of the government, with the biannual election of the party president (hence the Prime Minister) the event of major concern. Because the *habatsu* system has taken on quasi-institutional form since the late 1950's, conformity to its rules are required of any representative concerned with advancing his own political career. Finally, the multimember electoral system, which makes open competition between conservative party candidates within the individual constituencies inevitable, works to perpetuate factional rivalries. The Liberal-Democrats remain essentially a parliamentary party without a broad popular base or a strong national organization, and party leadership is recruited from those members of the Diet who can best operate in the complex and constricting world of the *habatsu*.

Major foreign-policy decisions have been deeply affected by conservative factional politics. Factions are essentially expediential groups, existing almost exclusively to gain political power in the form of cabinet and party posts. Therefore, apart from

those factions clearly on the periphery of power, a *habatsu* tends
not to become unequivocally identified with an issue regarding
which there is no general consensus, except when its leader seeks
to form or join a group to challenge the dominant "mainstream"
factional coalition of the Prime Minister.

The commingling of factional politics with foreign-policy-
making imposes serious restraints on the Prime Minister's capacity for leadership; for, as the head of a coalition, he must
seek at least the tacit agreement of the other faction leaders concerning not only the merits of policy but the current balance
of power within the party. Limits are also placed on the *kinds*
of policies that are undertaken. Initiative tends to be confined
to issues with minimum risk and controversy and having relatively calculable costs—which excludes all important international political matters. Moreover, by confounding domestic and
international considerations, the policy debate gives undue emphasis to the specific and short-term effects of each decision. Only
in the special "hothouse" international conditions in which
Japan has been able to operate can salutary results be produced
by this style of policy-formulation. Japanese foreign policy has
been successful because it has been restricted to issues free from
the imperatives of long-term strategic planning and decisive action required of a nation fully engaged in international politics.

A brief review of the major foreign-policy decisions since the
Occupation illustrates the inhibitions that have been placed on
positive leadership by this foreign-policy-formulation process.
The decision, in 1956, to normalize diplomatic relations with the
Soviet Union was preceded by two years of wrangling among
the conservative factions, during which the issue became fully
ensnared in the factional struggle for party control.[7] Indeed, by
mid-1956, Japan's Soviet policy came to be determined literally
by considerations of the intraparty battle rather than by international calculations. The decision to settle the issue was ultimately made only when the Prime Minister (Ichirō Hatoyama)
promised to resign, upon the signing of the agreement, to clear
the way for an immediate successor. In 1960, the American-
Japanese Mutual Security Treaty issue touched off the worst
political crisis of the postwar period. The crisis developed not

simply because of public and violent left-wing opposition, but because conservative faction leaders (notably Ichirō Kōno) opposed to Prime Minister Nobusuke Kishi chose to use this question to challenge his position in the party.[8] Again, the effectuation of the decision brought with it the downfall of the Prime Minister and a realignment of intraparty factions. Similarly, in the last years of the lengthy negotiations to normalize relations with the Republic of Korea, factional infighting among the Liberal-Democrats delayed the inevitable positive decision by Japan.[9] Only when public opinion shifted on what initially had been an unpopular move and the business community took a strongly favorable position did Prime Minister Hayato Ikeda force the issue. Although the government did not fall from power, factional uncertainties did destroy the opportunity for diplomatic initiative on this matter.

Prime Minister Eisaku Sato chanced to enjoy an unusually strong position within the party, for the three strongest rival faction leaders all died within several months after he came to power. Largely for this reason, he was able, in 1970, to proceed toward the reversion of Okinawa and to dampen controversy over extension of the Mutual Security Treaty free from the usual pressures of factional challenge. This exceptionally stable intraparty situation during the latter half of the 1960's also helped increase the importance of those elements of the bureaucracy and the formal party organs concerned with international affairs. It was a period of quiescence for the *habatsu*.

Division over relations with Communist China, and the related question of national security, brought into being in late 1964 and early 1965 two large intraparty groups quite different from the *habatsu* in structure as well as in purpose.[10] The Asia Study Group (*Ajiya Mondai Chōsakai*) and the Afro-Asia Study Group (*Ajiya-Afurika Mondai Chōsakai*) were established by individuals from different, often competitive, *habatsu* who shared a common interest in promoting a particular foreign-policy position. In general, the larger Asia Study Group has stood behind the official policy of close alliance with the United States and a strongly anti-Communist stance in Asia. In contrast, the Afro-Asia Group has pressed for a more independent international position for Japan, openly criticized the American role in Vietnam, and, above all, called for normalization of relations with China. Although primarily concerned with policy matters, these groups are broadly linked with the party factional alignment as well—the Asia group supporting the Sato "mainstream" coalition, and the Afro-Asia group comprising primarily representatives from factions opposed to the government for political as well as policy reasons.[11] Despite their connection with *habatsu* politics, these policy associations have been seen as potential bases for a party split or at least as harbingers of the eclipse of the personality-centered factions.[12] These groups and similar policy-defined organizations, such as the Dietmen's League for Normalization of Relations with Communist China—a motley multiparty group favoring early normalization of relations with Peking, established in late 1970 and nominally including a majority of Diet members[13]—do constitute fresh and important addenda to conservative foreign-policy-making, but their significance must be kept in perspective. Essentially, they are loose and informal associations, and they are more than balanced by the comprehensive claims of the *habatsu* system, the advantages of membership in the majority party, the impressive record of party discipline, and the shallowness of foreign-policy opinions of all but a marginal group of conservative Diet members. Although the politics of decision-making has not been much affected, these groups have greatly complicated both the substance of the party policy debate and the problem of policy leadership.

FORMAL INSTITUTIONS AND POLICY LEADERSHIP

During the past decade, the formal machinery for working out the details of Japan's foreign policy has expanded enormously. As Japanese overseas activities have grown in scope and variety, the various party standing committees (e.g., the Foreign Affairs Research Committee [Gaikō Chōsakai] and the Defense and Security Research Committee [Anzen Hoshōkai]), the periodic special committees specifically charged with foreign-affairs matters, and the more general Policy Affairs Research Council (Seimu Chōsakai) have all become more visibly important in the formulation of government policy.[14] Similarly, the contributions of not only the Foreign Ministry but particularly the staffs of the Ministry of Finance, the Ministry of International Trade and Industry (MITI), the Self-Defense Agency, and the Cabinet Research Office (Naikaku Chōsashitsu) have become integral and essential to the conduct of foreign affairs. This development eloquently bears witness to the widening scope of the nation's international activities and also raises a basic question regarding the style of decision-making and the substance of the goals pursued. Some critics of recent American foreign policy (especially toward Vietnam) have traced the ultimate responsibility for U.S. international behavior not to the conscious decisions of the President and his advisers but to the "vast foreign policy machinery of government" that "structures the decisions by setting out the choices."[15] Policy is thus seen as essentially the product of the process of decision-making, not the result of choice by political leaders. In a similar vein, one analyst of Japan discusses future allocations for defense and foreign aid in terms of competing domestic demands involved in the over-all budget-making process, thereby implicitly subordinating as a causal factor in policy-making any new political or strategic decisions by the government in response to altered international circumstances.[16] In a significant sense, Japanese policy is influenced by the complexity and momentum of the elaborate bureaucratic and consultative apparatus that is now central to decision-making. With the cultural imperative for consensus reinforcing the inherent tendency toward cautious accommodation of competing groups and views, the main effect of this development is to hinder still more decisive action and to increase the risks that a gap will appear between the policy needed for political and bureaucratic agreement and the policy best suited to the international situation. In short, expanded institutional procedures for foreign-policy formulation further check the likelihood of responsive and flexible leadership.

Gradual accretion of political power in the office of the Prime Minister, especially regarding foreign affairs, provides the main countervailing force to this tendency. More and more, the Prime Minister has come to exercise in fact the comprehensive powers that reside formally in the position. As the spokesman for the government and the representative of the nation in international negotiations, the Prime Minister's authority and visibility provide unique opportunities to draw public support for his views. Through skillful appointments, especially of the foreign minister and members on relevant party committees, he can do much to check opposition and to build intraparty unity on foreign-policy goals. Whether by design or not, each Prime Minister has assumed personal responsibility for, and identity with, one principal policy achievement during his administration,[17] and inevitably major foreign-policy decisions have fallen into this category. "Normalization of Soviet relations" (Hatoyama), "renewed security alliance with the United States" (Kishi), and "return of Okinawa" (Sato) have all come to be seen as keystones in the respective administrations. Because these critical decisions acquire a personal definition, the full prerogatives of office are employed to bring about their achievement—even if, as in the cases of Hatoyama and Kishi, this practice leads to the political demise of the Prime Minister. Thus, whether through shrewd political maneuvering or by a desperate assertion of political prerogatives, the Japanese Prime Minister is today able to bring about *a* decision regarding almost all critical international issues, the *habatsu* and institutional paraphernalia notwithstanding.

Business and Foreign Policy

Beyond the world of politics and government, the business community (*zaikai*) has had significant influence on foreign policy generally and toward Asia in particular, but the extent of its influence and the channels through which it flows are obscure. Business leaders are closely linked to the conservative party through their overt and covert financial support, through a sharing of basic political values, and through continuous and intimate personal contacts. Ties between the *zaikai* and MITI and the other government agencies that exercise close control over the day-to-day conduct of Japan's international economic activities are similarly close—inevitably so, given the overwhelmingly economic character of postwar foreign policy. Despite these connections, and despite the establishment of committees by the large business organizations to deal with specific foreign-affairs issues and continuing questions such as rearmament, there is no clear mutual understanding regarding the procedures through which business opinion should be brought into the policy-making process. Nor is there automatic agreement on the specific goals of the nation's foreign policy, beyond maximization of profits. The Japanese business world is complex and diverse, as are the attitudes of the various individuals and groups who speak out on international affairs. Consequently, as political and security considerations become involved with policies geared essentially toward maximizing economic benefits, it is as probable that these divisions within the *zaikai* will be aggravated as it is that the business community will simply rally around the flag.

The impact of organized business and individual businessmen on major Japanese foreign-policy decisions has varied. In the talks on normalization with the Soviet Union in 1956, and the events surrounding extension of the Mutual Security Treaty in 1960—both issues involving essentially political questions—the *zaikai* were unable to reach the policy process in a decisive way. However, at the end of the protracted negotiations leading to normalization of relations with South Korea in 1965, the leaders of the national business federations played a direct and significant role in working out the terms of the economic settlement that was crucial to the final agreement.[18] Any future moves toward an expanded political role for Japan in Asia will draw the business world more directly into the foreign-policy-making process, for it is precisely the immense growth of the Japanese material stake in East Asia, in which private enterprise has played the major part, that makes withdrawal from the political and military dimensions of the region's international relations more and more difficult. As the links between economics and politics grow, and as Japan moves toward full participation in power politics, the relationship between the *zaikai* and the Liberal-Democratic Party cannot but take on added importance and be placed under strain—thereby adding another uncertain element to Tokyo's policy toward East Asia.

PUBLIC OPINION

In addition to the spheres of politics and business, public opinion is the most important influence on the formulation of foreign policy. Indeed, its importance has been given unusually strong emphasis, partly because of the democratic ideals underlying the postwar political order, and partly because the contemporary political role of mass opinion contrasts sharply with that in the prewar period. Nevertheless, it is necessary to recognize at the outset that the Japanese public does not differ in politically significant ways from the public in Western nations, where the impact of public opinion on the conduct of foreign affairs is seen as complex but more limited.[19] To make even a cursory appraisal of the specific ways in which Japanese foreign policy is affected, a distinction must be drawn between "articulate opinion"—the overtly expressed views of important individuals, organized groups, and the mass media—and the "climate of opinion"—the broadly held attitudes of the general public.[20]

Articulate opinion has an activist dimension, and in Japan it has been employed primarily by the opposition, especially through demonstrations, policy pronouncements in the mass media, and interpellations in the Diet. These tactics have, of course, also been utilized on occasion by opposition factions within the conservative party and various interest and opinion groups. Both the style, and to a large extent the impact, of articulate opinion are basically shaped by the mass media, who report and distill the opinions expressed, provide much of the factual background immediately relevant to the issue at hand, and are able to present forcefully their own views to the policy-makers and the general public alike. These exchanges constitute the essence of the public foreign-policy debate, but whether they affect the decision-making process is a function of the dynamics of a party system continuously dominated by the conservatives, an electoral system in which personalities and domestic issues consistently take precedence, and an elite political culture (involving bureaucrats and conservative party leaders) that lacks a tradition of democratic decision-making. In the recent political history of

Japan, the government has paid scant attention to the critical expressions of articulate opinion in making major decisions,[21] leaving the conduct of international affairs essentially as the preserve of a narrow elite.

What is true about articulate opinion regarding influence on specific foreign-policy issues is also true about mass opinion. The overwhelming majority of the public in Western democracies is uninformed about, and uninterested in, foreign policy, and the views displayed in the vast number of polls regarding foreign affairs are shallowly held and expressed largely in response to prodding of the questioners. Japan falls in this pattern. As surprising as it may be to learn that one out of four Americans in mid-1964 was wholly unaware of the war in Vietnam,[22] it is no less surprising to find that, in mid-1967, one out of three people in Japan did not know that a Communist government controlled China.[23] This extreme lack of awareness, which finds repeated examples, and the amorphous, unarticulated form of mass opinion, assure that the public normally plays a passive role in the foreign-policy-making process, and that the Japanese Government, therefore, has wide latitude for policy leadership.

Foreign-policy goals are, however, shaped by the climate of opinion in two important ways. Policy-makers respond instinctively to attitudes that are integral to the social and political milieu of which they are members, such as the strongly negative Japanese attitude regarding Koreans and the powerful, albeit ambivalent, attraction to China. Even more important, as politicians they are influenced by the focus and tone of the general opinions manifested in polls, in election trends, and in the overall debate on foreign policy. An example of a general and undisciplined mass feeling (mood) with political import is the pacifism that has for so long prevailed in all strata of Japanese society and imposed limits on governmental action regarding rearmament. The equally broad and loosely structured sentiments of nationalism, universally acknowledged as rapidly expanding in recent years, also fall into this category. These moods in a basic sense transcend the conflicts over specific policies and are properly seen as constituting the consensus on which all foreign policy must rest without polarizing or destabilizing the whole political order. Japan is now in the throes of moving from a "pacifist" to a "nationalist" mood, and changes in the current climate of opinion regarding foreign affairs will touch in fundamental ways both general and specific Japanese policies toward Asia.

As Japan moves toward greater involvement in East Asia, control of foreign-policy formulation will continue to rest with the Liberal-Democratic Party or a conservative-dominated coalition, thus assuring perpetuation of the past diffuse style of decision-making. It is a style that precludes bold leadership, that makes virtually inevitable a passive and reactive international role at a time when the nation is ever more deeply involved in the region, and that assures that policy will proceed incrementally, on a case-by-case basis. The elitist nature of this process, therefore, places the government in a position to deal with short-term international exigencies with limited concern for internal political pressures; but, conversely, this risks provoking deep and long-term polarization of domestic politics. Even given a national mood more tolerant of activist international goals, it is hard to be sanguine about the prospect that Japanese political leadership will adjust smoothly to the swift variations characterizing the East Asian international dance.

4 Foreign Policy Goals and East Asia

East Asia holds a special place in Japan's contemporary international perspective. The actual importance of Asia for the Japanese has been obscured by the caution and ambiguity of the policies taken and the cacophony of the accompanying domestic political debate. To sort out and evaluate Japan's aims in the region, it is necessary to consider the policies adopted by the government, the various positions taken by politically articulate groups (especially the Liberal-Democratic Party elite), and the attitudes toward international affairs broadly shared throughout the society—the national mood. More and more, the involuted politics and cautious policies of Tokyo have become important and uncertain variables in the already complicated mosaic of international relations in East Asia.

A New Diplomatic Tradition

To a degree extraordinary for a country of its size and importance, Japan has conducted international relations without a foreign policy in the usual sense of the word. Ensconced behind the American alliance, the Japanese have avoided questions of security and power politics while aggressively concentrating on aims appropriate to an expanding international trading company, i.e., enlarging overseas contacts for the purpose of maximizing economic well-being. Not only have Japanese actions abroad resem-

61

bled those of a trading company rather than a nation, but the policy debate within the conservative party and among its many left-wing critics has been implicitly based upon assumptions appropriate to this perspective. To be sure, this debate has concentrated on the day-to-day problems of diplomacy and has been cast in the issues and the lexicon of contemporary global and regional politics, but until very recently there has been a consensus that defined Japan's international role in narrowly economic terms within the framework of a nation-state system.

If there is a prophet for this policy, it is not Marx or any contemporary figure but, curiously, Richard Cobden, a leading British proponent of free trade in the mid-nineteenth century. Cobden's prescriptions for Victorian England correspond closely with Japan's postwar priorities. His abomination of war and armaments and his derision of military intervention and of the balance-of-power concept in international affairs strike responsive and recurring chords in contemporary Japan.[1] Cobden's faith that free trade could serve as a sufficient cause for international harmony is only slightly beyond the main thrust of Japanese policy, and his equation of national welfare with increased productivity captures the essence of the postwar mood. By simply substituting "Japan" for "England" and "Asia" for "Europe," his century-old policy prescription reads like any number of position papers published by the Foreign Office during the past two decades.

> [Japan,] by calmly directing her undivided energies to the purifying of her own internal institutions, to the emancipation [and increase] of her commerce . . . would aid more effectively the cause of political progression all over the continent, than she could possibly do by plunging herself into the strife of [Asian] wars.[2]

More important than the coincidental similarity between the views of a Victorian liberal and contemporary Japanese foreign policy is the identity this gives to the latter in the Anglo-American diplomatic tradition. This tradition stresses the application of moral concepts in determining the goals of foreign policy, reluctantly accepts the existence of international power politics, and extends the belief in "progress" rooted in democratization and economic development from intra- to interstate politics. As Arnold Wolfers has convincingly argued, these predispositions in large part grow out of political experiences of the United States and Great Britain, especially the freedom from direct attack or invasion enjoyed by both countries prior to the shattering political and technological impact of World War II.[3] Japan, similarly insulated from the pressures of *Realpolitik* following catastrophic defeat in 1945, has understandably slid into a comparable approach to foreign affairs, one that its American "tutor" did much to promote.

Japan's postwar outlook constitutes a radical break with the premises and actions of its prewar diplomacy. At that time, Japan was deeply caught up in imperialist power politics in East Asia in a manner more in keeping with the continental European tradition, with its emphasis on compelling and impersonal forces that shape relations between states, the pervasive and continuous presence of conflict, and the necessity for substantial military capacities to carry out successful diplomacy. In the 1920's and 1930's, Anglo-American efforts to promote international peace through disarmament were categorically rejected by Japan as "too idealistic" for Asia.[4] Thus, Japan is now living with a fractured diplomatic tradition. This is of special significance, since the formulas of disarmament and the "outlawry of war" are even more utopian for the establishment of peace in Asia today than they were in the earlier era. For Japan, this situation presents a particularly agonizing and difficult problem; for, as the anomalous isolation from East Asian politics dissolves with the bipolar order, not just the policies but the fundamental assumptions underlying the policies of the past two decades will be challenged. For Japan to move from a largely apolitical and noninvolved position toward a political and interventionist one is likely to precipitate deep internal political cleavages—such as those the United States experienced first in the 1940's, in the move from isolationism to internationalism and, more recently, in the continuing, more bitter turmoil touched off by the indecisive and "immoral" war in Vietnam. Consequently, in considering the specific policies that make up postwar Japanese diplomacy, it should be borne constantly in mind that their full meaning must include their cumulative effect on the basic premises underlying the country's general posture toward the international system. It is very much an open question whether Richard Cobden alone can continue for long as the prophet for Japan's foreign affairs.

Postwar Goals

The broad themes of Japanese foreign policy since the end of the Occupation are modest in character and limited in number. Regarding the global system, they have centered on cultivating the alliance with the United States to provide for Japan's security and to fuel national economic development,* achieving a respected status in the world international order and developing economic relations with all nations, while gaining acceptance within the club of advanced industrial powers. Additionally, unique emphasis has been placed on relations with the countries of East Asia. Although these themes are most obviously manifested in the pronouncements of political leaders, the details of the picture are filled in by the aims implicit in the actions Japan has taken. In the same style employed by the conservative factions in intraparty politics, the nation has moved expediently in foreign affairs, without ideological or even policy commitments beyond vague slogans praising peace and propitiating the *status quo,* while allowing maximum room for maneuver on specific issues. A straightforward acceptance of the government's articulated goals provides only a partial representation of the direction of Japanese foreign policy. This point can be properly grasped only through a broad examination of the actual pattern of Japan's international behavior and the Japanese perception of it through the prism of domestic politics.

"Status" and "peace" have been the keystones of this policy. Reflecting the peculiar importance accorded to status within Japanese culture, and paralleling the successful diplomatic campaign during the Meiji period, which brought initial acceptance in the Western international system, a self-conscious effort has been conducted since the end of the Occupation in order, as Prime Minister Sato put it, "to occupy an honored place in inter-

---

* The Japanese-American alliance is treated separately and at length in Chapter 6.

national society."[5] Negatively, Japanese policy has involved an attempt to erase the stigma connected with the outbreak and conduct of the Pacific War. Positively, it has taken on concrete meaning through participation in various international organizations (especially the United Nations and the Organization of Economic Cooperation and Development [OECD]), in sponsoring international extravaganzas, such as the 1964 Olympics and "Expo 1970," and in cautious efforts at aid and cooperation legitimatized in terms of international brotherhood and humanitarian ideals.

Japan, a "great power" throughout the first half of the twentieth century, has taken as its postwar reference group the industrialized Western nations. International respectability has been successfully pursued by achieving economic well-being while gaining full and unqualified political acceptance among the global elite. Policies toward the poor and newly independent nations have been accorded lower priority. Despite the moral tone of Japan's diplomacy, no real effort has been made to identify with the Third World or with the causes that these countries have championed. Modest gestures in extending aid have been clothed in the accepted shibboleths of "development"; but, in reality, they have served primarily to cultivate markets and resources directly beneficial to Japan, and not to promote the broader international goals commonly associated with the North-South problem. In a manner befitting a rising member of the Victorian middle class, Japan has prudently sought status within its economic means, with minimal political costs and commitments.

Above all, Japan, in this quest, has specifically eschewed military competition and chosen the banner of peace. Indeed, throughout the history of modern international politics, no nation of comparable size and importance has effectively implemented an overtly pacifist position for such an extended period. This in itself constitutes a formidable barrier to any abrupt change of course toward an autonomous military role. In the immediate future, a *volte-face* from the pacifist tune that has been trumpeted for two decades would involve political risks prohibitively high for any government. Similarly, the timing and scope of any move toward a more independent security posture would necessarily be tempered by the web of political and economic interdependence with the global international community and the world economy. This is not to imply, however, that the future will simply be an extension of the past, devoid of change. Not only are there ample opportunities for Japan to become a regional power, but such options find support in the intense, albeit somewhat suppressed, concern for Asia that has consistently run through Japanese foreign policy in the postwar era.

Geographically, culturally, racially, and historically Japan is part of Asia. This truism needs restatement, because short shrift is given to the special importance of Asia to Japan in many discussions of the contemporary scene that emphasize the "modernizing" effects of prosperity and the strong ties that have grown between Tokyo and the distant but advanced nations in Europe and North America.[6] The burden of history alone tilts Japan's international perspective sharply in the direction of the neighboring region. From the war with China in 1894–95 until defeat in 1945, Japan engaged continuously in far-reaching military, political, and economic activities in Northeast Asia. Its position as a great power and its relations with the other great powers were defined in terms of its policies and capacities in this area. That is, Japan's status in the global system was a function of its position in the region, not the reverse. Since Japan's emergence as a modern nation-state, the country's diplomatic ideals have been most fully defined in terms of relations with the region, especially in the vague and romantic concept of pan-Asianism. In view of the muted and inchoate aims pursued since 1945, this Asian-oriented nationalism constitutes the only fully developed international mission in modern Japanese history.

Both the reality and vision of this diplomacy were shattered by defeat and the elaborate effort during the American Occupation to discredit completely the ideals on which it was based. It is common to view 1945 as a watershed in Japanese history, one marking political, social, and psychological discontinuities in the society. In some ways, this perspective is valid, and certainly the radical changes that have touched all aspects of the political socialization process make it necessary to distinguish between prewar and postwar generations. However, it is easy to exaggerate the break with the past, especially for the elite that has made foreign policy since 1952. These men were all nurtured in the highly developed nationalist tradition of the earlier era, which neither the agony of defeat nor the new circumstances of the post-1945 scene totally eradicated.[7] Furthermore, because age is strongly correlated with leadership, during the next decade or two the government will continue to be controlled by the prewar generation.[8] In the critical years immediately ahead, when Japan will confront the problem of a new, more independent international strategy in Asia, the destiny of the nation will be guided by men who straddle two contrasting diplomatic traditions.

EVOLUTION OF ASIAN POLICY

During the 1950's, policy toward the East Asian region was conditioned by internal weaknesses and uncertainties and by highly fluid international conditions. Japan, living under the cloud of the past war, deeply dependent on the United States in a bipolar world, and still a relatively poor nation, had only limited policy alternatives. Ensconced behind the comprehensive American alliance, Japan approached its international problems individually, without a cohesive set of goals, while according preeminent and unquestioned priority to economic recovery. The modest variations in policy toward Asia were more than anything a function of the personalities of successive Prime Ministers. In this period of rehabilitation, what is surprising is not that there was an absence of more positive commitments to Asia, but that, in the groping search for a new international *modus vivendi,* regional policy received as much attention as it did.

Throughout these years, normalization of political relations and a new base for economic (i.e., commercial) ties were the two topics around which Asian policy revolved. Overcoming foreign ill will caused by the war proved a long and onerous task. Under the terms of the San Francisco Peace Treaty, Japan was obliged to pay reparations to the recently occupied Asian countries. The amounts were to be determined through direct bilateral negotiations, and, under a generous arrangement designed to minimize the burden on Japan's economy, the payments were to be in Japanese goods and services. One effect of this settlement was to assure a certain continuity with prewar diplomacy by channeling attention toward, and establishing a material presence in, Asia. Reconciliation with the region became a primary goal for all early post-Occupation Prime Ministers. Good will trips were made to Southeast Asia by Shigeru Yoshida (1954) and Nobusuke Kishi (1957 and 1959), and reparation agreements were signed with Burma (1954), the Philippines (1956), Indonesia (1958), and South Vietnam (1959). Additionally, the Nationalist Government on Taiwan waived all reparation obligations regarding China when a peace treaty was signed in 1952, and a modest, war-related claim by Thailand was settled in 1954. Through these gestures, aimed essentially at righting past wrongs, Japan smoothly resumed normal diplomatic and economic relations with non-Communist Asia.[9] Nevertheless, Japan's role remained modest and peripheral. Positive contacts were restrained and formal—a whisper lost in the cacophony of the internal and international political turbulence of the postcolonial era—and the two most important regional problems—relations with China and Korea—were left in abeyance.

Policy toward Asia concentrated on what Foreign Minister Shigemitsu called "economic diplomacy," that is, promoting trade and economic cooperation in order to "stabilize" the region. Entry into the Colombo Plan aid program and the Economic Commission for Asia and the Far East (ECAFE) added a multilateral dimension to regional economic activities, but the scope of cooperation never extended much beyond reparations and commercial transactions. Both the spirit and the limitations of this economic diplomacy are exemplified by the aid scheme Prime Minister Kishi promoted during his first tour of Southeast Asia. Japan was to provide large-scale technical and industrial assistance—but the funds for the project were to be provided by the United States![10] Washington, however, quietly declined to underwrite another nation's aid program. In spite of serious inhibitions and the inevitably modest nature of the policies undertaken, Japan, by 1960, had developed the rudiments of a new pattern of economic and political interaction with non-

Communist Asia; the basic contours of this pattern remained remarkably intact during the ensuing decade.

The government of Hayato Ikeda (1960–64) is rightly noted for its low-profile approach to domestic and foreign problems. As the keynote to his diplomacy, Ikeda declared Japan to be, in company with the United States and Western Europe, one of the "three pillars" of the non-Communist world. Emphasis was thus given at once both to relations with the advanced Western powers and to special, albeit vaguely defined, national responsibilities in Asia.[11] Regarding the latter, Ikeda went further than any of his predecessors to link Japan's fate with that of the region. Spurred by the Sino-Soviet split, Japan increased its trade with China sharply and steadily, even though it continued to enforce the formula of separating politics from economics. Its relations with non-Communist Asia also progressed, with a notable expansion of trade, new aid programs, and good-will visits by the Prime Minister in 1961 and 1963. Ikeda's most important single legacy was decisive progress toward normalization of relations with South Korea, although the agreement was formally consummated a year after illness had forced his retirement. By laying the basis for extensive, long-term contact with its former colony, Japan was pulled further out of splendid isolation and closer to the turmoil of the continent. Moreover, the government came increasingly to recognize broader obligations in Asia, repeatedly encouraging political support of, as well as economic aid to, states in the region; for, "without stability in the Asian nations that border the Communist bloc, it would be hard to secure our own safety."[12] These were quiet, transitional years, with no fundamental changes in Japanese diplomacy and no serious external developments to provoke them; but even during this period of quiescence, the country was nudged significantly toward greater regional engagement.

A new phase in foreign policy came about almost simultaneously with the establishment of the government of Eisaku Sato in late 1964. From the first, Sato's philosophy and style of diplomatic leadership was the same as those of his predecessors, but a series of international events led the Japanese to become more deeply involved in East Asia and gradually forced reconsideration of their entire orientation to foreign affairs. In October, 1964, China successfully detonated a "nuclear device." The event immediately cast the question of Japan's security in a new light and subsequently magnified the uncertainties caused by the excesses of China's Cultural Revolution. Southeast Asia also took on decidedly larger dimensions in Japan's foreign policy following the rapid escalation of America's involvement in Vietnam in early 1965 and the spurt in Japanese contacts with Indonesia in the wake of the sudden political eclipse of President Sukarno later that year. Formal restoration of relations with South Korea in 1965 was immediately followed by a burst of commercial activities and governmental aid. Two themes stand out in the many and varied short-term actions that were taken in the latter half of the decade and in the accompanying domestic debate over long-term foreign policy goals: One reaffirms the special role of Japan in fostering economic development in the region; the other concerns the political and security problems with which the changing international milieu confronted Japan.

Economic diplomacy toward Asia took on more specific meaning in terms of both actions and aims. Japan became a leading participant in the many conferences and international organizations that were spawned to promote economic cooperation and a sense of regional unity among non-Communist Asian nations. On the multilateral level, Tokyo became the largest regional contributor (equal to the United States) to the Asian Development Bank, initiated a series of ministerial conferences to coordinate regional aid and planning, and joined the Asian and Pacific Council (ASPAC), an association founded in 1966 to foster political as well as economic interaction among member nations. Bilateral programs of reparations and aid were extended, and the Prime Minister visited South Korea and the countries of Southeast Asia during 1967. These actions, supplemented by the accelerated growth of trade, tied Japan *de facto* more securely to the region.

In recognition of this condition, an attempt was made to articulate a general rationale for the mounting number of discrete but related actions involved in this economic diplomacy. In 1967, Foreign Minister Takeo Miki's concept of an "Asian-Pacific zone'" brought together the loose strands implicit in past policies in a vision that made clear both the hopes and the dilemmas of his country's foreign policy at a crucial juncture in history. While proclaiming a special role for Japan in Asia distinct from that of the United States, particularly in promoting a new Asian consciousness, Miki at the same time saw as imperative the participation of the other advanced nations of the Pacific rim in efforts to foster the economic development of the region. The alternative to this line of action, according to Miki, was clear: If Japan did not boldly contribute to ameliorating the North-South problem in Asia by dissolving the basis for regional conflict through economic development, involvement in power politics was inevitable.[13] As the purposes of foreign policy became more clearly defined, the interconnections among economic, political, and security concerns were increasingly, albeit reluctantly, acknowledged.

China's successful development of nuclear weapons touched off the first serious postwar debate on security policy. The details of this debate will be elaborated subsequently,* but here it is important to note the unanimity with which the problem of defense was defined essentially in Asian terms. Some saw the Chinese as basically peace-loving and provoked only by American aggression in Asia. Others viewed China as an actual or potential threat from which protection could be provided only by the American alliance. On all sides, however, the target of concern for Japan's safety now shifted toward China, and the states on its periphery, and perceptibly away from the still important but separate issue of the Soviet Union. There was also a change in the intensity of interest as well as in the direction of threat. Not only was the potential nuclear menace of China more plausible, but, as the situation in Vietnam deteriorated in 1966 and 1967, the possibility of being drawn into a general Asian war raised new doubts about the limitations inherent in the unqualified character of the American alliance. Although, late in 1969, the government formally declared a "security interest" in South Korea and Taiwan and the negotiations regarding the return of Okinawa raised new questions about defense, no change was made in Japan's

* See Chapter 7.

basic security position. Yet, a new threshold of concern was crossed, and the continuing security debate has since been centered within this same regional framework.

With the heightened concern for security came a gradual change in the tone of Japanese diplomacy. Policy pronouncements came to be cast more in terms of specific national interests than of abstract moral goals, and emphasis shifted to defining Japan's independent responsibilities and needs. In a marked departure from previous administrations, Foreign Minister Etsusaburō Shiina noted that "competition [with China] for Asia has already begun."[14] As Japan edged toward a broader and more competitive international role, the internal debate sharpened over specific issues as well as ultimate goals, and policy focused increasingly on East Asia.

In recent years, implicit or explicit support has been given by various groups involved in foreign-policy-making to the Asia-first theme in official policy. Within the Foreign Ministry, there is an identifiable circle of individuals, centered mainly in the Asian Bureau, that consistently stresses a more pronounced regional concentration of diplomatic activities independent from those of America. Although still eclipsed by the so-called Anglo-American group, which places overwhelming priority on relations with the United States, the voice of those Gaimushō bureaucrats inclined toward Asia has grown much stronger since Japan has come to play a more active role in the region.[15] In less obvious fashion, the socialists have consistently preached a kind of Asianism as a means of establishing independence from the United States and promoting solidarity with "neutralist" nations and especially with China.[16] Also speaking from a left-of-center political position, the *Asahi Shimbun* has repeatedly pressed its own formula for a new Asian policy, emphasizing the importance of greater autonomy from America, of the promotion of regional peace through aid, and of "standing on the side of Asian nationalism."[17] Finally, although businessmen on the whole take a broadly internationalist position rooted in the realities of the global economy, it is both startling and significant that, in 1970, the president of Mitsubishi Trading Company, the largest such company in Japan, could say, "It is the right time for us colored

Asian races to unite again. I believe the concept of the prewar Greater East Asian Co-prosperity Sphere was right. We must just look to the interests of our own country."[18] Thus, a unique orientation toward Asia has demonstrable appeal across almost the full range of the political spectrum, especially in fulfilling the growing desire to play an independent international role.

Specific Policy Problems

From the perspective of Japanese politics, however, Asia is more a series of individual issues than an undifferentiated ideal. To convey an accurate impression of political awareness on this subject, it is necessary to ask which part of Asia is first, in official policy and in the foreign-policy debate. In broad terms, three areas may be distinguished: (1) China and Taiwan, (2) Korea, and (3) Southeast Asia.

Southeast Asia stands lowest both in policy priority and in the political consciousness of the Japanese. Despite the historical emphasis on pan-Asianism, Japan had only limited contact with countries in this area, outside of the wartime Occupation, until the spurt of economic and political activities of the past decade. Serious scholarly research regarding the region is still in its infancy, while the public image has been provided essentially by sporadic and fragmentary mass-media reports centered on the war in Vietnam. Indeed, although Japan has developed substantial international interests in Southeast Asia, this has not been fully or widely recognized within Japan. Time may bring awareness and involvement, but, in the near future, any security crisis in the area will tend to be seen more in terms of its implications for the credibility of U.S. commitments in the Far East than in terms of the actual importance to Japan of the particular country. Neither Southeast Asia as a whole nor any of its individual countries has yet acquired a position of intrinsic importance in Japanese politics similar to that of Korea or China.

Internationally, Korea is an indispensable link to Asia, and bilateral relations touch critical elements within Japanese politics in important ways. For the forty years prior to the end of

World War II, Korea was fully incorporated into the Japanese Empire, and this experience profoundly colors the contemporary situation. Japan was perhaps the most demanding of the colonial powers. Policy in Korea involved rigid suppression of all movements on behalf of self-government, an elaborate effort to stifle Korean culture, and the creation of a semideveloped but strictly "colonial" economy. Today, a sense of remorse and guilt exists among some Japanese, but the dominant attitude still embodies the hubris and condescension of the earlier era. This attitude is nurtured by the status of the sizable Korean minority in Japan, which is primarily the product of a forced migration during the height of the Pacific War to replenish the industrial labor force. Holding an unassimilated position not unlike that of the blacks in the United States, the Koreans not only contribute disproportionately to the lower classes and semicriminal elements, but a majority actively participates in the politically vocal and militantly Communist General Federation of Korean Residents in Japan (*Chōsōren*). This organization bitterly opposed the treaty normalizing relations with South Korea and was instrumental in prodding the Japanese Government into the politically embarrassing act of repatriating almost 100,000 Korean residents to North Korea. From several perspectives, Korea has a highly developed, extremely negative definition in Japan.

Nevertheless, this unfavorable image is more than counterbalanced by the almost universal acknowledgment that the political and security fate of Korea is inseparable from that of Japan as well as by the wide range of contacts with South Korea since 1965 that has drawn the two countries ever closer together. The Nixon-Sato communiqué of November, 1969, formally proclaiming Tokyo's security interest in South Korea, rests on widespread and long-standing recognition of, and concern for, Korea's inevitable special place in Japan's policy toward Asia. The *prima facie* historical and geographical reasons have been bolstered substantially by the *de facto* ties that have developed during recent years. Already, Japan is linked to South Korea, through trade, aid, and direct investment, to a degree unequaled by any other Asian nation, and such connections are expanding at an accelerated rate. Close and direct cooperation between the businessmen in each country has rapidly progressed, and Japan is now replacing the United States as the main prop of Korea's ambitious plans for economic growth. Overt political contacts have proceeded in more muted fashion and at a slower tempo, but common membership in multilateral regional organizations has supplemented regularized bilateral consultations on all matters of diplomacy. Surrounding and strengthening these more visible forms of interaction is a web of communications involving tourist visits, regularized cultural and athletic exchanges, multiple daily air and sea transportation connections, and the like, which has made South Korea as accessible and familiar to many Japanese as some of the more remote parts of their own country. Although remarkably ambivalent sentiments are involved, the Korean question has salience and meaning within Japan to a degree exceeded only by the issues of China and the United States. This fact cannot but magnify any problems that may arise from the current policy to strengthen cooperation with South Korea on all but the military level.

To a degree exceeded only by relations with the United States, the China problem has been central to the foreign-policy debate in Japan. Extraordinary emotional and symbolic importance surrounds this matter for all politically articulate groups. China stands at once as a revolutionary, nuclear-armed Asian power directly competing with Japanese interests, as the critical key to war or peace in the region, as the world's largest untapped market, and as a nation with which cultural-historical connections are so profound as to cast an aura over things Chinese that transcends immediate political-economic conditions. That the issue supersedes party lines is evident from the composition of the groups pressing for early normalization of relations with Peking—a motley coalition of nostalgic, conservative Sinophiles from the prewar era, opportunistic businessmen in search of the legendary China market, and left-wing Maoist revolutionaries. Because of the salience and definition this issue already has within Japanese politics, adjustment of Tokyo's external relations involving the two Chinas has been greatly complicated. Moreover, the intensity of concern has led to definition of the China problem narrowly in terms of Japan's relations with the two Chinese governments and to exaggeration of the capacity of Japanese diplomacy to affect the situation.

Japanese policy toward China has been conducted on two distinct levels. With the right hand, they have limited diplomatic recognition to the Nationalist Government on Taiwan, have sponsored the "important question" resolution in the U.N. General Assembly (thereby delaying Peking's admission to the world organization), and have cultivated extensive economic ties with Taiwan. With the left hand, Japan has established, through various cultural, political, and economic missions, more varied and extensive contact with the mainland than with any non-Communist nation. The result has been a kind of *de facto* "two-China" policy, involving an ostrich-like position regarding the uncomfortable political and security issues raised by the growing international power of Peking. In fact, the triangular relationship involving Tokyo, Taipei, and Peking graphically illustrates both the advantages and the inadequacies of the trading-company philosophy underlying Japanese foreign policy. Although the Nationalists and the Communists adamantly insist that there is only one China and that politics and economics are inseparable, and have sporadically imposed restrictions upon Japanese trade, Japan has steadily expanded economic relations and now is the leading trading partner of *both* Chinas. However, the spate of foreign moves to recognize Peking that began in late 1970 has forced Tokyo to face squarely a major political choice likely to involve substantial international economic and political costs, no matter what policy is adopted. This decision has become more difficult and internally divisive precisely because it has been so long avoided.

Japan is bound to Nationalist China by far more than economics. In 1952, as one of the American-stipulated conditions for the San Francisco Peace Treaty ending World War II, a separate peace treaty was signed with Chiang Kai-shek's government. For the Japanese, the latter treaty ended one of the ugliest aspects of the war (for which they felt a particular moral onus) and publicly established an obligation to support internationally the Taipei government. Another special and important link with Taiwan grows out of the legacy of fifty years of Japanese colonial rule over the island. This has been most visibly manifested in the attitudes of several leaders of the "Taiwan lobby" within the Liberal-Democratic Party, who have thus far been successful in promoting close relations between the two countries, and in the more broadly shared sentiment that the Taiwanese should be provided with at least the choice of whether or not they wish to join the Communist mainland. The recognition of a special security interest in Taiwan in the November, 1969, Sato-Nixon communiqué, which is consonant with the American goal of an Asian defense system under Japanese leadership, strengthened the commitment between Japan and non-Communist Asian nations and aggravated the fears of the Chinese Communists that Japan will indeed play a major military role in the region. In view of these circumstances, any Japanese move toward recognition of Peking will almost inevitably involve a "two Chinas" formula to salvage the political and economic interests of Taiwan.

Yet, there are strong incentives for Japan to move boldly toward *rapprochement* with the Chinese Communists. Every Prime Minister has recognized that Japan's policy toward Peking is the cornerstone for relations with all Asian nations. If, from an overall perspective, Japan's China policy has been schizophrenic, it has been prayerfully passive regarding Peking. Bilateral relations have been determined almost entirely by responses to Chinese policies or to the drift of world politics. China's criticisms of Japan have been monotonously consistent and have concentrated on opposition to the alliance with "American imperialism," on collaboration with the "Taiwan bandits" and the "American puppet regime in South Korea," and, more recently, on the rise of "Japanese militarism." What is likely to initiate change in Tokyo-Peking relations, however, is not a policy shift by the Chinese but the alteration of the climate of world opinion to bring China more fully into international society, and the pressure this trend places on Japan to acquiesce. Peking will also constitute the most important single influence on how Japan approaches the question of rearmament, and in this regard the very meaning of the threat that is posed will be fundamentally shaped by the pervasive internal political struggle over the China problem.

All Japanese political parties have been deeply touched by this question for some time. It was the issue of China policy that gave rise to the policy factions among the Liberal-Democrats in 1964–65, and these divisions have been encouraged by frequent "informal" visits of prominent conservative leaders to Peking and Taipei—an inevitable product of the *de facto* two-China policy. Reaching a satisfactory internal consensus will severely strain party unity and tax the leadership of the Prime Minister. The socialists, too, have made China policy an intra- and interparty political football. Since there is general agreement on the need to recognize the People's Republic, the socialist debate has centered on how fully Maoism should be accepted and on the tactics for politically exploiting the issue within Japan. Since the mid-1950's, it has become popular sport for socialist leaders to visit Peking, ritualistically denouncing Japanese and American imperialism and then having a heated intraparty wrangle about the real meaning of the words employed. The Japanese Communist Party (JCP) has greatly improved its internal unity and electoral strength since abandoning a pro-Chinese position in the mid-1960's. Now, however, when it is *de rigueur* among the left to support reconciliation with Peking, the JCP is in the awkward position of being labeled by the Chinese as one of the "great enemies" of the true Communist revolution, and it was barred as a sponsoring organization of the Dietmen's League for Normalization of Relations with Communist China. This surge of interest, and the Babel of voices regarding an issue that will be at best ambiguously resolved, insures that China policy will continue to be deeply affected by internal events and will bedevil Japanese diplomacy over a wide range of issues.

NATIONALISM

Nationalism is the dominant feature of modern Japanese history. More than in any other industrialized society, nationalism was self-consciously and effectively nurtured as the political vehicle for facilitating rapid economic growth, and it fired the activist and expansionist foreign policy pursued until 1945. Catastrophic defeat and the Occupation reforms discredited and undermined the nationalist ideals on which prewar policy and society were structured, and prolonged abstention from international politics has cut off all opportunities for a recrudescence in response to outside pressures. Thus, nationalism fell from a position of comprehensive dominance to become the *bête noire* of Japanese politics. Correspondingly, the groups and individuals directly advocating a nationalist reconstruction since the end of the Occupation have been extremists and romantics operating on the fringes of Japanese politics, with a very narrow membership base and an appeal more psychological than ideological. Japan has been living in a kind of nonnationalist era. Yet, the historical and psychological discontinuities implied in this pattern, the peculiarly homogeneous, insular, and involuted nature of Japanese culture, and the absence in Asia of the economic and political conditions conducive to the international and supranational collaboration found in Western Europe make extension of the recent past singularly improbable. The real questions are what sort of new nationalism will develop and how it will affect foreign policy. Broad answers to these questions have already been suggested.

Most frequently, speculation has focused on a nationalism born in the ashes of the current Japanese political order. A breakdown of the present system as the result of economic catastrophe, or a massive disenchantment with the ability of governmental institutions to cope with domestic and foreign problems, would indeed raise the specter of a radical, authoritarian, and militarily oriented movement more akin to European fascism than to the militarism of Japan after 1931. There are no immediate prospects for such a development from internal causes, and it could be precipitated only by a global international calamity of the proportions of the Great Depression. In view of the most rapid and massive upheavals in popular life experienced by any modern society, Japanese social and political stability has been remarkable. The psychic and social tensions brought on by altered working conditions, the rootless impersonality of urban living, and the discomforts of environmental decay have spawned periodic protest movements. In this respect, the most visible challenges to the system have been the violent acts of alienated

student radicals and the spectacular 1970 ritual suicide of novel-
ist Yukio Mishima, a brilliant, right-wing political activist, who
sought spiritual identity with anti-establishment youth. These,
however, are rumblings at the periphery of politics and do not in
themselves represent strong currents in the mainstream. Such
radical gestures of protest are relevant to the emergence of nationalism through whatever direct or indirect impact they have
on the current political establishment.

Postwar nationalism has not been rooted in societal malaise or
in the congruence of traditional values and prevailing political
ideals but, rather, has focused on the issues confronting the nation as a result of changes in the external world. Nationalist sentiments have been channeled through the pattern of legitimate
political authority and have moved forward, *pari passu,* with the
foreign policies of the government and the tone and temper of
the accompanying policy debate. All political parties, socialist
and Communist[19] as well as conservative, have claimed to speak
on behalf of nationalism in forwarding their policies and have had
an important part in delineating those issues most commonly
used to define Japan's autonomy: the thread of Asianism described previously, the clamor concerning an independent defense force, and relations with the United States. It was only in
the latter half of the 1960's, in the wake of growing self-
confidence that followed economic recovery and the tangibly
more important place that Japan held in the world, that these
issues came to be defined with an intensity reflecting an increased
sense of national consciousness and an emphasis on Japanese interests rather than vague, universal, internationalist ideals. Despite the immediate disagreements over policies regarding China
and rearmament, foreign policy has progressed with the more or
less general recognition that national interests have priority, even
if this leads to a competitive international role. Nevertheless, the
style of postwar nationalism (and the popular mood by which it
is sustained) is orthodox and restrained, finding direction primarily from international, not internal, forces.

Rearmament is the issue with the greatest potential for setting
into motion internal forces to disrupt the moderate nationalist
course the country has followed. The gap between the pacifist

climate fostered by the "peace" constitution and the need to expand Japanese defense capabilities is already such that any abrupt decision to accelerate rearmament or to deploy troops abroad would polarize opinion and bring forth vocal political forces from the right and the left. A policy shift of this sort could be brought about only by a sudden escalation in the perceived threat to Japan's security interests, in turn precipitated by an American strategic withdrawal from the region. Ironically, the rise of militarism on a nationalist tide within Japan, the fear of which is most strongly expressed by the Chinese and the Russians, is most likely to be generated by external, not internal, events and to have an anti-American coloration.

Given the nature of the current international system and Japan's place in it, the government could not easily undertake a foreign policy on behalf of expansionist aims or geopolitical ideals. At the same time, engagement in Asia may—short of neutralization of the region or an unprecedented and permanent outbreak of peace—eventually require the use of force as an instrument of diplomacy on behalf of Japan's material interests. Whether internal political forces will allow a policy of *Realpolitik* in support of such a limited international goal within the current rubric of moderation, or whether the nationalist pot will boil over, remains the critical unanswered question. Until the appearance of an internal or external catalyst, however, nationalism in Japan will remain latent, embryonic in structure and ambiguous in content—and a secondary influence on Japanese foreign policy.

For Japan, Asia holds a position of unique importance. From the very outset of the modern era, the nation's international identity has been established primarily in terms of relations with the East Asian region. This motif runs through the postwar era, albeit somewhat distorted and stunted by the economically skewed emphasis given to foreign policy. Yet, Japan has demurred from participating in the political tempests and uncertainties in the surrounding region. Like the snail in the Mock Turtle's song, it "would not, could not, would not, could not, would not join the dance." The finality of this disclaimer, however, is doubtful. In light of the strong regional predisposition and a reactive international role assured by the pattern of decision-making, the course of Japanese foreign policy will continue to be shaped to an extraordinary degree not by internal decisions but by external relations with East Asia.

5 Japan in Asia: The Entangling Web

A vast and complex web centering in Tokyo now extends throughout East Asia. It has been woven bit by bit without a comprehensive plan. At the center of this web lie two developments: Japan's spectacular economic growth, and the peculiar international conditions created by America's heretofore virtually unqualified military commitments to contain Communism in the region. The former inevitably led to rapid penetration of geographically near and historically familiar markets, while the latter resulted in a concentration of contacts among non-Communist regional states. Because this pattern of interaction came into being in a largely spontaneous and undirected manner, it is rarely seen or considered as a whole—especially by the Japanese politicians, diplomats, bureaucrats, and businessmen responsible for its construction. Although a general design is lacking, each strand—trade, bilateral aid, multilateral international institutions—has its own rationale, and together they display the assumptions and principles on which the meaning and durability of the entire structure depend. Elaboration of these various links between Japan and East Asia and an appraisal of the foundations on which they rest lay bare a basic question confronting Japanese foreign policy: Will this web continue to provide nourishment for its proprietor or will it become a snare in which the spider itself is brought into violent struggle?

The answer depends to a great extent on whether and how these largely economic ties are given meaning in political and security terms. Given the gravity of the implications, this issue has been accorded surprisingly little attention, despite a mounting regional concern about Japanese economic domination and an impending security vacuum once the Nixon Doctrine is fully implemented. To be sure, achievements buried in the details of trade statistics and balance-of-payments accounts are of an intrinsically different order from the stentorian threats and ominous uncertainty of China's foreign policy. Moreover, the Japanese have made little effort to play up their expanding regional position because of the still unpleasant echoes of the Greater East Asian Co-prosperity Sphere, and because even indirect reference to a possible role in *Realpolitik* carries high domestic political risks. However, the web linking Japan to the regional subsystem has already attained politically significant proportions for all the parties involved, and it demands scrutiny as one of the fundamental realities of the new East Asian international order.

REGIONAL COMMERCIAL RELATIONS

East Asian Trade

Japan has operated as a highly successful trading company; it is in the area of trade and, more recently, in investment that the most tangible and important contacts with East Asia have been established. Despite extensive governmental direction of Japan's international economic activities and the integral role foreign aid has played in regional economic intercourse, the flow of capital and goods has been fundamentally directed by the forces of the global market place ås perceived in Tokyo. This outlook has encouraged consideration of the economic dimension of Japan's foreign policy as a separate and discrete entity (a focus that the government has publicly been wont to promote) and has further obscured and understated the political implications of these activities. Any effort to assess the full meaning of commercial relations for Japan's international role must be prefaced by a straightforward description of the relevant statistics on aggregate trade and investment with both the region as a whole and with individual East Asian countries.

The magnitude and distribution of Japan's trade with East Asia vividly underscore Japan's position of pre-eminence. As previously indicated (Table 3), Japan has moved far ahead of the global industrial powers to become the leading trader in the region as a whole and is expanding its share of the market at a far greater rate than that of any other nation. Even more importantly, the Japanese are now the primary trading partner of every major non-Communist nation in the region except South Vietnam (Table 4). In 1968, Japan was involved in more than 31 per cent of the trade of these countries and thus held a position of primacy that was so great, merely in terms of volume, as to provide enormous influence on the stability of virtually all of their economies. Moreover, the proportion is expected to expand rapidly in the coming decade, placing Japan in an ever more dominant position. Before examining this pattern of commerce, two other aspects of Japan's general regional trade role deserve clarification: the importance of East Asia in Japan's total trade picture, and the degree of continuity from the pre–World War II pattern to that of today.

Despite the trends toward regional trade dominance, the present and potential importance of Japan as the leading trader in East Asia has often been questioned. The argument, cast entirely in economic terms, gives special emphasis to the fact that Japan, as a developed global power, has interests that naturally lie in strengthened relations with the other industrial powers, as well as to the fact that trade with East Asia has not grown as a percentage of the nation's total trade. There has, indeed, been a notable shift in the direction of Japan's exports from developing to developed nations, with the industrialized countries of the West absorbing 55 per cent in 1968 as against only 35 per cent in 1956.[1] Imports from the developing countries have actually fallen slightly during this same period (from 60.7 per cent in 1956 to 56.2 per cent in 1968), so that over-all trade with economically developed states has risen by a smaller, though nevertheless significant, amount, from roughly 50 per cent to 56 per cent. These changes simply provide specific illustration of global trade patterns between industrialized and underdeveloped nations. Primary-goods economies have increasingly lagged behind the developed countries both in internal growth and in the expansion of international transactions.[2] In view of this situation, the stable proportion of Japan's total trade that has been held by East Asia (Table 6) is properly seen as an impressive exception to the general trend. Since 1958, this trade has risen in absolute terms almost 550 per cent (from $1,046 million to $6,868 million), and its proportion in Japan's total trade has gone up slightly from 17.7 per cent to 18 per cent. Even if the special stimulus provided to East Asian economies since 1965 by American expenditures related to the Vietnam war is taken into account, the region has clearly maintained its important position in spectacularly increased Japanese trade.

The sharp disparity between prewar and postwar Asian trade is commonly cited as further evidence of Japan's global rather than regional economic orientation. This is only partially correct. Even a cursory examination of the aggregate data reveals that

TABLE 6

JAPAN'S TRADE WITH THE EAST ASIAN REGION,[a] 1958–70

Year	Amount (in millions of U.S. dollars)	Per cent of Japan's total trade
1958	1,046.1	17.7
1959	1,171.1	16.6
1960	1,486.4	17.4
1961	1,604.4	16.0
1962	1,667.8	15.8
1963	1,932.1	16.6
1964	2,381.0	17.4
1965	2,970.4	19.1
1966	3,623.2	20.1
1967	4,018.4	19.4
1968	4,665.7	19.0
1969	5,719.8	18.5
1970	6,868.4	18.0

[a] Includes Burma, Cambodia, Communist China, Nationalist China, Indonesia, North Korea, South Korea, Laos, Malaysia, the Philippines, Thailand, Singapore, North Vietnam, and South Vietnam.

SOURCES: International Monetary Fund, *Direction of Trade Annual*, 1963–67; March, 1969; June, 1969; and Ministry of Finance, Japanese Government, *The Summary Report: Trade of Japan*, 12 (1970).

there is far greater continuity with the prewar era than is evident from a gross comparison of current trade statistics with those of the 1930's. This point becomes clear if the appraisal is made from a region-wide perspective, with a distinction drawn between Northeast Asia (China, Taiwan, and Korea) and Southeast Asia. In terms of trade, Japan is now more extensively related to Southeast Asia than at any time in its recent history. As shown in Table 7, the average of Japanese trade with the main nations of Southeast Asia in 1966–70 is approximately 50 per cent greater than the comparable average for 1934–36, the last years before the war in China distorted trade figures. Despite numerous and formidable political and economic obstacles, Japan has to a large extent replaced the former colonial powers and greatly raised its stake in the area.

TABLE 7

PREWAR AND POSTWAR JAPANESE TRADE PATTERNS IN ASIA

(In per cent of Japanese trade)

Year	Southeast Asia[a]			Northeast Asia[b]		
	Imports	Exports	Total	Imports	Exports	Total
Prewar						
1934	5.5	11.0	8.0	33.6	40.7	37.0
1935	6.1	8.8	7.4	35.1	41.2	38.3
1936	7.6	8.1	8.0	34.9	44.4	39.1
Average	6.4	9.3	7.8	34.5	42.1	38.1
Postwar						
1966	10.4	12.3	11.4	6.2	9.9	8.1
1967	10.4	13.4	11.8	4.9	10.4	7.5
1968	10.1	12.1	11.1	4.2	11.4	7.8
1969	10.2	11.8	11.0	3.7	11.0	7.5
1970	10.0	10.5	10.2	4.1	10.9	7.3
Average	10.2	12.0	11.1	4.6	10.7	7.6

[a] In the prewar period, this includes British Borneo, Burma, French Indo-china, Indonesia, Malay States, the Philippines, Singapore, and Thailand; in the postwar period, Burma, Cambodia, Indonesia, Laos, Malaysia, the Philippines, Singapore, Thailand, North Vietnam, and South Vietnam.

[b] In the prewar period, this includes China, Korea, and Taiwan; in the postwar period, China, Nationalist China, North Korea, and South Korea.

SOURCES: International Monetary Fund, *Direction of Trade Annual*, 1963–67; March, 1968; March, 1969; Bureau of Statistics, Office of the Prime Minister, *Nihon Tokei Nenkan (Japan Statistical Yearbook)*, 1935–37; and Ministry of Finance, Japanese Government, *The Summary Report: Trade of Japan*, 12 (1970).

Prewar trade with China, Taiwan, and Korea was, of course, enormously greater than it is now (Table 7), and this precipitous decline has led to the comparatively diminished economic importance of East Asia for Tokyo. However, in Northeast Asia, prewar Japan operated in a uniquely favorable milieu that included imperialist and colonial prerogatives—circumstances both artificial and no longer possible, which produced trade that only in the loosest sense could be called international. In the wake of devastating defeat for Japan, revolution in China, and war in Korea, relations among these nations were variously clouded and disrupted for more than a decade and a half after 1945. During the 1960's, however, Northeast Asian economic links with Japan showed remarkable growth. Abetted by the ever deepening Sino-Soviet split, the prosperity of Taiwan, and the development of normal ties with a politically stable and economically revitalized South Korea, Japanese trade with these countries has more than doubled since 1965. Total trade in 1969 reached roughly $2,370 million, approximately equal to that of Japan with the entire European Economic Community and Great Britain. Economic relations with Northeast Asia (especially the two Chinas) are extremely vulnerable to changes in the political winds; but, short of a major external upheaval or a decision by Tokyo to participate in power politics, Japan will consolidate its position as the leading trading partner of these nations much in the pattern of recent years. Consequently, to say that Japan is no longer as Asian-centered economically as it was in the prewar period is really to say that Japan's relations with its former colonies and with China have drastically altered. Within the radically different contemporary Asian landscape, the Japanese have established themselves as the dominant economic power.

Distribution and Composition of Trade

Economic benefit has been the guideline for Japanese trade, but its regional distribution manifests a political bias through concentration in non-Communist countries. It is not surprising that the flow has been tilted in one direction, but the degree of bias is startling. In 1969, trade with non-Communist regional nations having a combined GNP of approximately $47 billion reached $5.1 billion—well over *seven times* the trade with the Asian Communist bloc, whose GNP totaled roughly $58 billion. This trade distribution, which is reinforced by other forms of contact, is so skewed that even sudden and dramatic *rapprochement* with the Chinese Communists (who, effectively, are the Communist bloc) could not alter, in the immediate future, its basic structure and the pull it exerts on the direction of Japanese foreign policy.

Political conditions have also significantly affected the ebb and flow of trade within the non-Communist segment, as is graphically illustrated by three recent developments. American expenditures related to the Vietnam war have stimulated the growth of the economies of allied nations (notably South Korea, the Philippines, Taiwan, Thailand, and South Vietnam) and thus directly contributed to the surge of Japanese exports to these countries.[3] Normalization of diplomatic relations in late 1965 led to a quadrupling of Japan–South Korea trade over the next four years. Similarly, Japan's trade with Indonesia doubled during this same period as a result of the political coup in 1965 and subsequent policy shifts by the military government toward broader foreign contacts and internal economic development. With the continued expansion of Japan's economic stake in the region, similar local political changes and attendant side effects will take on greater importance and further complicate this web.

Economically, the most distinctive feature of Japan's East Asian trade is the consistently large surplus that has been generated—a surplus that reached $1.5 billion in 1970. Because there are wide variations in bilateral trade balances, this enormous deficit is borne almost entirely by four or five countries. The uneven distribution of trade reflects, above all, the peculiar composition of Japan's imports from the region. Raw materials constitute the bulk of these imports, and nations endowed with primary goods needed by the Japanese economy have been more than able to balance their bilateral accounts. Indonesia, Malaysia, and, until very recently, the Philippines have regularly run up sizable trade surpluses. In each case, more than 60 per cent of their exports have been concentrated in one or two primary commodities: timber from the Philippines, petroleum from Indonesia, timber and iron ore from Malaysia.[4] Future demand for these goods will expand with the growth of the Japanese economy, thereby allowing these nations to minimize or to avoid the trade deficit problems that plague their neighbors. In 1969, the remaining regional countries outside the Communist bloc, principally South Korea, Taiwan, Thailand, and Singapore, together showed an incredible deficit of approximately $2 billion out of trade totaling only $2.8 billion. Moreover, the conditions underlying this extraordinary imbalance are more or less chronic, due to the limited appeal of the main exports of these countries (e.g., light manufacturing products and selected foodstuffs) in the Japanese market and the large and growing demand for Japan's principal exports in their developing economies.

East Asian nations now rely on Japan for nearly 40 per cent of their total imports, which constitute roughly one-quarter of Japan's exports. These remarkable totals have come about even though Japan has not given the region top priority as an overseas market because of the risks and limitations inherent in uncertain political and economic conditions there. In their successful drive to achieve global economic prominence during the 1960's, the Japanese concentrated on cultivating trade with developed and stable nations, treating East Asia as a "secondary market . . . stressed only when the domestic economy slowed."[5] However low in priority in the global economic perspective viewed from Tokyo, Japan's trade efforts in the region were far more aggressive than those of any other nation. The heavy machinery and chemical products, which have become the mainstays of Japanese exports, ideally complement the needs of the area's developing economies. Accordingly, more than 70 per cent of the exports to every country in the region have centered on the capital equipment needed in the early stages of industrialization. This demand, and Japan's competitive advantages in meeting it, will assure trading leadership despite continuing huge imbalances in bilateral accounts, illustrating how economic forces alone work to pull Japan into the network of East Asian international relations.

China

Trade with China holds a unique place in Japan's postwar international economic relations. Ostensibly, it has been built on the principle of separating politics from economics. However, this approach is categorically rejected by Peking, and Japanese trade policy in fact has been strongly colored by domestic and international political pressures that have continuously focused on Peking. Relations with China are the touchstone of Japan's policy toward Asia, and the deep internal political and emotional divisions over this issue have inevitably had an impact upon the extensive bilateral commercial contacts that have developed. At the same time, many sectors of the Japanese business world are particularly affected by the pull of the legendary China market, and the Chinese Communists also have compelling economic incentives to import the attractively priced and high-quality products of Japan's industry. Consequently, behind the statistical picture of Sino-Japanese trade lies a complex set of political and economic influences.

Since the establishment of the People's Republic of China in 1949, trade between the two countries has fallen into two distinct periods. Through 1960, trade tended to be quite modest and was shaped primarily by political decisions in Peking. It rose to its highest levels in 1956 and 1957, when China's foreign policy featured the peaceful coexistence line. An abrupt shift occurred in 1958 with the abortive Chinese effort to topple the Kishi government and influence the general election by suddenly canceling all orders in a recently signed trade pact.[6] Only token exchanges took place during the following three years, but the split with the Soviet Union and the attendant decline in Sino-Soviet trade ushered in a new era in China's relations with Japan.

Tokyo held an advantageous position as Peking was forced to turn to non-Communist industrial nations for the products needed for its economic development plans. By 1965, the Japanese had become the main supplier to the China market. As seen in Table 8, the level of bilateral intercourse soared from $23 million to $621 million in the five years that Japan became the leading trading partner of Peking. In 1966 and 1967, Japan

TABLE 8

SINO-JAPANESE TRADE, 1958–70

Year	Japan's trade with China (in millions of U.S. dollars)			Per cent of total Japanese trade			Per cent of total Chinese trade		
	Exports	Imports	Total	Ex-ports	Im-ports	Total	Exports	Imports	Total
1958	50.6	54.4	105.0	1.8	1.8	1.8	2.8	2.9	2.9
1959	3.7	18.9	22.6	0.1	0.5	0.3	1.0	0.2	0.6
1960	2.7	20.7	23.4	—	0.5	0.3	1.0	0.1	0.6
1961	16.7	30.9	47.6	0.4	0.5	0.5	2.0	1.3	1.7
1962	38.5	46.0	84.5	0.8	0.8	0.8	3.0	3.9	3.4
1963	62.4	74.6	137.0	1.1	1.1	1.2	5.0	6.1	5.5
1964	152.7	157.8	310.5	2.3	2.0	2.1	12.6	15.4	13.9
1965a	245.3	224.7	470.0	2.9	2.8	2.8	16.5	18.7	17.6
1966	315.2	306.2	621.4	3.2	3.2	3.2	18.2	18.2	18.2
1967	288.3	269.5	557.8	2.8	2.3	2.5	19.3	17.6	18.4
1968	325.5	224.2	549.7	2.5	1.7	2.1	16.9	29.5	22.6
1969	390.8	234.5	625.3	2.4	1.6	2.0	16.2	31.5	23.0
1970	568.9	253.8	822.7	2.9	1.3	2.2	n.a.	n.a.	n.a.

a The difference between the import and export figures cited here and those cited in Table 5 is due to using Japanese trade figures in this table and Chinese trade figures previously to keep consistency in the sources of the data.

SOURCES: International Monetary Fund and International Bank for Reconstruction and Development, *Direction of Trade Annual,* 1958–62, 1963–67; *Direction of Trade,* March, 1969, June, 1969; *Far Eastern Economic Review Yearbook,* 1969–71; Dick Wilson, "China's Economic Prospects," in Ruth Adams, ed., *Contemporary China* (New York: Vintage Press, 1966), p. 193; and Ministry of Finance, Japanese Government, *The Summary Report: Trade of Japan,* 12 (1970).

slightly increased its proportion of China's total trade, but the absolute amount temporarily dipped as a result of the dislocations of the Cultural Revolution. As internal conditions stabilized in China, trade once again began to expand rapidly and reached $823 million in 1970.

Considering the various international economic and political obstacles that have stood in the way, this is a notable record of growth. Membership in the Western alliance has been a major inhibition for Japan. Under the restrictions of COCOM (Coordinating Committee for Export Controls to Communist Countries), which the Japanese have scrupulously followed, only a highly selective list of "nonstrategic materials" could be exported to China. In addition to this overt limitation, the United States has occasionally sought to discourage the rapid expansion of trade with the Chinese Communists, even when the Japanese dealt only in approved goods.[7] Because Japan has had extensive commercial dealings with both Taiwan and Peking, but diplomatic relations only with the former, trade has been a natural weapon for both Chinas to use against Tokyo when political issues have spilled over into their triangular relationship. Taiwan has repeatedly threatened and occasionally employed sanctions against Japan, but trading contacts with the mainland have been continuously conducted under a cloud of political threat and invective.

Trade with Peking has proceeded through two channels: direct contracts with "friendly" Japanese firms (more than 80 per cent of the trade) and the so-called memorandum trade, involving an annual formal agreement between representatives of the Chinese Government and a quasi-official Japanese delegation. The ritual required for negotiating this memorandum is drolly analogous to the kowtow ceremony required of all foreigners facing the emperor in traditional China. A delegation including leading business leaders and conservative politicians has regularly signed a communiqué condemning in florid terms the "rise of Japanese militarism" and "U.S. imperialism" and endorsing the other current propaganda shibboleths related to Sino-Japanese affairs, thus repudiating the entire foreign policy of Tokyo and displaying on behalf of trade an attitude of national political self-abnegation that would have made a British East India Company representative blush in the heyday of imperialism.[8] As part of this "annual humiliation"—as the communiqué is called by Japanese critics—three political principles (essentially, rejection of the "two-China plot" and abrogation of the Japan–Nationalist China Peace Treaty), and the political conditions required of any Japanese company wishing to trade with Peking, are set forth. The latter require that Japanese enterprises not have large investments in Taiwan or South Korea or be affiliated with American firms. In the past, these requirements have been circumvented by working through third parties; but, as the large

Japanese corporations with established and extensive interests in Taiwan and the Republic of Korea (e.g., Toyota Motors) move into trade with China, the dilemmas posed by insistence on the inseparability of politics and economics will become more acute.

The most important impediment placed by the Japanese Government in the way of trade with the mainland has been the restriction on the use of loans from the official Import-Export Bank. In 1963, the Bank did provide financing for the export of a synthetic fiber plant, but, in response to strenuous objections by the Nationalist Government, former Prime Minister Yoshida sent a letter in mid-1964 to Generalissimo Chiang Kai-shek promising that such funds would not be used again in trade with Peking. For the next eight years, Japan adhered to the substance of the Yoshida letter, and trade with Communist China was financed with the somewhat more expensive credits from commercial banks until this practice ended early in 1972 in direct response to President Nixon's visit to Peking.

Sino-Japanese trade has flourished, with one partner asserting the inseparability of politics and economics and the other rejecting this principle, and the actual pattern of bilateral relations graphically illustrates how difficult and complex it is to separate these two levels of international interaction. Despite the obviously political tone of Peking's policy, trade with Japan has developed essentially for economic reasons (indeed, out of necessity) in the shadow of bitter anti-Japanese invective and Tokyo's continued close alliance with the United States. Conversely, political considerations have been integrally involved in Japan's "exclusively economic" policy. Virtually every move for increased trade has involved, either directly or indirectly, a decision by the Japanese Government, including the extension of private credits as well as Import-Export Bank loans. It is through the sanctioning of expanded trade ties and the frequent and varied "unofficial" missions to the mainland that *de facto* political acceptance of Peking has become a leading feature of Japan's foreign policy in Asia. The two countries generally complement each other economically in a manner that leaves substantial latitude for future growth of trade, but limits are imposed by the restricted appeal of Chinese exports in Japan and by the political uncertainties regarding the Communist regime. Because the Chinese are likely to continue to pursue national economic self-sufficiency to an extreme degree (the current ratio of imports to GNP approximates 3 per cent, far lower than that of any other major nation), considerable room will remain for manipulating trade for political ends. These factors leave the future pattern of economic ties more conjectural than is normal in bilateral relations of this sort. Politics and economics are in this case integrally related, and the dimensions of Sino-Japanese trade will ultimately depend on the broader competition between the two nations as major regional powers.

Regional Investment

Unlike other industrialized societies, Japan has not expanded its overseas investment greatly until recently. The Japanese have followed a rather narrow path of economic nationalism, impeding foreign investment in their own economy and, with a few notable exceptions, investing cautiously and selectively overseas —especially in East Asia. The capital needs of the world's fastest-growing economy have been more than sufficient to absorb its resources, but several major overseas investments were, in fact, made primarily to develop raw materials: oil in the Persian Gulf; iron ore in India and Australia; and timber in Alaska, western Canada, and Southeast Asia. By the latter part of the 1960's, Japan's enormous prosperity, and the new capital and needs it generated, had markedly altered the situation. Powered by the ever greater need for raw materials, a large balance-of-payments surplus, and an increasingly acute labor shortage at home, the steadily growing flow of foreign investments is generally expected to swell during the next few years to an annual rate of $2–$3 billion. How this expansion involves East Asian nations is critical both to the economic development of the region and to the future role of Japan in international politics.

Political as well as economic factors have contributed to Japan's highly uneven past record of investment in East Asia. The raw materials of highest priority have not been made available to Japanese industry in abundance, and the conditions providing the kind of long-term security required for substantial investments have been virtually unobtainable because of political turbulence throughout the region. Full-scale relations with Indonesia were not possible until 1967, when President Suharto reversed the anticolonial, exclusivist policies of the Sukarno era by welcoming economic contacts with all nations and offering formal protection through the Foreign Guarantee Law to those seeking direct participation in the nation's economy. Despite manifold connections with the Republic of Korea, only since 1966 has a normal flow of contacts developed and only since early 1970 has there been a framework for unfettered, direct private investment.[9] Trade with the Philippines has reached almost $1 billion annually, but Manila has yet to approve a commercial treaty with Japan providing the guarantees essential to full, normal bilateral ties. The investment climate in Malaysia, Singapore, Taiwan, and Thailand has been comparatively free from legal and bureaucratic restrictions, and the forces of the economic market place have perforce led to more normal Japanese economic involvement in these countries. It is in the context of past local restraints, the general climate of political and economic uncertainty, the enormous capital demands of Japan's domestic economy, and the only recently eased regulations of the Finance Ministry that the current, relatively modest level of Japan's regional investment should be appraised.

It is difficult to present a detailed, comprehensive picture of Japan's current investment in the region with an eye to understanding the future pattern. In part, this is because the future is likely to be quite different from the past. Major momentum in this direction is just now under way and the previous inhibiting conditions are likely to continue to be removed. Even a description of the current structure of investment presents formidable difficulties. An opaque veil shrouds the specific overseas activities of Japanese enterprises, especially the operations of the trading companies. Investment takes place in many ways—through full control, joint ownership, technical participation, direct capital investment, commercial loans, and numerous variants of these forms. Under the best of circumstances, it is difficult to move through the relevant statistical thickets, while the accuracy of the data from many of the developing countries is questionable. Rather than distort a complex and only partially known situation by presenting fragmentary details, a glance will be taken at the records of Japanese investments in Indonesia and South Korea, two nations in markedly different domestic and international circumstances with which Japan has recently expanded its economic ties. Some feeling can thus be provided for the style of past actions and the direction of change in two countries that have special importance for Japan in the East Asian region.

Japanese businessmen moved boldly and rapidly in pursuit of the opportunities made suddenly accessible in the potentially abundant but still murky economic waters of Indonesia. Other nations were similarly drawn in the wake of the Suharto government's efforts to bring internal economic order and attract foreign capital to one of the least developed and resource-rich areas of the world. More than two-thirds of the $1.34 billion of foreign capital invested in Indonesia from 1967 to 1970 was predictably concentrated in extractive-type industries, particularly in mining and logging ventures.[10] All of the major investing countries directed the bulk of their capital in this fashion—except Japan. The two leading countries, the United States and Japan,* both invested in fifty-three different enterprises; but, of the $374 million in American capital, more than 85 per cent was in large work contracts with the Indonesian Government, with three mining ventures alone involving $228 million. Although $75 million of the $157 million Japanese total is tied up in a similar project to develop nickel, the remainder consists primarily of small joint ventures ($3–$6 million each) in manufacturing—arrangements that pull Japan deeply into the day-to-day operations of the Indonesian economy. However ideal a base may be thus provided for future expansion, if this broad trend of involvement is continued, Japan will inevitably be brought into local economic problems in ways that will make the future internal political stability of Indonesia a matter of increasing priority to Tokyo.

* Actually, the Philippines ranked second and invested roughly $100 million more than Japan, but almost all of this amount was concentrated in two lumber projects, one for $235 million. The nation simply lacks the capacity for a balanced and sustained overseas investment effort.

An element of political risk will grow hand in hand with the rapidly growing business commitments, especially since they are supplemented by an extensive aid program.

Japan's investments in South Korea cannot be separated from the extraordinary growth in all forms of bilateral economic contacts since normalization of diplomatic relations in late 1965 —the aid program, the government and private machinery (e.g., the businessmen's Korea-Japan Economic Cooperation Committee) for regularized consultation on economic matters, and the high level of trade. The Japanese have benefited from the extremely rapid growth of the Korean economy since the mid-1960's as well as from gaps created by steady reduction of the huge U.S. aid program. Forces of the market place supplement the evolving policies of economic cooperation between the two governments. In addition to governmental grants and loans, the normalization agreement committed Japan to $300 million in commercial loans, a figure that was subsequently raised to $500 million. At the same time, Seoul placed tight restrictions on direct foreign investment (requiring that the ownership of all enterprises be shared with a controlling Korean partner), so that less than 10 per cent of all private foreign capital entered in this way during 1965–69.[11] The United States and Japan contributed more than 90 per cent of the foreign investment made during these years—$76.6 million and $48.7 million, respectively. These figures compare with the $266 million in commercial loans extended by Japan and the $240 million offered by the United States. The loans took on a quasipublic form, in that they were negotiated under close scrutiny of the Korean Government and coordinated with its economic development plans. With the relaxation of foreign investment controls in 1970 and the rising costs and acute shortage of labor in Japan, the flow of private capital to South Korea should spur ahead despite the threat by the Chinese Communists to boycott any Japanese firm making investments of this sort. The most distinctive feature of bilateral commercial relations is the depth to which political considerations have already become enmeshed—and the increasing difficulty Tokyo will have in disentangling economics from politics.

Except in Taiwan, where the cloud of a political settlement

between Tokyo and Peking looms very large, and in the war-torn countries of Indochina, the prospects for future Japanese investment in the other non-Communist countries in the region are bright. The incentives for a sizable influx of Japanese capital are particularly high in Singapore and Thailand,[12] where there is relative political stability and a great need to rectify the bilateral trade imbalance. Whatever pattern may develop, the initiative and dynamism will come from the Japanese side, from the international requirements of a new economic superpower in the context of the global economy. Moreover, investments in the East Asian region are intrinsically different from other overseas commitments, for they inevitably carry with them implications and risks that go beyond economic considerations and touch the political and security aspects of Japan's foreign policy as well.

The Political Legacies of Economic Interaction

Japan's position as the dominant trader and a major investor in East Asia has developed almost entirely as a by-product of the nation's growth into a major international economic power. The involvement has lacked conscious or comprehensive design and has sprung essentially out of the forces of the market place— quests for customers, materials, and profits. To the extent that there has been a rationale, it has been that of the trading house, the pursuit of economic gain independent of political considerations. It is now both appropriate and imperative to explore some of the implications of the resulting pattern of commercial interaction for regional interdependence and for Japan's future international role.

Economically, Japan remains quite independent of East Asia. Becoming an industrialized global economic power brought it greater economic autonomy. In one sense, the Japanese are becoming increasingly less dependent on international trade to maintain their economic well-being. Like all industrial countries, Japan now has a far smaller portion of its national product involved in trade than it did in the pre–World War II period. Among basic reasons for this are, first, the favorable downward trend of prices of primary goods that are the main imports and, second, a shift in the economy to products and services that require less import content per yen of product. In fact, the ratio of imports to GNP has remained between 8 and 10 per cent for more than a decade, a figure well below that of almost all European nations. Not only is Japan in aggregate less dependent on trade, but multiple sources of raw materials have been developed on a worldwide basis. In response to the 1970 crude-oil price rise forced by the collective action of the producing countries, a joint government-business program was initiated, accelerating still more the cultivation of globally dispersed supplies. By establishing multiple primary-goods sources, the accessibility of critical materials will be enhanced and vulnerability to unilateral external economic pressures correspondingly reduced. This policy is both commercially prudent, in view of the probability of increasing collusion among underdeveloped nations to obtain higher prices for their resources, and diplomatically shrewd, since it reduces economic ties with the East Asian region and the political pressures that *pari passu* accompany such links. Consequently, no matter how much the trade, investments, and imports of critical raw materials (e.g., petroleum) involving East Asia may grow, it is most unlikely that an economic imperative will emerge that *alone* will force Japan to undertake independent military actions.

The size and distribution of economic intercourse with East Asia also leave Japan wide room for policy maneuver. No single country takes much more than 3 per cent of the total of Japanese trade. Conversely, however, Japan in no case takes much less than 25 per cent of bilateral trade and is involved in more than 30 per cent with virtually all major non-Communist nations in the region. A decision by Tokyo regarding trade can have a profound impact on any of these countries without seriously hurting the Japanese economy, but no nation in the region has the capacity to bring truly significant pressure on Japan. The great inequality involved in the bilateral relationships and the asymmetry of the trade and investment flow make it inappropriate to describe the regional web in terms of interdependence.[13] As the economic Gulliver of East Asia, Japan can take a firm position regarding those nations in which it has the greatest security interest. Thus, at first glance, the absence of any overriding economic necessity would seem to make it both feasible and rational to remain aloof from the political and security issues within the region.

Japan is, however, a peculiarly vulnerable economic super-power. Unlike the United States and the Soviet Union, the nation is almost totally dependent on imports of a number of raw materials (e.g., oil, iron ore, nickel, and bauxite) that are absolutely essential to operate a modern economy and for which there are no ready substitutes. This vulnerability is well illustrated by the circumstances surrounding petroleum supplies. In effect, all of Japan's oil is imported, some 90 per cent from the Middle East, and storage facilities can accommodate supplies for only three to four months. For Tokyo, the situation today is economically far more precarious than it was in 1941, when the imposition of an oil embargo triggered the military plunge into Southeast Asia. Gradual development of alternative power sources (especially nuclear energy) and intensified efforts to cultivate new and dispersed oil supplies—in East Asia, North America, and the seas adjoining Japan—can alleviate the problem only partially, at best. For the foreseeable future, a massive flow of oil from abroad will remain a matter of national economic survival. With similar conditions prevailing in regard to other critical goods, Japan clearly has a fundamental dependence on foreign trade that is somewhat obscured by the previously noted structural changes in the economy associated with the high level of industrialization and a large GNP. At the very least, these conditions will raise short-run pressure to expand the Japanese Navy by way of increasing the security of the merchant fleet and of the lifeline it provides.

Japan's basically precarious international economic position makes the country highly susceptible to external events. Dependence on imports for essential resources poses a serious problem in strictly economic terms. Steady supplies of materials such as iron ore and coking coal have been secured for the next decade through long-term contracts guaranteeing purchases in steadily expanding quantities. The amounts specified in these contracts are predicated on continued growth of both Japan's economy and exports at the extraordinarily high levels of the recent past. Even if the domestic economic house is kept in order, such a long-term assumption about the global economy has a peculiarly Pollyanna quality. Any serious slowdown in world trade (however temporary), far more a return to the protectionist world of the 1930's, would have unusually severe repercussions in Japan, especially regarding the balance of payments. Inevitably, these economic necessities force a heightened concern for international political developments, particularly regarding the underdeveloped countries that have served as the main suppliers of primary goods and that have provided, in the East Asian region, a substantial market for Japanese products. Japan is thus enmeshed in the flow of world trade in ways that at once serve as a rein on any autonomous *Realpolitik* actions and make international *political* stability essential for the nation's economic well-being. Statesmen in Tokyo will find it increasingly difficult to distinguish and deal separately with economic and political issues in formulating Japan's foreign policy.

Similarly, despite a growing capacity to remain economically independent from East Asia, there are, in fact, severe limitations on the extent to which autonomy can be extended. To be sure, there is no economic *necessity* for Japan to trade in East Asia, and, if the nation embarks upon a great-power role in international relations in the region, it will ultimately do so for political reasons. Economic relations may not determine Japanese foreign policy in the region, but they nevertheless will serve as a powerful supplementary influence. The degree of that influence is made clearer if the extensive and growing trade and investment are seen in the context of Japan's foreign-aid program and its web of formal and informal contacts with other Asian nations.

FOREIGN AID

The evolution of Japan's aid program parallels in striking fashion the essential features of the nation's foreign policy. To an unusual degree, aid has been integrally tied to the expansion of trade and the growth of the country's general international economic position. The program has grown in a piecemeal fashion without clear coordination by the government and largely in response to international trends during the "development decade" of the 1960's. No clear-cut goals have been articulated beyond an undifferentiated commitment to economic cooperation on behalf of peace and stability. How the modest and fragmented policies that are followed specifically conduce to political stability in the recipient nations has never been made clear. Partly because of the *ad hoc* and pragmatic fashion in which it has developed and partly because of the special priority given to relations with East Asian nations, Japan's overseas assistance has had, to an overwhelming degree, a regional concentration. Now, as newly affluent Japan simply moves to comply with the aid standard suggested by the Organization for Economic Cooperation and Development (OECD) for donor nations, these features of the limited program of the past have assumed new importance. If the OECD aid target of 1 per cent of GNP is met as pledged by 1975, the flow of Japanese assistance will sharply expand to $4 billion annually. On that scale, all of the issues heretofore avoided will have to be directly confronted—the composition of aid (grants versus loans), the direction of flow (regional versus global dispersion, non-Communist versus Communist targets), and the short-term effectiveness of the program in promoting peace. Japan has suddenly come of age as a major contributor of foreign aid.

Bilateral Reparations and Grants

Reparations to Asian nations as redress for damages inflicted in the course of the abortive attempt to extend the Japanese Empire throughout the region constituted the first effort at assistance to developing countries. The obligation to make such payments (which only in the loosest sense can be termed "aid"), as well as the right to pay in Japanese goods and services, was established as part of the San Francisco Peace Treaty ending the Pacific War. Settlements with Burma, Indonesia, the Philippines, and South Vietnam were reached through bilateral negotiations during the 1950's, while in the next decade smaller "economic cooperation grants" were given to Cambodia, Laos, Malaysia, Singapore, and Thailand in lieu of reparations (Table 9). A supplemental ten-year grant was extended to Burma in 1965 to bring the initial bilateral grant into line with the larger rep-

TABLE 9

REPARATIONS AND REPARATION-RELATED GRANTS
TO ASIAN NATIONS

(In millions of U.S. dollars)

Country	Reparations		Economic development grants	
	Period	Amount	Period	Amount
Burma	1955–65	$200.00	1965–77	$140.00
Cambodia	—	—	1959–62	$ 4.0
Indonesia	1958–70	$223.3	—	—
South Korea	—	—	1966–75	$300.0
Laos	—	—	1959–61	$ 2.8
Malaysia	—	—	1968–70	$ 8.2
Philippines	1956–75	$550.0	—	—
Singapore	—	—	1968–70	$ 8.2
Thailand	—	—	1962–69	$ 26.7
South Vietnam	1960–64	$ 39.0		
Total		$1012.3		$489.9
Grand Total				$1502.2

SOURCE: Foreign Ministry, *Sekai no Ugoki* (*Trends of the World*), no. 2 (1971), pp. 28–29.

arations settlements that had subsequently been reached with the other major Southeast Asian nations. The $300 million grant accompanying the normalization of relations with South Korea as indemnity for the prolonged Japanese colonial occupation is properly seen as a reparations gesture, despite the aid classification it is given by Tokyo. More than $1.3 billion of the $1.5 billion total of these commitments has been paid, and this is a major portion of the capital flow from Japan to underdeveloped countries. Indeed, apart from an extremely modest technical-assistance program and small emergency grants, discharge of these reparation obligations constitutes the *only* bilateral grant aid extended by Japan during the postwar period.

The process through which Japan has liquidated international debts from its imperial past has had a number of important effects on the way in which the nation's foreign policy has moved. Reparation payments inevitably extended beyond economic considerations, in that the primary purpose was to eradicate legacies of political ill-will as well as material damage. Further political coloration was added by the peculiar international circumstances of the 1950's and 1960's as these grants came to be directed only to non-Communist Asian governments and left in abeyance what could prove the largest reparation claim of all—that from Communist China. Moreover, the concentration of aid in an area congruent with the Greater East Asian Co-prosperity Sphere provided a certain *de facto* continuity with the emphasis of prewar diplomacy and reinforced the regional focus in other aspects of the country's foreign policy.

The reparations program did not lead Tokyo to confront the problems of development aid that came to concern other international powers during this period, but it did serve to lay the foundation for the ensuing rapid expansion of economic and diplomatic ties. In effect, the grants served as a "tied" aid program, that is, one in which the recipient nation is required to use the money to purchase goods from the donor. But the discretion as to what was provided ultimately has rested with the other East Asian nations, thereby relieving Tokyo of responsibility for a development strategy and producing widely varying results in the different countries. The most important effect of the reparation grants, which have been relatively effective and scandal-free, is not their direct impact on the development of East Asian nations but the entrée provided Japan into an area harboring strongly anti-Japanese feelings. Ironically, the success of the formula for redeeming past wrongs hastened the return of the Japanese to the region and paved the way for their economic ascendancy. The harvest that Japan has reaped from a modest input has been great, indeed. However, because the entire reparations program was, in essence, a passive discharge of obligations, few guidelines for expanded aid in keeping with Japan's vastly expanded resources seem to have been derived from this experience. Despite frequent government intimation of similar grants to promote economic cooperation,[14] virtually no additional gestures have yet been made as the previous commitments have been greatly reduced.

Beyond reparations, the only assistance grants of continuing, major consequence have been for technical cooperation programs, which, since 1962, have been administered by the Overseas

Technical Cooperation Agency under the supervision of the Foreign Ministry. The range and scale of these activities have steadily expanded and now encompass such endeavors as overseas technical-training centers, a tiny Japanese counterpart of the Peace Corps, and a training program in Japan that has accommodated more than 13,000 individuals from developing nations.[15] This technical assistance corresponds with the ideal of aid set forth by international organizations, for it is structured to allow the government to take initiatives regarding basic economic and social problems in collaboration with the recipient countries. Although the annual budget has expanded fivefold over the last eight years to $23 million, it has consistently taken only 2 per cent of the official flow of aid and is extremely small in relation to the current capacities of the country to extend assistance. What is most distinctive about the current technical-aid program is not its composition, but the fact that more than 60 per cent is concentrated in the same East Asian nations that have received reparations.

Creditor or Donor?

What Japan calls economic cooperation and aid essentially involves expanded credits for commercial purposes mainly in the East Asian region. By far the largest proportion of Japanese aid is in the form of private or government loans, which are directly or indirectly tied to the development of export markets or critical imports. During 1970 alone, the amount of assistance extended to developing countries rose 44 per cent to $1,824 million and constituted 0.93 per cent of GNP.[16] At first glance, this seems an impressive achievement, and the government was quick to proclaim that its recent pledge to raise the ratio of aid to GNP to 1 per cent by 1975 would be reached ahead of schedule. However, even a brief glimpse at the composition of this assistance casts doubt on the real meaning of the figures. Of the total aid, 75 per cent ($1,366 million) consisted of either government or private loans to finance deferred payment exports and direct Japanese investments. The balance ($458 million) was classified as official developmental assistance (grants and loans concerned with development as distinct from commercial purposes), but this figure made up a lower proportion of the total aid than in the previous year and *included* reparation grants and loans. Additionally, *all* of the loans extended were tied to the purchase of Japanese products, and the grant component constituted only one-third of this aid—against an average of roughly two-thirds for the sixteen nations on the Development Assistance Committee of the OECD during recent years.[17] Thus, the sharp rise in Japanese aid in large part simply reflects the fact that trade with and investment in developing nations rapidly expanded during 1970.

Loans emanate from three basic sources: the Import-Export Bank of Japan, supervised by the Ministry of Finance; the Overseas Economic Cooperation Fund (OECF), under the direction of the Economic Planning Agency; and private commercial banks. The Import-Export Bank, which is wholly owned by the government, has operated since 1950 for the purposes of promoting Japanese trade and facilitating overseas investment by providing long-term credits under terms somewhat more favorable than those offered by commercial banks. From the inception of the aid program, the Bank has also been responsible for official development loans (e.g., the special yen credits granted to some Asian nations instead of reparation grants), but, since 1965, this task has been increasingly shared with the OECF. The latter organization was established in 1961 to demonstrate Japan's "active posture toward economic cooperation more clearly,"[18] but its scale of operations remained small and its functions of granting export credits and investment loans overlapped with those of the Import-Export Bank. However, following the $200 million loan agreement accompanying the normalization settlement with the Republic of Korea, the main business of the Fund shifted to intergovernmental loans directed almost exclusively toward Asian nations (notably Indonesia and South Korea) on terms substantially easier than those of the Bank, and the volume of its operations has grown significantly. Private credits, which in 1970 comprised 37 per cent of the "aid," simply involve bank financing of Japanese commercial transactions with the poorer nations at the prevailing domestic interest rate. These loans also may be subject to governmental approval (usually by the Ministry of International Trade and Industry and the Ministry of Finance), as, for example, the $300 million in private credits promised South Korea in 1965. Although the machinery for extending credits is variously touched by the government, there is no strong coordination or policy leadership. In consequence, loans to developing nations have been generated by the needs of Japan's international economic expansion, the fulfillment of reparation-type obligations, and token gestures in response to aid policies set forth by the United Nations and other international organizations.

The distortions in this passive and commercially oriented aid program have come increasingly under criticism from both advanced and underdeveloped nations,[19] but, frequent government statements notwithstanding, it will be difficult to change the past pattern. Given the momentum of Japan's trade expansion and the internationally competitive power of Japanese products, export credits will continue to take an unusually high proportion of the official aid flow. This will certainly place out of reach for the immediate future even the U.N. specified goal of 0.7 per cent of GNP in official development assistance. Moreover, as long as economic forces are the predominant factor in determining the direction of loans, these credits are not likely to gravitate to social overhead (rather than industrial) projects, and loans will continue to be used by Tokyo to cushion the effect of huge trade deficits that a number of East Asian countries run with Japan. Outside pressures, from international organizations and other industrialized countries, have led Japan reluctantly to accept "in principle" the need to untie aid loans,[20] but this concession has not yet produced concrete policy changes; how fully it will be implemented remains conjectural. Some improvement has occurred in the terms of loans to developing nations, but Japanese credit still stands as the most costly offered by any industrialized country. Finally, the regional concentration of Japan's assistance—a matter of criticism for several years now—is the natural consequence of the tendency to use aid to cultivate overseas markets and the prominent place that reparations have held in the over-all picture. Despite some gesture to allocate aid on a global scale, since the mid-1960's virtually all the special initiatives taken by Japan in the field of economic cooperation have tended to emphasize East Asia. From the perspective of foreign aid, Japan also appears as an Asian trading company.

Aid to East Asia

The degree to which the aggregate flow of Japan's aid is concentrated in the region is indeed extreme. During the past decade, Japan has consistently sent more than 60 per cent of its total aid to East Asia and, as early as 1967, extended a greater absolute amount of assistance to the region, excluding Vietnam, than did the United States.[21] Including all categories of aid, the five recipients of the largest amounts in 1969 were all Asian nations: South Korea ($219 million), Indonesia ($109 million), the Philippines ($93 million), Nationalist China ($92 million), and Thailand ($69 million).[22] Underlying and reinforcing both the trend evident from these figures and the web of trade ties previously considered have been the many bilateral and multilateral conferences and organizations for regional economic cooperation of recent years.

Beginning in early 1965, the coincidental settlement of long-standing aid negotiations and the sudden turn of events in Vietnam and later Indonesia resulted in a series of actions that pulled Japan more fully into the field of economic cooperation in East Asia. Some appreciation for the extent to which Japan's foreign policy was turned by these developments is provided merely by a chronology of events. In April, the ten-year $140 million reparations-extension grant was made to Burma and a $150 million special yen credit was given to Taiwan. Two months later, the Japan–Republic of Korea Treaty was signed, involving $800 million in grants and loans. Plans were then laid by the government for the first Ministerial Conference on Southeast Asian Economic Development, which was convened in April, 1966, and which represented the first diplomatic initiative taken by Japan in this field. In June, 1966, Japan became a charter member of the Asian and Pacific Council (ASPAC). After several emergency grants and loans to the new Suharto government, Japan took the lead in smoothing the way for resolving the international financial problems of Indonesia by convening a conference of Jakarta's non-Communist creditors (the so-called Tokyo Club). In November, 1967, the Asian Development Bank was inaugurated, with a Japanese as president and Japan and the United States as the largest contributors.[23]

The regional focus established at this time has persisted and developed, but the implications have remained somewhat clouded, because none of the multilateral organizations has yet acquired major international importance, and because Japan's commitments to them have remained limited or ambiguous. The Ministerial Conference on Economic Development has become an annual affair and has led to a small Southeast Asian Agricultural Development Fund and the initiation of several technical-assistance projects, but Japan has resisted repeated requests from the other member nations* for expanded direct aid. Despite gradually widening activities, the Asian Development Bank remains essentially a device for channeling extraregional capital into the development of East Asia, and there are no immediate prospects that its programs will assume truly fundamental significance in international affairs in the area. ASPAC is made up of the most stanchly anti-Communist nations in the region,† and Japan has often sought to temper the political cast of the pronouncements at the annual meetings. It has made only token aid gestures. For Japan, the importance of membership in these as well as in the many other regional multilateral aid projects (e.g., Colombo Plan, Mekong River Development Project, Asian Productivity Organization) lies not so much in the impact of each explicit commitment but in the implicit and cumulative effect these actions have on the international perspective of Tokyo in the context of the nation's range of activities in foreign affairs. The inevitable political and psychological meaning of the intensified interaction between Japan and the non-Communist states can be circumvented only if the goal of Japanese economic aid is realized—that is, if prosperity engulfs the region to dissipate domestic conflicts and create international harmony.

---

* Members of the Ministerial Conferences include Indonesia, Malaysia, Singapore, the Philippines, South Vietnam, and Thailand, as well as Japan.

† South Korea, South Vietnam, Nationalist China, Thailand, Malaysia, the Philippines, Japan, Australia, and New Zealand.

Economic Development and Political Stability

Basic to the aid program and the economic cast of Japan's general foreign policy is the assumption that prosperity can, indeed, prove the solvent of political conflict in the East Asian region. This position of economic determinism is ideologically in keeping with Marxism, the "inverse Marxist" rationale on which much of the American aid program has rested (i.e., economic development will create conditions that would make Communism unnecessary)[24] and also with the revised form of optimistic Victorian liberalism that has grown out of Japan's own postwar experience. Further, it is a policy consistent with the short-term diplomatic imperatives of a demilitarized power in an era when the need for rich nations to aid the poor has acquired an unquestioned moral status internationally. In the words of Prime Minister Sato, "By stabilizing a country economically, a way to co-prosperity and coexistence will be opened. This is the way to abide thoroughly by peace. Japan wishes to move forward along this course."[25] The critical questions, however, remain unasked and unanswered: How can economic aid *qua* economic aid be used to achieve the *political* goals of stability and peace? More basically, does economic development necessarily conduce to a peaceful pattern of domestic political development and to international harmony?

If economic growth does, indeed, lead to political stability, then there is a special incentive to provide all possible assistance to East Asian nations, for the region has displayed greater potential for rapid short-term growth than any other developing area. Despite pockets of extremely high population density, the land-labor ratio is not the drawback that it is in South Asia. Outside of Burma and the nations of Indochina, all the countries have demonstrated a capacity for sustained growth, with South Korea and Taiwan having the most spectacular records of achievement. Consequently, it is particularly appropriate to ask what kind of international political order will emerge if the most optimistic possibilities for development (i.e., a sustained real growth rate of 8 or 9 per cent) are fulfilled.

Although it is commonly believed that success in achieving a high rate of economic growth will minimize the possibilities for political unrest and insurrection, little concrete historical or contemporary evidence is offered in support. The symbolic importance of economic progress may, in some instances, be substantial, but it is doubtful that, in the short run, the tangible benefits will significantly affect the political strength of a regime. Indeed, a sharply accelerated growth rate (high enough to affect fundamentally the popular living standard within two decades) is potentially a very destabilizing influence.[26] Rapid growth breeds a large number of people who change status (*nouveaux pauvres* as well as *nouveaux riches*), creating an environment in which extremist political movements prosper. At the same time that urbanization, education, and altered working conditions are undermining the traditional and the familiar, the absolute increase in wealth does not reach the incomes of the masses in the short run, except in bare subsistence economies. Consequently, the immediate impact of the development process may well be to increase the level of social frustration of the masses and to undermine political stability. Not only, therefore, is it questionable to predicate domestic political stability on economic growth, but, in a basic sense, this puts the cart before the horse; for a substantial amount of political stability is a precondition of economic development. There is no automatic process of stable and peaceful social and political change that can be set into motion even by the most extensive aid and trade actions that Japan (or the United States and Japan) might undertake.

Another assumption concerning the salutary benefits of economic development that is implicit in the Japanese approach is that regional economic cooperation will mitigate if not eliminate fractious, nation-centered political rivalries. Again, this seems badly wide of the mark in East Asia, where substantial economic integration is out of reach. The scope of East Asian economic cooperation will ultimately be a result of *political* decisions by the elites of the various countries in which the benefits of economic rationality from a region-wide viewpoint represent only one consideration. No matter what the levels of cooperation and interaction, the new order in East Asia will be made up of discrete nation-states with the asymmetry of interests and proclivity to conflict inherent in any nation-centered system. If a united Europe has proved elusive despite the successful Common Market, then the prospect for greatly increased political coherence in non-Communist Asia is dispiriting. Japan will remain the leading nation among the non-Communist nation-states of Asia, even in the face of successful regional economic development.

As constituted at present, the web linking Japan to Asia cannot in itself bring international harmony or even serve as the base for coping diplomatically with the full range of issues that will inevitably arise. Trade and aid have drawn Japan deeply and inextricably into Asia, but they cannot offer an immediate solution to chronic international political problems. Japan's foreign policy must move beyond its narrowly economic orientation, and it is for this reason that the U.S. alliance and Japanese security policy regarding East Asia have such great importance.

6　The Japanese-American Alliance: An Asian Pandora's Box

An era of close and special ties between the United States and Japan is ending. From the conclusion of World War II, through the American Occupation, the bipolar world of the 1950's, and the multipolar but Vietnam-dominated world of the last decade, Japan has been a defense satellite of the United States, a distinctly junior economic partner, and a kind of protégé in free-enterprise democracy. In recent years, however, there has been a sharp rise in the intensity and frequency of conflict over specific issues, such as military bases and trade, and new dilemmas for Japanese security have been posed by the uncertainty of future U.S. commitments in Asia. In consequence, delineation of Japanese-American relations has become a task reminiscent of the myth of Pandora, for the box is open and hitherto intimate and felicitous conditions of the past are now, and increasingly will be, tormented by the troubles of international politics in the nuclear age—for which the most appropriate remedy may well be Hope.

Until recently, the fundamental importance of the Japanese-American alliance was obscured by more dramatic events in East Asia and by the modest and passive role of Japan in international affairs. Two major wars on the Asian mainland, the rise of China, the tensions attendant upon the liquidation of former colonial empires, and direct American military actions and commitments to contain Communism in Asia have overshadowed the infrequent conflicts between the United States and Japan and underscored the latter's almost complete security dependence. However, the sharply increased international weight of Japan, changes in global strategy developing in the wake of Vietnam, and a more complex world order have produced a changed picture. In addition, there have been growing Japanese claims for a more autonomous international role, which above all involves adjustment of relations with the United States.

In the Vietnam-spawned debate over American foreign policy, one of the few points on which all the participants have agreed is the central importance of Japan for future international stability in Asia. Japan is now seen as strategically equivalent to Europe, and the extreme instability of international politics in Asia clearly creates problems for Japanese-American relations vastly exceeding those that have troubled the Atlantic alliance during the past decade. Current security ties are mutually acknowledged to be unsatisfactory. The United States sees them as "unequal" in view of the modest scale of Japanese military commitments, while Japan sees them as "unequal" in terms of the peculiarly dominant position held by America. The situation must change, even if the risks are very high. As Herman Kahn has said, "Japan, not China, will be the most important country in Asia during the next decade." Japanese-American relations may well prove the key for peace or war in this region.

BILATERAL RELATIONS

To an unusual degree, American policy toward Japan has given emphasis to bilateral, nonmilitary relations. Economic, cultural, and political contacts between the two countries have expanded enormously, with a minimal amount of conflict. The very success of these policies has led to a curiously skewed but widely supported vision of the nature of Japanese-American relations. This vision gives scant attention to security policies (which have been predicated on quite different grounds), downplays the potential for conflict implicit in expanded patterns of bilateral interaction, and links the alliance with fulfillment of a moral (i.e., democratic) potential, regarding which the United States has a tutelary role. Japan's ties with the United States are in this sense very special, indeed, and the basis for this relationship grows directly from the experience of the Occupation.

Political Relations

The six-year Occupation of Japan (1945–51) provided the United States with the opportunity to give concrete meaning to the liberal ideals for creating international peace in the name of which the war had been fought. "To insure that Japan would not again become a menace to the United States or to the peace and security of the world," the headquarters of General Douglas MacArthur instituted sweeping reforms of demilitarization and democracy. Not only was the Japanese war machine dismantled, but Article IX of the new, American-drafted constitution renounced war "as a sovereign right of the nation and the threat or use of force in settling international disputes." With this gesture of utopian bravado, the Occupation gave legal sanctity and symbolic dignity to pacifism and renounced what is acknowledged as the elemental requisite for a state's participation in international politics. Demonstrating his capacity for hyperbole and exemplifying the profound idealism underlying American policy of that time, General MacArthur grandly announced, "Japan today understands as thoroughly as any nation that war does not pay. Her spiritual revolution has probably been the greatest the world has known."[1]

Concrete actions were taken to insure that this spiritual rebirth was not chimerical. In keeping both with a New Deal-style reformist zeal characteristic of the early years of the Occupation and with the Wilsonian notion that defects in the internal political structure of states are the basic cause of war, a full-scale "democratization" of economic and social as well as governmental institutions was undertaken in ways that were "deemed likely to stress the peaceful disposition of the Japanese people."[2] To a degree without parallel in modern history, the United States directed a process of nation-rebuilding with the explicit aim of shaping a country's international behavior. From the outset, the American-Japanese alliance was placed on a unique level, standing as a kind of test of the most basic beliefs of the American diplomatic tradition.

America has served as a kind of political-cultural stepfather to Japan, and this is evident in the scope and tone of American policy. Occupation reforms projected the United States so deeply into all aspects of Japanese society that most of the dramatic breaks with past political and social practices that have emerged in the postwar years are in some way seen (by Japanese as well as Americans) as "Made in America." U.S. aid, trade, and technology have been major factors in Japan's spectacular prosperity. This development, in turn, had added meaning, in that a basic theme in contemporary American diplomacy is the belief that sustained economic growth conduces to peaceful international behavior. Finally, the successful and self-conscious effort to broaden political and cultural contacts with the Japanese people as well as with their government (the "people-to-people" approach), a policy reaching its apogee during the tenure of Edwin Reischauer as ambassador, represents a diplomatic style in keeping with the Occupation orientation and strengthens the paternalistic cast of bilateral relations.[3] Like the father who rejoices in the self-image seen in a successful son, the United States has tended to view the alliance as ultimately resting on principles, with political-economic conditions transcending narrow calculations of self-interest. This has added a special glow to the successes of the past but has also served to place American relations with Japan on a uniquely moral plane—a position not unlike that which characterized our relations with China in the years prior to the Communist takeover. Any future conflicts with the Japanese will be affected by this posture, with its inherent potential for rigidity and sanctimonious overreaction that has on occasion characterized American cold-war policies.

The pervasive presence of the United States has profoundly influenced Japanese politics and the style and emphasis of Tokyo's foreign policy. Most basically, the greatly expanded scale of bilateral interaction, noted in the past for cooperative achievements, has also multiplied the occasions for conflict. This will be a fact of increasing importance as Japan moves toward a more politically independent and economically competitive interna-

tional role. In addition to the many explicitly international contacts and the ubiquitous evidence of cultural diffusion, the
United States is given a central place in the domestic political
scene by the featured treatment accorded American contemporary events by the mass media—especially regarding foreign policy and business activities touching Asia. The Japanese public
is provided with coverage of U.S. national politics and international activities that frequently rivals that offered on similar
events involving Japan. Similarly, the shrill and unbroken anti-
American campaigns by the Japanese left, in which unarmed
neutrality is offered as a substitute for the present policy, have
insured that every issue involving the alliance is accorded dramatic attention and have magnified the salience of American influence in all areas of policy. Despite the fact that the socialists
have never posed a real political threat to the ruling party, this
obsessive concern has heightened the intensity and narrowed the
focus of the Japanese foreign policy debate, so that a kind of
bilateral myopia regarding the United States has come to prevail.
Conjunctively, the level of concern in this debate, both pro- and
anti-American, has centered not so much on concrete conflicts of
interest as on the grand issues of peace and democracy—matters
of principle with strong emotional and ideological overlay. In a
basic sense, a mirror image of the American attitude toward Japan exists, for a strong moral cast underlies much of Japanese
policy toward the United States—even if this policy has, in fact,
coincided with calculated self-interest. Today, at the end of a
prolonged period of intimacy, during which Japan has emerged
once again as a major world power, it is understandable but
ironic that conservatives and leftists alike measure international
autonomy and nationalism in terms of movement away from the
American axis.

Economic Relations

The web of economic intercourse between the two countries
places limits on any sharp change in relations and has important
implications for possible political conflict. Japan is heavily dependent on trade with the United States. Since 1958, the Ameri-

TABLE 10

UNITED STATES–JAPAN TRADE, 1958–70

(In millions of U.S. dollars)

Year	U.S. exports to Japan	U.S. imports from Japan	U.S. trade surplus/ deficit	Per cent of U.S. total trade	Per cent of Japan's total trade
1958	843.8	670.8	173.0	4.8	29.6
1959	968.0	1,028.7	—50.7	5.9	30.7
1960	1,345.2	1,148.5	196.7	6.9	31.2
1961	1,742.1	1,054.8	687.3	7.8	31.6
1962	1,415.5	1,358.0	67.5	7.3	30.5
1963	1,846.4	1,498.1	348.3	8.2	29.5
1964	2,018.0	1,768.0	250.0	8.3	28.7
1965	2,083.5	2,414.2	—330.7	9.2	29.4
1966	2,371.4	2,964.5	—593.1	9.5	29.4
1967	2,699.9	2,998.7	—298.8	9.7	28.3
1968	2,953.9	4,056.9	—1,103.0	10.3	29.5
1969	3,461.8	4,869.0	—1,407.2	11.4	29.1
1970	4,652.0	5,875.0	—1,223.0	12.7	30.5

SOURCES: International Monetary Fund, *International Financial Statistics* (Washington, D.C.: July, 1970); International Monetary Fund and International Bank for Reconstruction and Development, *Direction of Trade Annual,* 1958–62, 1963–67 (Washington, D.C.: February, 1969; March, 1969); U.S. Department of Commerce, *Foreign Trade,* FT 455 (1969 Annual), Washington, D.C.: FT 990 (May, 1970); Japan Customs Association, *Bōeki Nenkan (Trade Yearbook),* 1970; U.S. Embassy, Tokyo, "U.S.-Japan Bilateral Trade, 1970" (mimeo.).

can share of Japan's total trade has remained stable at approximately 30 per cent (Table 10). In contrast with the remarkably constant proportion of Japanese trade taken by the United States, the Japanese have steadily increased their part of the American total from 4.8 to 12.7 per cent during this same period. From one perspective, these figures provide striking evidence of how Japan has improved its relative position in bilateral trade. At the same time, they make clear that the Japanese still hold a highly inferior trade relationship vis-à-vis the United States, which imposes an important qualification on the previously noted trend toward global economic tripolarity. In 1970, America took 30.7 per cent of Japanese exports, but this was only 14.4 per cent of total U.S. imports. Similarly, although the Japanese relied on America for 29.4 per cent of their imports, this constituted only 10.9 per cent of U.S. exports. The $10.5 billion volume of bilateral trade is impressive, and Japan was by far America's largest overseas trading partner. However, the asymmetry makes it as inappropriate to describe this relationship in terms of "interdependence" as it is to characterize in similar terms Japan's trade relations with the states of East Asia. A trade decision by the United States may have a profound impact on Japan without seriously disrupting the American economy, while a Japanese trade initiative may have only a minor effect on the United States. Since this condition will persist in the immediate future, the United States will continue to have substantial leverage for pressure on political as well as economic matters. Thus, despite a sharply greater capacity for independent international action as a result of economic growth, Japanese dependence on the American market will constrain any radical *Realpolitik* maneuvers.

This one-sided aspect of the trade relationship also raises the possibility that serious bilateral conflict may be generated by the successful lobbying of narrow interest groups in the United States, as is well illustrated by the protracted dispute that broke out in 1969 over the regulation of the import of Japanese textiles. During the 1960's, Japan and other low-cost Asian producers took an increasingly larger share of the American textile market. Although a source of concern within industry circles, the issue gained political consequence only in 1968, when Presidential aspirant Richard Nixon promised relief to Southern textile manufacturers if he should be elected to office. After his election, to redeem this political debt while at the same time maintaining an essentially free-trade posture, President Nixon sought an agreement through direct personal negotiations with Prime Minister Sato. For complex and somewhat obscure reasons, the tentative agreement reached in November, 1969, was never implemented, and the whole matter foundered on the shoals of domestic politics in both nations until it was finally resolved in the fall of 1970 on American terms. Sato failed to persuade Japanese textile industry leaders on the merits of the quota system proposed by the United States, and, in the ensuing wrangle of far more than a year's duration, the issue came to be seen in Japan not merely as a trade dispute but as a kind of national insult. In the United States, protectionist forces, buttressed by a domestic economic slump and a neo-isolationist political mood, used the occasion to press for legislated controls over not only textiles but a host of other products as well. The result was an unexpected challenge to Presidential leadership on trade policy, and resolution came only in the wake of U.S. initiatives to alter the postwar international monetary system and to devalue the dollar. Thus, as a result of an incident initiated by a single American pressure group, the whole atmosphere of bilateral relations was befouled, despite the efforts of political leaders in both countries to limit the scope of the controversy. The episode underscores the inseparability of political and economic relations and points to the future potential for conflicts as Japan further develops as a major competitor in both domestic and international markets.

Another serious problem has developed regarding the bilateral balance of payments, which, since 1965, has shifted heavily in Japan's favor. The issue remained obscured for several years partly because of the previously noted basic dependence of Japan on American trade and the remarkable sevenfold expansion in economic intercourse between the two countries since 1958. By 1971, however, the imbalance had become so large and the causes so persistent that the question could no longer be ignored. As seen in Table 10, the deficit incurred by the United States, starting in 1968, has annually run considerably above a billion dollars. Indeed, in 1969, the over-all bilateral balance of payments (including American military expenditures and the capital and current account transactions) pushed the deficit to more than $2.2 billion.[4] This deficit was a central factor underlying the dramatic moves by President Nixon in August, 1971, to strengthen the basic place of the United States in the global economic system. These moves have brought temporary relief, but unless the competitive advantages that have given Japan a chronic surplus in international accounts disappear, or the general American balance-of-payments problem is truly resolved, the risk of protectionist action by the United States will remain. Even if there is alleviation of the grievances of the past five years—tardy and selective liberalization of imports into Japan, the "dumping" of goods into the U.S. market at depressed prices, and Tokyo's seri-

ous restrictions on capital investment in Japan—the pressures
within America to rectify (with punitive legislation if necessary)
a perennial deficit are not likely to diminish in the near future.

International economic disputes are susceptible to calculation
and compromise in ways that conflicts over political and security interests are not. Negotiation may indeed bring the needed
accommodations, but the scope and intensity of Japanese-American economic differences have reached a level that involves the
very foundations of the alliance.

During the past two decades, elaborate and highly effective
channels of communication have been developed between the
Japanese and American governments to deal with all aspects of
their relations. There have existed for some time regularized
procedures (e.g., the annual cabinet-level consultative conferences) and more irregular but long-established patterns of consultation on economic, military, and diplomatic matters. The
past record of anticipating and diffusing potential conflicts and
the machinery established for this purpose constitute a significant legacy for the future. Bilateral relations, however, have proceeded successfully not so much because of effective bargaining
techniques as because of an essential congruence of interests on
matters of defense as well as nonsecurity issues. Indeed, if the
past is a guide to the future, it will be the question of security
that ultimately defines the nature of American-Japanese relations. This issue, of necessity, transcends direct relations between
the two countries, encompassing the global commitments of the
United States and the rapidly shifting tides of international politics in East Asia.

SECURITY ROLES IN ASIA

The guidelines of past American security policy toward Japan
cannot serve as the basis of the future alliance. Most basically,
the strong U.S. commitment to active military support of non-
Communist nations on the Asiatic mainland will no longer be
tenable during the next decade. This is peculiarly significant for
Japanese-American relations, for past security policy toward Japan has been determined not by bilateral considerations but by

the general American policies toward containing Communism in East Asia. Consequently, any limitation on U.S. commitments in Asia raises fresh questions about the automatic identity of American-Japanese security interests and Japan's continued abstention from all concerns of military *Realpolitik* in the region. The dimensions of the problem this poses for the Japanese-American alliance are clear from a review of the past record and an examination of the probable points of conflict over major security issues currently outstanding.

Bilateral Security

American security obligations regarding Japan and East Asia have developed in a piecemeal, *ad hoc* fashion in response to the specific needs involved in meeting the threat of Communist expansion and in liquidating the wars in Korea and Indochina. The first major change in policy toward Japan occurred in 1948. With the emergence of the cold war and the mounting triumphs of the Communists in China, the United States abruptly reversed course, dealing with Japan not as a defeated aggressor and primary threat to peace but as a major and essential ally. Occupation efforts, which had previously stressed democratization and demilitarization, now emphasized political stability and economic rehabilitation. Further change came with the outbreak of the Korean war, as a cautious step toward rearmament was made by the establishment of a small "police reserve" (which later became the Self-Defense Forces). The integral relationship between American security policy toward Japan and general strategy toward Asia was clearly manifested in the 1952 Peace Treaty, in which the central objective came to be not settlement of issues related to the Pacific War but securing an alliance with Japan to check Communist expansion in Asia.[5] A bilateral Security Treaty was made effective simultaneously with the Peace Treaty, and provision was made in it for continued deployment of the large numbers of troops already in the country as a result of the Occupation and for the logistical needs of the Korean war. Thus, the foundation of the American-Japanese security alliance, as well as the attendant specific military arrangements, grew out of the vastly expanded U.S. commitments in East Asia resulting from the cold war.

Drafted in the midst of the Korean war and in the shadow of the 1950 Treaty of Friendship, Alliance, and Mutual Assistance between the Soviet Union and China, the American-Japanese Security Treaty of 1952 (and the accompanying Administrative Agreement) gave emphasis to the use of American forces in Japan to meet any military threats in the region. American troops could be used in any way that Washington felt would "contribute to the maintenance of international peace and security in the Far East." Japan was prohibited from granting military bases to a third power without U.S. consent, and, despite a pledge against "territorial aggrandizement" in the Atlantic Charter, the United States insisted on retaining control of Okinawa and various smaller Pacific islands as "strategic territories."* Japan returned to international politics totally committed to and dependent on the Western bloc, a logical if not indispensable position in view of the international milieu and its own demilitarized and weak economic condition. However, it was a position effectively chosen by the United States, not the Japanese, and it underscored the passive and dependent nature of Japan's role in the alliance.

Revision of the Security Treaty in 1960 occurred prior to the open Sino-Soviet split and was again predicated on cold-war assumptions that the Communist monolith posed the security threat in Asia, which the United States bore the full responsibility of meeting and containing. Although this revision remedied some of the more glaring infringements on Japanese sovereignty (e.g., responsibility for internal security was returned), and although there was an explicit effort to emphasize reciprocity and partnership, Japan remained a military protectorate of the United States and American troops stationed there were to continue to be used to maintain security throughout the Far East. The Japanese did seek to avoid involvement in military operations beyond their territory, but the United States would consent only to "prior consultation" (not a veto) regarding combat

* Prime Minister Yoshida rejected, however, the demand of Special Ambassador John Foster Dulles that Japan play an active military role in regional defenses—a position the Japanese still support.

deployment of Japan-based American troops and the introduction of nuclear weapons in emergency situations. Almost before the ink was dry on the revised treaty, the United States began to promote modifications in Japanese policy more in keeping with the rapidly changing strategic realities in Asia that centered on China's development of nuclear weapons following the Soviet break and the profound impact of the war in Vietnam on all aspects of international politics in the region.

During the past decade, American policy has attempted to prod Japan into playing a larger role in East Asian international affairs, while the United States continued to deal with all military conflicts. On the most general level, the aim has been to move the Japanese into a leadership position in Asian economic and political affairs under a military "partnership" featuring an American nuclear umbrella. This policy assumed that the United States would continue to remain deeply engaged militarily in the region, both on nuclear and conventional levels, that there was and would continue to be a basic identity of Japanese and American security interests, and that the economic and political dimensions of international politics could be effectively separated from security matters. All of these assumptions are already being subjected to serious challenge.

Vietnam and the Nixon Doctrine

The war in Vietnam has had several effects on this policy. On the one hand, the enormous U.S. military and political investments in the war, a *reductio ad absurdum* of cold-war globalism in the eyes of many critics, has created the kind of implausibly exorbitant commitment to Asian security implied in American policy toward Japan. This has prolonged the Japanese withdrawal from all concerns of *Realpolitik* and has allowed the measured but steady expansion of their conventional forces to occur free from any tangible security threats. The stalemate in the war has demonstrated that the United States, despite its vast diplomatic, economic, and military resources, lacks the capacity effectively to control international conflict in the region. It has also provoked bitter divisions within the United States, forcing a general reassessment of American foreign policy and making highly improbable any military ventures in East Asia in the near future. Thus, Vietnam at once insured the short-term success of American policy toward Japan and demonstrated the infeasibility of America's general Asian policy, which involved a policeman-type obligation toward conflicts in the region.

These developments led to the Nixon Doctrine. It is not a fully developed policy position but rather involves a response or set of responses to new international conditions and a shift in the mood in American politics away from the internationalist principles on which the nation's diplomacy has rested since 1945. Substantively, this policy implies a departure from the past emphasis on expanded Japanese activities in Asia only in the economic and political spheres. Now, Japan is also seen as playing an active and stabilizing security role in the region, but the dimensions of this role are left indeterminate and obscure.[6] More generally, the "Doctrine" lays bare the dilemmas resulting from the uncertainties of international developments in East Asia and the concomitant incapacity of the United States to set forth a blueprint of its future behavior. Although both the rhetoric and the actions relevant to America's future intentions are ambiguous, the new posture ultimately rests on a singularly optimistic assessment regarding the stability of politics in the region following a reduction of the U.S. military presence—a remarkable shift from previous aims and experiences. The United States has pledged to deploy at least token forces for an indefinite period in Vietnam and in most other allied countries, but the number of troops and bases is being greatly reduced and the mission of the remaining military units is very unclear. While avowing that all past commitments will be honored, Secretary of State William Rogers has nevertheless stated that "we are not going to fight any major wars on the mainland of Asia again."[7] President Nixon has gone still further, expressing doubts that, after Vietnam, "we will ever have another war."[8] To structure policy on the expectation that past commitments will be salvaged by the sudden cessation of all major military conflicts in this inherently unstable and warprone region, or on a prophetic vision of perpetual peace, is to build on a foundation of sand. For Japan, with substantial and long-term interests in the region, the fresh and dubious strategic assumptions of the American position raise new and difficult choices, regarding which it will be increasingly difficult for the United States to provide "credible" responses.

In recognition that China is the critical key for peace in Asia, American policy toward Peking has correspondingly undergone a significant change. For two decades, China was seen as an immediate and formidable threat to the region, one that necessitated direct and substantial U.S. military commitments on China's periphery. The suppositions underlying the *détente* implied in the Nixon Doctrine now display the other extreme. Peking is seen as a paper dragon, lacking the capacity and the desire to pursue an expansionist foreign policy in the immediate future. This broad swing of the pendulum, reversing the fundamental assumptions of past policy, is, above all, symptomatic of the groping by the United States for a new strategic stance in Asia. Moreover, this change has far more basic significance than the improvements in Sino-American relations since mid-1971 or than the broadened contacts that would flow from normalized diplomatic ties. The results of this shift are unclear, but, unless China proves to be a truly ineffectual power or suddenly abandons its place at the vanguard of revolutionary forces, a competitive international environment centering on Peking will persist in East Asia—with a greatly diminished American role.

America's Regional Interests

The United States will without question remain a Pacific power. What is unclear is the kind of power it will be. Future American involvement in Asia will not grow simply out of military calculations or the patchwork alliance system; it will emerge from consideration of the full range of the nation's political and economic interests in the area. Since a central issue of the Vietnam controversy within the United States is whether the nation has a vital "national interest" in Southeast Asia, it is instructive to examine the past pattern of aid and the scope of the U.S. economic stake in the region against the background of deepening Japanese involvement.

For the underdeveloped countries of East Asia, economic relations with the United States are very important, indeed. Among

TABLE 11

TRADE OF EAST ASIAN COUNTRIES WITH THE UNITED STATES AS
A PERCENTAGE OF THEIR TOTAL TRADE, 1968

(In millions of U.S. dollars)

Country[a]	Exports[b] Amount	%	Imports[b] Amount	%	Total Amount	%	Rank[c] (total trade)
Burma	0.8	1.0	12.1	7.5	12.9	5.3	10
Nationalist China	269.6	37.5	387.5	43.3	657.1	39.0	1
Indonesia	174.5	24.1	169.2	25.5	343.7	24.8	2
South Korea	198.8	43.2	510.5	34.5	709.3	36.5	1[d]
Malaysia	240.1	21.4	53.6	8.2	293.7	16.5	2
Philippines	435.9	53.0	436.3	34.1	872.2	41.5	1
Singapore	28.6	9.6	101.5	10.3	130.1	10.1	4
Thailand	81.0	19.0	186.2	18.3	267.2	18.5	2
South Vietnam	1.6	9.1	270.5	38.3	272.1	37.6	1

[a] Cambodia and Laos are not included because the volume of American trade with them was too small to be of statistical significance.

[b] As reported by the United States.

[c] Preliminary reports for 1970 indicate that the United States now is the second largest trading partner of Nationalist China and the Philippines, with Japan in both instances taking over first place.

[d] Japan had an identical amount of trade with South Korea.

SOURCES: International Monetary Fund and International Bank for Reconstruction and Development, *Direction of Trade Annual, 1963–67; Direction of Trade,* February, 1969; May, 1969; July, 1969; September, 1969; November, 1969; February, 1970; and *Far Eastern Economic Review Yearbook,* 1969.

all the larger nations, America alternates with Japan as the first or second most important trading partner (Table 11). This trade is one-sidedly favorable to the United States, which in 1968 enjoyed a $672 million balance-of-payments surplus. Moreover, the composition of trade* makes it unlikely that this imbalance will be speedily redressed. With the United States able to supply categories of imports that are expanding at a high rate, and with four of the countries already conducting more than 35 per cent of their total international transactions with America, the regional trade dependence of the past will continue.

At the same time, East Asia outside of Japan remains of pe-

* America imports primary goods, such as rubber, tin, lumber, and oil, and low-cost textiles in exchange for technologically advanced industrial products essential for the rapid economic-development plans of all Asian nations.

ripheral economic importance to the United States. During the 1960's, U.S. trade with these countries rose from $1,588 million to $4,078 million, but this total has consistently approximated only 5 per cent of the nation's annual foreign trade. Comparable figures for Japanese trade grew even more and were 40 per cent greater than those of the United States. More important, during the last five years, an average of 19 per cent of Japan's annual total trade was absorbed by the region. Private American investment in East Asia (especially in Indonesia) is spurting ahead, and there are now possibilities of huge offshore oil fields in several locations. Nevertheless, there are not—nor are there likely to be —economic incentives commensurate with the material and political costs incurred in waging two wars and in maintaining a military establishment of the size that has been sustained over the past two decades. From the perspective of the region, the United States will remain a leading economic power in the Pacific, but Japan is already a much larger one, and the linkages between American economic interests and security policy are likely to remain at best tenuous.

The changing scope and structure of U.S. commitments in the region are further elucidated by a profile of the flow of American foreign aid since 1962 (Table 12). In the early 1960's, the United States was still operating as a cold-war superpower, extending sizable economic and military aid to promote the security of non-Communist states. At that time, security was broadly defined, in the words of then Secretary of Defense Robert McNamara, as "economic, social and political development."[9] As such, aid occupied a critical place in the strategy for containing Communism. Distribution of the aid, however, was, in fact, more narrowly correlated with the immediate military threat, and, in 1962, approximately 70 per cent of all assistance was sent to South Korea, South Vietnam, and Nationalist China.

In 1969, the absolute amount of economic as well as military aid to East Asia exceeded that of seven years earlier, but this was because of the extraordinary and temporary expenditures connected with the war in Indochina. Regarding the other countries in the region, the pattern of distribution and the intent of American assistance have considerably changed. Prosperity, in part

TABLE 12

U.S. FOREIGN AID TO EAST ASIAN STATES, 1962–69

(In millions of U.S. dollars)

Country		1962	1963	1964	1965	1966	1967	1968	1969
Burma	E	0.9	15.3	1.2	3.8	0.3	0.2	0.2	0.2
	M								
Cambodia	E	29.1	20.0	3.4					
	M	9.4	12.8	0.4					
Nationalist China	E	28.4	38.6	2.1	0.4				
	M	174.9	82.5	81.9	75.1	97.8	90.4	60.2	36.0
Indonesia	E	22.8	36.7	10.4	3.2		31.1	35.8	56.2
	M				0.2		2.6	5.3	5.5
Japan	E	0.4							
	M	70.6	14.6	11.3	18.5	1.6	0.4		
South Korea	E	125.7	127.8	109.5	122.5	146.8	114.7	75.2	45.4
	M	218.7	204.1	149.6	129.7	157.5	160.0	260.0	141.9
Laos	E	27.5	38.1	41.2	50.6	55.2	56.5	62.9	52.0
	M	74.6	23.5	*	*	*	*	*	*
Malaysia	E								
	M				0.1	0.2	0.2		0.2
Philippines	E	4.0	3.3	3.4	3.0	3.7	11.3	9.1	5.6
	M	27.3	20.9	24.6	23.7	21.9	26.6	21.2	18.9
Thailand	E	34.0	17.4	12.9	39.7	43.4	53.3	46.7	35.5
	M	81.0	73.5	*	*	*	60.0	*	*
South Vietnam	E	124.3	143.3	165.7	225.0	593.5	494.4	400.0	314.0
	M	176.5	211.5	214.5	*	592.2	*	*	*

E: AID foreign assistance, which includes development loans, supporting assistance, technical cooperation, development grants, and contingency funds.

M: Military assistance.

*: Data classified.

SOURCES: *Foreign Assistance Program: Annual Report of the President to the Congress,* 1962, 1963, 1964, 1965, 1966, 1967, 1968, and 1969.

stimulated by previous large-scale aid, led to the end of economic assistance to Nationalist China in 1965 and to the phasing out of support to South Korea in 1970. Substantially increased funds are currently being given to Indonesia to facilitate the massive reconstruction of the economy begun after the political demise of President Sukarno in 1965. The immense war-related assistance extended to South Vietnam, Laos, Thailand, and, more recently,

Cambodia already consumed 77 per cent of the total economic grants in 1969 and, undoubtedly, a still larger proportion of the partially classified military aid.

It remains unlikely that the present scale of aid will be sustained after the war in Indochina winds down, no matter what support may be required to help East Asian nations "increasingly shoulder their own responsibilities so we can reduce our direct involvement abroad."[10] The bloom has faded in Congress from the whole concept of foreign aid, largely because of the domestic bitterness engendered by the Vietnam conflict. In the 1970's, grant aid will not be available for use with the scope and flexibility possible in the 1960's. Guidelines for past assistance programs to East Asia were established overwhelmingly in terms of U.S. security interests in the region. Now that the nature of these interests is being redefined and their scope reduced, the future of American aid stands in a state of limbo. A selective reduction would dilute still more general U.S. commitments to the region and accent further the rapidly expanding foreign aid efforts of Japan.

Security Issues

Whether American and Japanese security interests will always remain congruent in these circumstances is *prima facie* highly dubious, but American strategic experts have shown a notable reluctance to acknowledge and/or confront this development. The logic of expanded Japanese power together with American frustration in Vietnam have prompted some (e.g., George Ball and George Kennan) to suggest a strengthening of our link with Japan, accompanied by an effective withdrawal from any military effort to "balance power" on the Asiatic mainland. Another widely supported position, most forcefully advocated by Edwin Reischauer, urges continued alliance with a Japan transformed into a more "responsible partner" through greatly augmented conventional military capabilities. Both positions imply Japan's continued acceptance of ultimate security dependence on America, presuppose that the Japanese will not be confronted with a security threat with which the United States could not and would not deal, and presume an active but nonmilitary Japanese foreign

policy. On the most general level of response, let us note Robert
Osgood's remark that "it would be one of the great anomalies of
history if a state with the potential power, the extensive foreign
interests, and the long-run security problem . . . of Japan should
indefinitely entrust the military protection of its interests to another state."[11] There are two fundamental alternatives: extension of the *status quo,* providing Japan with "a unique opportunity to prove that a nation can be great without possessing
commensurate military force"[12]; or a move toward an autonomous
military posture. The likeliest alternative, and the problems it
may pose for conflict within the American alliance, is suggested
by a consideration of the four basic security issues currently facing
the Japanese: the threat of Communist China, the defense of
South Korea, the status of American bases and the return of
Okinawa, and the problem of rearmament.

China. Communist China is viewed by both Japan and the
United States as the greatest security threat in Asia, but the differences in the nature of this threat, as perceived in Tokyo and
as perceived in Washington, are so significant as to be a major
potential source of conflict between the two countries. Two basic
considerations have underlain American efforts to isolate and
militarily contain China during the past two decades—the global
commitment to contain Communism and specific policies to
stabilize the international situation in East Asia. Ten years of
polycentrism and the widening of the Sino-Soviet split have made
imperative more flexible and muted policies of containment, and
the stalemate in Vietnam has made all but inevitable a great
reduction in future U.S. conventional military involvement in
Asia. Unless emphasis is given to the still highly conjectural
Chinese nuclear threat to the continental United States, the likelihood of conflict between America and China is destined to de-
crease. Conversely, for Asia, and especially for Japan, reduction
of the American presence will heighten the concern over security
from China.

What possible security threat can the Chinese pose for Japan?*

* It is assumed that any direct attack by the Soviet Union against Japan
would automatically provoke an American response, and that the Russians will
move cautiously toward expanding military involvement in Asia.

If the Japanese continue to limit their security zone solely to their home islands and to accept *in toto* the American nuclear guarantee, there is not likely to be a clear or present military danger to them from China, or from any other country, that could not be met by their own modest conventional defense forces. Yet, the Japanese Government has acknowledged since 1965 that China poses a security threat to Japan, and that this threat has a nuclear dimension. Moreover, a Chinese nuclear attack would certainly not be directed against Japan *in vacuo* but would involve Sino-Japanese conflict over an "outside issue" or over the conditions of alliance with the United States; that is, it would most likely take the form of nuclear blackmail.[13] Thus, a China threat is tied to Japanese engagement in Asia, either through autonomous commitments integrally involving security considerations or through Japan's alliance with America. Japanese involvement in war through alliance with the United States is increasingly less probable, in view of continued strong resistance by the Japanese to direct involvement in American military moves and the increasing reluctance of America to make them. The option of total withdrawal from Asian security problems assured by the scope of past American actions cannot be held open much longer for the Japanese. Without isolation, a real or perceived threat from China could be avoided only in the highly improbable event that international conflict is purged from Asia or that the Chinese effectively withdraw from regional politics. A Japan engaged in Asia could not be expected to depend entirely on American security policy in dealing with Peking, both because of the long-term unacceptability of such dependence to the Japanese and because the vicissitudes of international politics virtually preclude an absolute identity of interests for the two allies. The pressures for an independent military posture may well prove irresistible.

Korea. In the November, 1969, communiqué announcing the American return of the Ryukyu Islands, Japan explicitly acknowledged a "special security interest" in Korea and Taiwan. This was the first formal public statement in the postwar era implying a broadened security role for Japan, and it elicited unusually strong reactions from both the Chinese and the North

Koreans. Japanese security interests in Korea are rooted in compelling geographical, economic, and political considerations. American interests are also strong; but the reversion of Okinawa in 1972, the reduction of American bases and troops in Japan, a significant reduction of U.S. forces in South Korea, and the still uncertain implications of an impending general military cutback in Asia, all point to a reduced capacity and commitment to defend Korea. Conjecture about the likelihood that the Japanese will replace the United States has been refuted by both Seoul and Tokyo; indeed, such a possibility is quite unfeasible in the immediate future. Yet, the persistence of the Korean security problem illustrates in clear and specific terms the pressures for an autonomous military role for Japan and the dilemmas of expanded Japanese-American security collaboration in a post-Vietnam Asia.

A major check on the outbreak of another war in Korea has been the deep involvement of the United States and the Soviet Union with the respective sides. The resulting cold-war type of confrontation has brought the usual constraints found when the superpowers directly face one another. This situation is changing. Even if, after Vietnam, the United States remains ultimately committed to defend Korea, it is very uncertain whether a full-scale "limited war" in the style of the 1950's would or could be undertaken. If a full-scale conventional war broke out between the North and South, it would be virtually impossible to restrict the combatants to Koreans alone, particularly if an advantage were gained by the Seoul government. Furthermore, even if the Soviet Union and the United States were prompted by global strategic considerations to forestall or limit any outbreak of hostilities, it is far from clear that the Chinese, with narrower strategic interests and a more immediate concern for the military importance of Korea, would be so constrained. In any open conflict of this sort, the critical pawn in the ensuing strategic game would be Japan, a nation essential to the effective conduct of a conventional war by the United States and immediately susceptible to a nuclear threat from China. Any Chinese effort to neutralize Japan in this way would directly test the credibility of the American nuclear umbrella and, whatever the result, bring the Japanese face-to-face with the realities of power politics in contemporary East Asia. This or a similar, equally plausible scenario would raise basic and difficult questions regarding the status of American bases and the nature and timing of rearmament issues, which have already served as sources of conflict in the Japanese-American alliance.

Military Bases and Okinawa

No matter what formal arrangements are devised, every military crisis in Northeast Asia will almost certainly lead to a domestic political crisis in Japan regarding the nature and use of American bases. Beyond their strategic value, these bases have peculiar importance for the political foundations of the alliance. They will continue to serve as lightning rods for anti-American protest over a variety of issues. This aspect has been given much emphasis in the past and cannot be expected to diminish as the anti-Americanism of the left persists and as nationalist sentiment grows. It is also important to recognize, however, that American military forces stand as a symbol of continued U.S. interest in defending Japan. Any serious cutback of these forces could be interpreted as a signal of a reduction in this commitment. As suggested by the response to the reversion of Okinawa with a drastically curtailed American military presence, further policy change in this direction is bound to precipitate strengthening of the Japanese Self-Defense Forces, leaving uncertain whether this will result simply in a broadened sharing of the defense burden or provide the impetus for Japan's development of security capacity fully independent of the United States. The permanent deployment of American nuclear weapons in Japan currently is not—nor is it likely to be—allowed by the Japanese, but the credibility of the U.S. nuclear umbrella is linked to the commitment implicit in the presence of conventional bases. A serious reduction of them will undoubtedly increase the pressures for the establishment of a Japanese nuclear capacity. Thus, on the political plane, the bases leave the United States with a difficult choice: retain them at the risk of stoking anti-American and nationalist sentiments; or reduce them and raise the pressure for an autonomous Japanese defense policy.

Strategically, the case for maintaining the bases is increasingly weak. With the development of high-speed air and sea transport, the need for the peacetime presence of American conventional forces in Japan has evaporated. If, in fact, the bases are cut back to skeletal proportions, as is widely expected by the mid-1970's, they would become useful only in emergencies—emergencies that will almost certainly arise on the Asiatic mainland or Taiwan, not in Japan. From Tokyo's viewpoint, the main effect of the American forces, apart from the hostage value regarding nuclear support, will be to implicate the Japanese in military actions in Asia at a time and place not exclusively of their choosing. Despite the limited and shrinking strategic value to the United States of bases in Japan, a conflict could well arise from their specific use in dealing with one of the chronic security problems in the region, such as Korea.

Okinawa has held a special place on the agenda of problems outstanding between Japan and the United States. Article III of the San Francisco Peace Treaty placed this island and the others in the Ryukyu chain wholly under American jurisdiction. Full authority over their disposition was vested in the Department of Defense, and Okinawa was transformed into the largest base in East Asia, the keystone to U.S. military activities throughout the region. In effect, the island became a fiefdom of the American military. It was administered by an army general (the High Commissioner), and, because the bases were totally free from any restrictions, they were stanchly defended as a *sine qua non* for effective strategic operations in East Asia. The political risks and inconsistencies involved in this policy were substantial. To facilitate the conduct of operations to contain Communism, full democratic rights were denied to 1 million people and quasicolonial occupation was prolonged in territory over which Japan held "residual sovereignty." The uncertainties and logistical needs created by the Vietnam war further postponed consideration of the issue from a broad, diplomatic perspective. Only in the latter part of the 1960's, when local sentiments in Okinawa took a sharp turn toward immediate reversion and irredentist feelings in Japan attained politically significant proportions, did the United States move to liquidate the last major legacy of World War II. With reversion in May, 1972, this problem finally was resolved, but the diplomatic costs of reaching settlement were exorbitant. Because narrow military considerations were given disproportionate weight for so long, a political issue was allowed to develop in a way that encouraged bilateral conflict over a wide range of matters at the very time when the entire alliance, and the strategic principles on which it rests, came under serious strain.

Rearmament

If Japan is to participate effectively in power politics in Asia, with China as its main rival, nuclear weapons must be developed, especially in view of the cloud of uncertainty that will surround gradual American military disengagement from the area. In the foreseeable future, the only threat to Japan will be nuclear. A conventional invasion is unthinkable and, in any event, would assure American intervention in ways that a nuclear threat (linked to another military or political act) would not. To be sure, it is difficult to justify the development of nuclear weapons in terms of any strategic calculus narrowly concerned with the physical defense of Japan proper, as many American and virtually all Japanese strategic analysts point out. However, the incentives for developing such weapons are rooted in a vision of security that extends beyond the home islands and an assumption that, in a world where the major international actors are nuclear powers, some nuclear capacity is essential for pursuing a successful foreign policy by other, nonnuclear means.

A posture that would maximize the possibility for continued Japanese noninvolvement in Asia, avoid the uncertainties of American nuclear support, and meet immediate, narrow security needs would consist of nuclear weapons and limited conventional forces. By strongly promoting the Treaty on the Non-Proliferation of Nuclear Weapons, the United States is raising the one security issue on which Japan may ultimately be forced to break sharply and openly with American policy—an alternative clearly implicit in the long and sharply phrased statement issued by the Foreign Ministry when Japan signed the treaty. Emphasizing the inherent inequities for the nonnuclear powers, Tokyo made clear that Japanese ratification was contingent, among other things, on "concrete measures of nuclear disarmament . . . by *all* nuclear powers."* The nuclear option, in short, will be kept open, particularly as no serious technical or budgetary obstacles stand in the way. Japanese expansion of conventional capacities, strongly encouraged by the United States, is significant not so much in terms of the marginal increment provided for defense of the home islands as in terms of the positive effect on the national commitment to, and the technical ability for sustaining, a military establishment.

International conditions require that the basis of the American-Japanese alliance change. In the wake of America's greatest foreign-policy misadventure, which unequivocally demonstrates the intractability and instability of international politics in East Asia, basic and long-term strategic considerations of the magnitude faced in the late 1940's are now critical to Japanese-American relations. What in the past was effectively determined by statesmen may be increasingly beyond their reach in the future. Conflicts between the two nations now seem destined to be primarily defined by events in this region that are beyond the control of either country. This situation cannot but result in a divergence of American and Japanese policies in Asia, a change that will be further abetted by the renascence of nationalism in Japan.

At first glance, there is little new either in the Japanese political situation or in the government's policies to indicate an imminent shift regarding the American alliance. For one thing, it is almost a certainty that the pro-American Liberal-Democratic Party will remain in power for years to come; for another, the current political rhetoric of government leaders continues emphatically to define Japan's national interest largely in moral and/or economic terms within the framework of the Mutual Security Treaty. Furthermore, despite sporadic leftist outbursts, the public mood appears to endorse this direction and the low-keyed approach to foreign affairs. Yet, a glimpse beneath the surface reveals several cracks in the alliance that could lead to profound changes. The absence of consensus on policy goals and a decision-making process that precludes bold leadership bar any Gaullist-style defiance of the United States. But they also assure

* See Appendix C.

that future relations with America will proceed without the moderating effects a strong policy direction could provide, and that the basic course of Japan's foreign policy will develop incrementally in narrow circumstantial terms. In sum, the dynamics of Japanese internal politics make relations with the United States particularly susceptible to the shifting tides of international politics and the drift of American foreign policy.

Like Pandora and Epimetheus, Japan has been living in a child's paradise free from danger and conflict, thanks to the American alliance and American commitments in East Asia. Continued trust in the United States cannot perpetuate this utopia, for America demonstrably lacks the capacity of the gods to insure international harmony. In this era of nuclear multipolarity, the problems of war, revolution, and uncertainty are evils conspicuously evident in the international milieu in which the United States and Japan must live. The partnership in paradise has ended, and the hope can only be that conflict will not result in unbridled competition.

7 The Security Problem: The View from Within

The way is now open to consider the most important aspect of Japan's foreign affairs, the problem of national security. In a fundamental sense, Japan's posture in this field has been remarkably simple: Beyond the American alliance, there has effectively been no strategic policy regarding external threats or regional conflict. Security has been defined in the narrow sense of preserving national territorial integrity, and government defense measures have been aimed, first, at maintaining *internal* order[1] and, second, at supplementing American forces to cope with a conventional invasion—a contingency that has been singularly implausible since the early 1950's. Under the rubric of the peace constitution, independent concern for matters of *Realpolitik* has been eschewed *in principle* as well as in fact by the government and the opposition alike. Although the security issue has been an inter- and intraparty political football and a central feature of the nation's foreign policy, the entire domestic debate has occurred in a vacuum free from immediate concern for international realities. The debate has thus focused on abstract moral concepts, such as pacifism, disarmed neutralism, and undifferentiated anti-Communism, or has been cluttered with details regarding transient issues, such as visits of nuclear-powered warships and local incidents regarding American bases. In the midst of unrelieved regional tension and turmoil, Japan has withdrawn into a self-contained pacifist cocoon with a defense budget that has consistently taken a far lower percentage of its GNP than in any comparable nation. Recently, however, the insulation of this cocoon has been significantly weakened by the uncertainties of future U.S. military commitments in Asia and the growth of the international web emanating from Tokyo. This development has prompted new concern within the country for security. At the same time, the ambiguity and confusion that surround the entire Japanese position on defense have led to growing concern in other nations about the real direction of Japan's policy and have provoked warnings from the United States, as well as China and the Soviet Union, about the possible revival of militarism. Japan, albeit reluctantly, stands at a strategic crossroads, and to understand the dimensions of the decisions facing Tokyo it is necessary to look beyond the past policies and programs explicitly concerned with defense. The landscape of the *Alice in Wonderland* world of Japan's security policy can be seen in proper perspective only within the framework of the broad trends in politics and economics relating to the new international milieu in East Asia set forth in the preceding discussion.

In considering the evolution of Japan's defense policies, the domestic political influences and the external environment must be scrupulously distinguished and evaluated separately. Normally, a nation's strategic policy reflects a dynamic balance between internal and international considerations, but in Japan this relationship has been disrupted. Prolonged withdrawal from all power politics has led to a perspective on defense that is derived almost solely from the politics and ideals peculiar to the conditions *within* the country during the postwar period. A defense plan that, in the words of the Defense White Paper of 1970, "smashes all historical precedents" by allowing the nation "to become a big economic power but not a big military power"[2] displays a self-centered myopia that has consistently tinged Japan's cautious measures to build up its military capacity. The scope of U.S. military commitments in East Asia made the muted Japanese gestures of the past feasible and appropriate, but there is universal recognition that the needs of the future will demand change to deal with the contours of the new regional environment and the changing direction and form of security threats the country will confront. At least initially, the direction of new policies will be stimulated by the international environment. Viewed on the screen of the external strategic setting, some of the most critical issues, especially the question of nuclear armaments, already have taken on vastly different proportions from what they have within the context of the domestic scene.

Japan has opened few doors leading to a workable defense policy beyond dependence on the United States, but remarkably few remain closed either. By keeping all options open, a properly flexible policy is within reach, but only if the imperatives of an expanded defense program can be made consonant with the national mood and accommodated in the decision-making process. How Japan will develop a national security policy suitable to the new East Asian international order is quite unclear, but the answer to this question is fundamental to the prospects for war or peace in the area and to the viability of the postwar domestic political system.

OFFICIAL DEFENSE POLICY

The Constitutional Issue

The departure point for considering the development of Japanese defense policy is the anomalous peace clause (Article IX) of the American-drafted constitution:

> Aspiring sincerely to an international peace based on justice and order, the Japanese people forever renounce war as a sovereign right of the nation, and the threat or use of force as a means of settling international disputes.
>
> In order to accomplish the aim of the preceding paragraph, land, sea and air forces, as well as other war potential, will never be maintained. The right of belligerency of the state will not be recognized.

This declaration left Japan adrift in a world of conflict, bereft of what has been universally recognized as an inherent right of sovereignty for all modern nation states, and, with the emergence of the cold war and the outbreak of fighting in Korea, made it more or less inevitable that the country would become a defense satellite of the United States. Domestically, this utopian experiment became the most dramatic symbol of the new constitution and gave rise to a legal and moral smoke screen behind which the defense program has stumbled ever since. Although the peace clause was sporadically questioned by several conservative leaders, particularly during the 1950's,[3] the basic principle on which it rests has not been directly and effectively challenged. In consequence, the government has operated in a pacifist milieu and has been continuously on the defensive in all efforts to develop a security policy. Indeed, the very legality of the military forces (created in mid-1950) is still questioned by the political left, and today the articulation of clear and positive national strategic objectives continues to be extremely difficult—thereby helping to prolong the fiction that the country can ignore military conflicts while fully participating in the international system in all other respects. Above all, the idealism embodied in this article has given all matters of defense a peculiarly moral cast and drawn this question deeply into the problem of constitutional revision and the values underlying the very foundations of the postwar political order. Ultimately, it is the emotional and political legacies of Article IX that stand as the main imponderables for the future direction of defense policy, but the legal dimensions further complicate an extraordinary situation.

Whether Article IX serves as a legal prescription for total pacifism is still a matter of dispute. *Prima facie,* it would appear that it does, since the wording is unambiguous, and it is included in the corpus of the basic law of the land. Most intellectuals and the socialist left support this strict interpretation and have flailed official policy as both illegal as well as immoral.[4] A much looser interpretation of the article, however, has been followed by the government and the Japanese courts, one that permits the maintenance of self-defense forces and treaties to insure the country's security. As expressed by the Supreme Court in the landmark *Sunakawa* decision, Japan *as a sovereign state* has an "inherent right of self defense" and is entitled to take the measures appropriate to this end. A similar view was taken by the late Professor Kenzō Takayanagi, chairman of the official Commission on the Constitution from 1957 to 1964, who saw the peace clause not as an ordinary legal provision but as a "political manifesto . . . a world ideal which cannot be realized by Japan alone but by the joint endeavors of all nations."[5] This court interpretation has given the Diet full discretion to determine whether there will be armed forces, as well as the nature of their capabilities. For a decade now, the issue of the constitutionality of the defense program has remained relatively quiescent, but the conspicuous legal ambiguities have continued to feed discontent both on the pacifist left, which sees the current interpretation as flagrantly inconsistent with the basic law, and on the nationalist right, which views the progressive rearmament of Japan under the peace constitution as sheer hypocrisy. In effect, the Supreme Court's interpretation of the constitution, on which the defense program has been built, has removed virtually all legal restraints on the direction in which this policy can move, but the full implications are as yet only partially recognized.

For a security program predicated on the "inherent right of self defense," the critical legal point is the determination of what are defensive as distinct from offensive capacities. Inherently, this principle provides no clear policy guidelines and the question cannot be answered with precision. In the nuclear era, it is absurd to define defense in terms of response to an attack; but then a force sufficient to deter such an attack clearly must have "offensive" potential. In what sense can a missile or a fighter-bomber capable of repulsing a strike from abroad remain a purely defensive weapon? In the past, the Japanese managed to downplay these matters, because only conventional external threats were considered and the force level was restricted to serve a purely supportive role to the United States. These conditions are now changing. As long as the legal prerogative for self-defense was limited by the slow rate of military expenditures and a refusal to dispatch troops overseas, the constitutional ambiguities involved were ignored by other nations. When, however, the Defense White Paper of 1970 blandly asserted that "it is within the scope of legal theory to possess . . . small-size nuclear weapons,"[6] demonstrating that the conservative government saw no real constitutional limit on "defensive" rearmament, many countries displayed concern over Japan's security policy for the first time since 1945.

As a consequence of Article IX, pacifism not only has become an important political issue but is deeply implicated in the most basic attitudes held by individuals regarding the state—that is, in the very foundations of citizenship. Beyond the numerous opinion polls predictably demonstrating the popular appeal of peace, there is astonishingly wide and strong support among the media and the intellectuals for the rather bizarre notion that the post-war generation has been literally "socialized for peace" in the political order created by the new constitution.[7] In a similar vein, the government has seen the current policy of building a more autonomous defense as essentially requiring "a new spiritual foundation among the people . . . a [new] sense of patriotism."[8] This peculiarly introspective quality of both positions can be attributed at least partially to the exaggerated concern displayed in the constitution (and early Occupation policies) for the internal political structure of Japan as the major potential cause of war in Asia. In any event, the development of security policy is entangled with the basic principles and attitudes of citizenship in the new political order in ways that intensify and exaggerate divisions within the society on this point. This has ominous implications for the future. Reconsideration of the meaning of Article IX was prompted in the early 1950's by external developments in East Asia (especially the Korean war and the rise of China), and stimulus for any new national consensus on defense is also likely to be created as a result of changes in the international environment. An externally generated move toward full-scale rearmament without constitutional revision would risk serious domestic political polarization as well as *de facto* discredit of the basic law. Alternatively, a successful referendum revoking Article IX* would provide the Japanese Government with another historically unique mandate, a popular, open-ended endorsement of the right to make war. In the imperfect contemporary world, the peace constitution is at best a mixed blessing.

Pattern of Policy Development

For the past two decades, Japan's approach to defense has been remarkably unvarying and subdued, an example *par excellence* of

---

* Amendment of the constitution requires support of at least two-thirds of the Diet and a popular majority in a national referendum, which means that, under the pattern of representation prevailing since 1955, the conservatives would need the support of at least one of the minor parties.

what in Tokyo is called *māmā seisaku*—a stand-pat policy. The principles on which this policy has been built remain platitudinous and vague; the strength of the military forces has grown at a rate determined essentially by the annual bureaucratic struggle to piece together a budget; and the *point d'appui,* full and unqualified U.S. support, has remained, at least until mid-1971, an assumption beyond question. New problems, especially regarding nuclear weapons and more autonomous defense forces, have steadily gained in importance since the mid-1960's, a result of the dramatic changes in the external environment and of a more gradual shift in the domestic mood. Nevertheless, the government, while indicating that some change is appropriate, has proceeded within the same basic parameters as in the past, leaving unclear when and how the era of low-profile *māmā seisaku* will end.

The military forces of postwar Japan were brought into being by General Douglas MacArthur in response to conditions created by the Korean war, a gesture rectifying the disarmed pacifism that he personally had done so much to foster. In July, 1950, a 75,000-man National Police Reserve was authorized to maintain internal security in place of American troops then caught up in duties related to Korea. With the end of the Occupation in the spring of 1952, the forces were somewhat expanded, a small naval arm was added, and over-all jurisdiction was assumed by the National Defense Agency.* Finally, in July, 1954, the basic framework within which the armed forces still operate was established with the passage of the Defense Agency Establishment Law and the Self-Defense Forces Law.

Although in basic purpose and function these forces remain remarkably the same at the present time as in 1954, their size and capabilities have grown significantly. From 1954 to 1958, the combined strength of the three branches of service (Ground, Air, and Maritime Self-Defense Forces) grew from 146,000 to 214,000, while the number of American troops in the country fell from 210,000 to 77,000. Since 1958, the Self-Defense Forces have been developed under three consolidation plans that have gradually expanded their size and sharply raised the quality and quantity

* The National Defense Agency became the Self-Defense Agency in 1954.

of equipment. In 1970, the over-all strength stood at approximately 250,000 men, 180,000 of whom were in the Army (the total of American troops had dropped to 38,000). The modest level of Japan's forces is further qualified by the absence of a conscription system and by a very limited reserve-forces program. With 200 ships (totaling about 137,000 tons), the Japanese Navy is equipped to deal almost exclusively with coastal defense and antisubmarine warfare, while the Air Force now has 920 modern jets and several Nike missile units.

Notable improvements in the quality of equipment and in the level of firepower are provided for in the Fourth Defense Plan (1972–76).[9] The total cost of this program is currently projected at $14.4 billion (2.4 times the previous plan), and its annual expenditures will exceed the defense budgets of all nations except the five nuclear powers and West Germany. Although the details are not yet settled, the proportion of domestically produced materials in the new plan is expected to increase sharply to 90 per cent, enhancing Japan's independence from the United States. The acquisition of 176 American Phantom fighter-bombers and a notable expansion of naval capacity will make the Japanese military among the best-equipped conventional forces in the world, and strain still more the distinction between "defensive" and "offensive" capabilities.

The development of the Self-Defense Forces, despite the fact that they are structured around five-year programs, displays two characteristics of Japanese foreign policy generally—a lack of clear, long-term goals involving more independent actions by the nation and an emphasis on domestic over external considerations. The very comprehensiveness of dependence on the United States has allowed the defense plans to develop in a kind of international vacuum, in which the direction and temper of expansion have been treated more as a budget than as a strategic question. For example, the Defense White Paper of 1970, written at a time of mounting international uncertainty for Japan, fails to broach a single strategic issue and in essence stands as weapons-procurement review. The scope of the American alliance and the trading-company style of Japanese diplomacy lie behind the extraordinarily modest level of military expenditures. These costs have at no time reached even 1.8 per cent of GNP, and this ratio has steadily fallen over the last eight years to .8 per cent—a record completely out of line with the comparable expenditures of the other major industrial powers, which in 1969 ranged from 3.5 per cent (West Germany) to 8.6 per cent (the United States).[10] This performance, and the parallel drop in the percentage of the defense budget in total government spending, are not best explained in terms of pacifist opposition to rearmament or of the imperatives of rapid economic growth—the reasons most commonly cited in Japan. Rather, the basic causes lie in the dynamics of decision-making and in the low priority (indeed, almost inadvertent attention) that has been accorded to the question of external defense. Without any independent strategic goals beyond holding operations for the United States, and with no immediate political incentives for establishing any, even the limited appropriations requests of the Defense Agency have been grist in the mill of the Finance Ministry and more powerful elements of the bureaucracy and reduced to proportions in line with other ministries' demands. Again, the economic planners have basically influenced the political, in this case the strategic, priorities of the nation's foreign policy.[11]

Since past security policies have been well suited to the circumstances Japan has faced since 1952, at first glance neither the peculiar pattern of defense decision-making, nor the extremely limited and one-sided nature of the strategic goals, nor the level and structure of the military forces, provide a basis for concern. However, the success of these policies is seen more properly as a function of the uniquely favorable external milieu rather than as a shrewd strategic calculation by Japanese leaders.[12] During the past two decades, Japan has lived in an international environment that, strategically, has been almost continuously dominated by the United States. Moreover, in the pervasive conflict and tension in Asia during these years, *no* defense policy (or one of minuscule budgets and ambiguous purposes) was the best policy. These circumstances transformed into virtues the fundamental immobilism of defense decision-making and the tokenism of official actions and brought into being an inertia that will make change to a more activist position more difficult. Except in the highly improbable event that these unique international conditions are extended into the future, it is doubtful that Japan can continue to proceed in a direction in which weakness and non-involvement will prove to be wisdom and budgetary criteria will establish appropriate goals for defense.

In the latter part of the 1960's, the government recognized the necessity for a change in security policy both in words and in action. It was implicit in the cautious approach taken toward ratification of the Treaty on the Non-Proliferation of Nuclear Weapons and in the broadening of Japanese security interests to include South Korea and Taiwan. Explicitly, it underlay the new concept of "autonomous defense" (*jishu bōei*) that was introduced as a supplement to the 1957 "Basic National Defense Policy," which exclusively emphasized the United States—Japan security system. In this new approach, the cornerstone of the nation's security, at least in the short run, would continue to be based on "collective defense" with America, but emphasis increasingly was to be shifted to developing more independent military capacities. Whether such capabilities are ultimately to be fully autonomous, or whether autonomy implies security objectives different from and possibly conflicting with those of the United States, has been left indeterminate. Indeed, *jishu bōei* has been given vague and widely varying definitions, such as: "the people's mental attitude . . . patriotism,"[13] "the autonomous development of [military] equipment," and "air and sea supremacy necessary for the defense of Japan."[14] Probably the most elaborate official attempt to outline this concept was made in early 1970 by Yasuhirō Nakasone, then Director General of the Defense Agency and a conservative politician whose vision of defense has undergone frequent changes of hue.[15] Three of his "five principles of autonomous defense" simply reaffirmed the sanctity of the peace constitution, civilian control over the military, and the imperative to provide for defense of national territory—all shibboleths of government policy since the Self-Defense Forces were established. However, he ventured into controversial ground in proclaiming (1) that Japan would neither make, possess, nor introduce into the country nuclear weapons, and (2) that, within the Japanese-American security arrangement, it would be necessary "to supplement

Japan's resources for national defense." These "principles" are notable because, in effect, they are ambiguous policy recommendations about which there are sharp divisions within and outside the Liberal-Democratic Party.

Openly raising the issue of nuclear weapons, if only to affirm the so-called three nuclear principles as an inviolate premise of Japanese policy, constitutes an important departure from the past. Indeed, the concern manifested regarding the nuclear question is of greater significance than the substance of the proposal set forth. The latter is properly seen simply as part of Nakasone's personal view of Japan as a "middle-range nonnuclear power"—a hazy and much disputed view that was subsequently openly rejected by the Prime Minister himself.[16] In fact, since the progress of China's nuclear program, the official Japanese position regarding such weapons has gradually changed from one of unqualified rejection to one of keeping open all policy alternatives. Understandably, the question of nuclear policy remains a matter of controversy and concern among the conservatives, as is abundantly manifest in the ambiguity of the 1970 Defense White Paper, which both sets forth the three nonnuclear principles and notes the possibility of armament with tactical nuclear weapons. "Autonomous defense" may or may not lead in a nuclear direction; the critical factor will be the credibility of America's nuclear umbrella.

Nakasone's final "autonomous defense" principle implies that the alliance with the United States must be continued, but under new conditions that give Japan an expanded role. At the most general level, this is compatible both with the long-standing pressure from Washington for a higher level of conventional armament by Japan and with the needs created by the general American military cutback in Asia. It also is in keeping with the modest tempo of growth envisioned for the Self-Defense Forces. This approach makes sense, if Japanese and American security objectives are identical and Japan continues to adhere to a purely "defense military posture"—a euphemism for the isolationism made possible in the past by U.S. actions. However, for Tokyo, the main thrust of the Nixon Doctrine is to create uncertainties about what future U.S. security priorities in Asia may be. To develop autonomy *within* the American alliance, this stumbling block has been avoided by raising the question of the compatibility of security interests to a vacuous level of abstraction. Thus, the critical issue has not been faced. To attempt to structure an autonomous defense by augmenting Japan's military resources without clearly formulated strategic objectives is to build blindly, to fashion a policy without substance. This is precisely the direction in which the government has moved.

On the surface, the evolution of the nation's security policy has proceeded smoothly and successfully, but a closer look at the anatomy of this policy reveals that the supporting structure is fundamentally flawed. Partly, this is due to the manner in which the issue has been approached. On the one hand, the approach has been too abstract, dealing at length with the question of whether Japan has the *right* to defense policy at all and not with what the policy ought to be. On the other hand, defense policy has been too specific, focused narrowly on the military aspect of potential security issues without reference to the broader political, economic, and psychological dimensions of the country's foreign affairs—What can Japan do if South Korea is subject to a massive attack? Answer: Not much or nothing. Similarly, the government has been wont to consider in a direct, *in vacuo* manner such sweeping and complex questions as "the rise of militarism" and "going nuclear." Ultimately, of course, the extraordinary nature of Japan's defense policy is the outgrowth of the peculiar external and internal political conditions that have led the Japanese to remain aloof from power politics. How fully the vacuum in strategic planning may prove a liability as the nation is drawn into full participation in international relations is better appreciated once the place of the defense question in the broader domestic political setting is made clear.

DOMESTIC POLITICS AND DEFENSE POLICY

Japan has been insulated from any real direct threats from abroad, and both the intellectual debate on defense and the conflicts over security issues among and within the political parties have been shaped almost entirely by internal considerations. For ideological as well as political reasons, the opposition parties early made matters of defense the focal point for challenging the ruling party—as well as for contention among themselves. Once caught up in the currents of domestic politics, the security question has taken on definition and a self-sustaining momentum of its own. The resulting public and partisan debates have been substantively so abstract and ambiguous that a straightforward, frontal approach to them would confuse rather than clarify their import. Because our purpose is to consider the influence of internal politics on Japan's defense posture, no attempt is made to elaborate all of the twists and turns that the overt dialogue on strategy has taken. Rather, stress is placed on the basic trends of opinions expressed by the political parties, the changes in mood of mass opinion, and the shift in emphasis in the debate in the mass media and among the so-called defense intellectuals since the mid-1960's. An understanding of these broad changes in the climate of opinion regarding defense, and of how they are related to the capacity of the government to adopt different future policies, is far more significant than the specific content of past security policies and proposals.

Political Parties

The party debate over the security problem has been structured around four major issues: (1) the Japanese-American Security Treaty, (2) the status of the Self-Defense Forces, (3) the nature and meaning of the "threats" posed by China and the Soviet Union, and (4) nuclear weapons. A review of the positions the various parties have taken regarding these issues sheds some light on the probable direction of the domestic political response to the changing strategic conditions that Japan now faces in Asia.

The Conservatives. In a basic sense, the position of the Liberal-Democratic Party can be equated with official government defense policy. There has, in fact, been consensus on the need for the Mutual Security Treaty and on the principle of collective defense. Similarly, there is almost unanimous agreement within the party that the Self-Defense Forces should be gradually strengthened, that this can and should be achieved without constitutional revision, and that there is a need to educate the public to a greater awareness of national defense needs. On the whole, Liberal-Democratic Party leaders have not been willing to speak out boldly on defense, because the American alliance has made unnecessary any real change of front, and because the emotional atmosphere surrounding the whole issue of security has rendered the domestic political risks prohibitively high. However, the conservatives have never been of one mind on this matter, and, since 1965, disagreements have become progressively more open over the full range of defense policy and particularly regarding the threat posed by China. Although these differences have remained relatively muted, especially concerning nuclear weapons, a defense dialogue has developed within the party that will critically influence the future direction of the nation's foreign policy.

Liberal-Democratic politicians rarely offer any but carefully qualified and ambiguous statements on defense, but it is possible to distinguish two groups among them with broadly different views. The most important is the "rightists," whose members are drawn mainly (but not exclusively) from the mainstream Sato factional coalition, which dominated the party from 1964 to 1970, and who have served as the core of the Asian Study Group. More than any other important element on the Japanese political scene, these men see a meaningful defense strategy as resting primarily on the calculus of international power politics. This realism regarding the international system is combined with a strong anti-Communism, which leads to a special concern for strengthening the military alliance with the United States and a sense of immediacy regarding the threat posed by China as well as that posed by the Soviet Union. The right wing (*Soshinkai*) of this mainstream group is genuinely concerned about a Communist-led internal insurrection and sees the prevention of such an eventuality as a major task of the Self-Defense Forces.[17] Although generally opposed to the Treaty on the Non-Proliferation of Nuclear Weapons and insistent on keeping open the nuclear option, almost all the leaders of the conservative right have shied away from advocating a truly autonomous defense posture and have insisted on proceeding hand in hand with the United States, even in the face of the mounting uncertainties caused by the Nixon Doctrine.

Common misconceptions persist regarding both the policy posture and the political strength of this group. Because the more extremist members (e.g., Minoru Genda, first chief of the Air Defense Staff) frequently articulate outspoken opinions on defense, the group as a whole and especially its most visible leaders (e.g., Nobusuke Kishi and Okinori Kaya), are often dismissed as ideological anachronisms. More properly, however, they should be seen as shrewd, flexible nationalists willing to accept the responsibilities of full participation in power politics—at a time when Japan is being nudged in the direction of *Realpolitik*. Contrary to widespread belief, the conservative "right" retains a broad, suprafactional base and includes many younger Diet members. Beyond vague ideological affinities, it is defined by the complex web of interpersonal relationships fundamental to politics within the Japanese conservative establishment,* and this inhibits bold or extreme policy positions. Although it is possible to discern elements within the right wing of the Liberal-Democratic Party that incline toward an independent defense posture sustained by a new nationalism, what is most distinctive about these men is the degree to which their approach to security matters is circumscribed by internal political considerations and by international constraints, especially the American alliance.

The second and less important group of Liberal-Democratic politicians is composed of antimainstream factions. Although the defense issue has been regularly employed by the minority factions within the party to attack the Prime Minister and allied *habatsu* leaders, no strong and consistent substantive criticism of strategic policy has been provided by any group among the Liberal-Democrats. During the latter part of the 1960's, however, significant intraparty differences surfaced regarding the nature of the Chinese threat and approval of the Treaty on the Non-Proliferation of Nuclear Weapons. The China issue drew the greater attention and was used extensively by faction leaders seeking to topple Sato from power, especially after the

* From September, 1970, until June, 1971, I was in contact on a formal and informal basis with politicians and advisers to this group, and these paragraphs are largely based on the materials and personal impressions gathered during that time.

American *volte-face* in 1971. This issue was defined broadly in terms of general relations with Peking, but many of the conservatives urging a more conciliatory approach (e.g., Takeo Miki) were openly skeptical about Chinese aggressive intentions and military capacities. Partly as a result of this position and its implications for peace in the region, many of these same individuals were the most outspoken proponents of ratification of the Non-Proliferation Treaty. Nevertheless, even in the heat of these controversies, no person with a significant political base or aspirations to power has taken a bold, clear-cut, and critical stand on defense policy. All the critics have equivocated,[18] and their shifting positions are best understood not as changes of deeply held policy convictions but as short-term tactical maneuvers for political purposes. The expediential nature of this process has further insured that no policy options are irrevocably closed.

There are several implications for Japanese foreign policy rooted in the peculiar character of the conservative defense dialogue. Substantively, this debate is remarkably open-ended, with a notable lack of well-developed opinions on specific issues, far less on the long-term strategic problems that the nation must face. At the same time, international changes have given new immediacy to issues of defense and brought into being a consensus regarding the general need for a more self-reliant military role. Under these circumstances, external events, especially any serious doubts that emerge regarding the credibility of the United States, will shape to an unusual extent the direction of opinion regarding national security. In these fluid conditions, moreover, the risk is extremely high that an issue such as ratification of the Non-Proliferation Treaty will become ensnared in and distorted by the factional struggle for party power, a tendency that is encouraged by the opinions and tactics of the opposition parties.

The Opposition. Questions of defense have been of central concern to all the opposition parties, and this has given broad definition to mass opinion as well as structure to the debate in the mass media and intellectual journals regarding the security question. Despite many differences within and among these parties regarding details, the two most significant effects of their actions have been to fuel anti-American feelings and to enhance and give political identity to pacifism. The Japanese Socialist Party, the Japanese Communist Party, and the Kōmeitō all have demanded immediate abrogation of the Mutual Security Treaty and the establishment of some sort of neutralist policy.[19] Because the first two parties have tended to see international reality through a Marxist prism, they have inevitably viewed the capitalist United State as "imperialistic and aggressive," while the Kōmeitō has given emphasis to the American alliance as a snare likely to drag Japan into a major Asian war. In contrast, the Democratic-Socialists see some utility in the Security Treaty and wish simply to amend its provisions to assure that American troops are stationed in Japan only under "emergency circumstances." Much of the public partisan clamor against the Security Treaty has been provoked primarily by periodic campaigns (most notably when the Treaty was revised in 1960) to exploit this issue for tactical domestic political reasons—and the conservatives will remain vulnerable to such attacks, with their implicit nationalist appeal, as long as close military collaboration with the United States continues.

All opposition parties but the Social-Democrats favor dissolution of the Self-Defense Forces, and their combined efforts to attack the government by focusing on the peace issue have greatly bolstered the pacifist mood as a factor in foreign-policy-making. The proposals for transforming the present armed forces vary widely: substituting a kind of domestic public works corps (socialists), developing a token national guard to be eventually incorporated into a United Nations police force (Kōmeitō), and establishing a new "people's army" under Communist leadership (Japanese Communist Party). Far more important than these visionary plans are the cumulative effects of unremitting campaigns over the past two decades on behalf of the peace constitution and disarmed neutralism. These have forced the conservatives into a highly defensive stance regarding all military questions and, at the same time, have kept alive a climate of opinion sustaining a moralistic cast to the security debate long after the bitter legacies of defeat have been replaced by new concerns of the postwar domestic and international orders. The very fact that the issue of disarmament has become so integral to domestic partisan machinations will make extremely difficult easy transition to security responsibilities beyond passive territorial defense, no matter how strong the international imperatives. Although militarism is thus inhibited by the peculiar definition the peace issue has acquired in the postwar party system, this has also had the dubious result of casting the whole question of defense in starkly black-and-white moral terms.

The risk of war with the two major neighboring Communist powers has been used extensively for domestic political effect by all the minority parties, primarily because of the "threat" rooted in the alliance with America and Japan's own military potential. Neither the socialists nor the Kōmeitō ascribe any aggressive intent to Peking, while the Japanese Communists (anathema to the Chinese) and the Democratic-Socialists press for early normalization of relations as a means of reducing military tensions in East Asia. The Soviet Union is viewed similarly, albeit with far more circumspection and wariness. If, as is advocated, the American alliance is terminated or drastically diluted, Japan will have to cope with military threats in a more or less autonomous fashion, unless international harmony is rapidly established. Although the subject is rarely broached, rearmament has been recognized and accepted by most opposition leaders as possibly an unavoidable course of action. Indeed, it is acknowledged that the development of independent military capabilities, possibly including nuclear weapons, might well be required if the country were forced by international circumstances to establish a national defense posture.[20] Beneath a morally tinted, rhetorical smoke screen, a similar pragmatic nationalist orientation underlay the unanimous opposition of these parties to the signing of the Treaty on the Non-Proliferation of Nuclear Weapons in 1970. Three reasons were cited as critical: (1) the discrimination in the treaty against the nonnuclear powers, (2) the likelihood that it would freeze the satellite relationship with the United States (with the "nuclearization" of Japan through deployment of American weapons at Washington's discretion), and (3) the Treaty's failure to place limits on either the superpowers or the nonsignatory nations, especially China.[21] This position is implicitly based on a nation-centered, interest-oriented approach to international affairs, no matter what idealist verbal garb it wore for domestic political consumption. All opposition parties but the Democratic-Socialists at present minimize or deny any military threat from the Soviet Union or China, but whether this benign attitude will persist is contingent upon the outbreak of peace in Asia following American military disengagement. Should international events fail to follow this utopian scenario, the Japanese left as well as right will ultimately turn naturally to a nationalist defense policy.

Because the defense issue will continue to be a focal point of partisan competition, and because of the salient place that pacifism has come to hold in the lexicon, if not the attitudes, of many party politicians, any major decision regarding strategic policy will be inhibited by Japanese domestic politics. Although the past partisan debate over security policy has been tailored to fit the body of domestic politics, not only the conservatives but all the parties acknowledge that "external events" may lead Japan to accept new and major responsibilities for national defense. The parties differ widely on the causes of tension and war in Asia, but the door for rearmament remains open, pending the emergence of international conditions that leave Japan free from external threat. The essentially open-ended approach of all political parties to defense strategy takes on added importance in light of the relatively limited import that public opinion and the business world have on the direction of Japanese defense policy.

Business and Defense

Although the Japanese business world is far more directly integrated into government policy-making than its U.S. counterparts, Tokyo is still far from having an Oriental equivalent of the much-maligned, and vaguely defined, American military-industrial complex. Needless to say, defense-related industrial concerns have pressed hard to maximize their own profits and bring about an expansion of the over-all defense budget. Indeed, since 1961, Keidenren, the leading national business federation, has had a number of standing committees concerned with government programs for weapons procurement and the role of business in the various defense plans. These committees now cover the full range of weaponry, and, since the mid-1960's, their activities both in research about and in coordination of business policies, as well as in liaison with relevant government officials, have enormously expanded.[22] In addition to this orthodox kind of lobbying by the national federations and individual firms, business leaders have become more and more vocal regarding the basic goals of the nation's security policy. Emphasis has been on promoting greater self-sufficiency in weapons production, but increasingly the fundamental aims of the country's strategic policy have been called into question, and a more independent posture, including autonomous and nuclear defense capabilities, has been advocated. These opinions deserve careful attention because of the closely knit character of the upper echelons of the *zaikai* in Japan, and because the most notable advocates have been drawn from the center of the business establishment.[23]

On the whole, however, the Japanese business world has been extremely cautious regarding a more autonomous military role for Japan. Necessarily, the largest corporations are fundamentally internationalists, anxious to preserve the global economic framework and the accompanying collective security arrangement within which they have prospered so well. At least until mid-1971, the dominant business interests have been particularly solicitous of American policy aims because of the critical importance of the U.S. market as well as the defense umbrella that has served Tokyo so well for so long. Additionally, the *zaikai* have been wary of the material costs and domestic political risks that any massive move toward rearmament would entail. Today, even more than in the late 1920's and early 1930's, the Japanese business establishment stands as a constraint on an autonomous militarist policy, but its interest-based, albeit commercial, approach to foreign affairs ultimately tends toward a nationalism that is compatible with more independent security capabilities.

Within the Japanese Government, there is no center analogous to the Pentagon in which the interests of the active military and the civilian defense establishment are found in powerful concentration. The military has remained remarkably peripheral to the civilian-dominated policy-planning process within the Self-Defense Agency. Furthermore, as was previously noted, the Agency holds a comparatively weak position within the bureaucracy in bargaining for a slice of the annual appropriations, to which its steadily declining share of the budget bears evidence. Without a clear and strong locus of power within the government regarding defense, there are severe limits on businesses seeking to bring direct pressure for greatly augmented military expenditures. Indeed, the absence of a clear point of access for influence has contributed to a business approach that focuses broadly on defense policy *per se* as much as on concrete projects. The military component of the "complex" is at best a weak and underdeveloped dwarf.

Once a decision to expand military expenditures greatly is made, a close business-government cooperative arrangement seems probable, and this may well feed upon itself to give momentum to a rearmament program. However, this will be the result, not the cause, of rearmament. The decision to rearm will grow not out of the machinations of a Japanese military industrial complex but from a policy-making process dominated by the ruling party and broadly rooted in the prevailing climate of opinion.

Public Opinion and Defense Policy

Mass Opinion. Public opinion has been ascribed a uniquely influential role in shaping Japan's defense policy. Deep and widespread support for pacifism and a profound popular aversion to nuclear weapons (a "nuclear allergy") are commonly cited by politicians and commentators alike as among the most notable features of the postwar Japanese political scene. Correspondingly, there has been extensive polling on the subjects of defense and peace, and it is possible to delineate in some detail the history of mass opinion on these matters. There are, however, clear but rarely observed limitations on accepting the results of these polls at face value because of the dubious assumptions regarding political awareness and actions on which the polls implicitly rest and because of the way in which the survey questions are framed.

Polls in Japan have given a distorted profile of opinions held by the public. Issues tend to be approached with excessive simplicity (e.g., "Do you favor American bases in Japan?") or complexity (e.g., "Which formula do you favor for Japanese security?" Choose from four subtly different alternatives including "armed neutrality" and "a four-nation nonaggression treaty"). Responses to queries of this sort provide insight into little more than reactions to proddings on matters that the *questioner* sees as important. Proper framing of questions is of special relevance for the many polls that have dealt in a direct and undifferentiating way with the issue of peace, since there is obviously a strong bias among all individuals on behalf of "peace" in the abstract. To place the repeatedly high levels of popular support for Article IX and the present constitution in proper perspective, it is useful to cite the results of a poll in February, 1967, showing that 60 per cent of the people had not read the constitution at all, 34 per cent were totally unaware of its contents, and only 47 per cent thought it "supported peace."[24] This low information level of the Japanese public regarding such a widely publicized subject casts further doubt on the meaning of detailed surveys regarding the issues of security and peace. The use of the results of such polls, except on the most general level of analysis, is extremely hazardous.

Behind the frequent assertion that there is a highly developed and politically potent mood for peace in Japan lie the assumptions that the opinions of the masses are intensely held and serve as central influences on popular political behavior. The latter assumption is *prima facie* suspect because of the complex process through which mass opinion is translated into policy influence, while the former postulates a level of commitment far exceeding that displayed by public opinion in Western nations. The limited evidence that is available on this latter point concerning Japan shows that this is not the case. A series of semiannual polls conducted in Tokyo in the mid-1960's indicated that only 20 to 30 per cent of the people in this urban setting were even "seriously concerned" about defense or the constitution—far below interest levels shown regarding domestic "rice and soy sauce" issues.[25] In the absence of contrary data, it seems correct to locate the roots of pacifism in the topsoil of public opinion rather than in the subsoil of the national temper. At the very least, the inconclusive nature of the evidence makes it prudent to avoid conjecture about the short-term political implications of survey results (e.g., the "credibility gap" regarding government foreign policy[26]) and to concentrate instead on data that sketch in broad strokes an aspect of the changing dimensions of the national climate of opinion.

The most striking changes in the mass mood have been not in regard to specific issues of defense policy, such as the Mutual Security Treaty, reversion of Okinawa, and American bases, but in the general attitude toward the Self-Defense Forces. From 1955 until 1965, roughly the first decade after the armed forces were formally established, their popular image improved remarkably, despite a continuing controversy over their constitutionality and unrelenting attack by the left-wing parties. During this period, the proportion of people who actively favored or accepted the presence of these forces rose from 70 to 85 per cent, while those flatly opposed dropped from 18 to 8 per cent.[27] Once such popular acceptance was established, the most interesting development in mass opinion regarding the Self-Defense Forces has been an increasing recognition that their primary function is defense of the country. In a 1965 poll, 40 per cent of the sample saw the main purpose as national defense, 28 per cent as the maintenance of internal security, and 15 per cent as disaster relief.[28] A similar survey in 1970 saw the same order, but 50 per cent then listed military defense as the primary purpose, totally overshadowing the next two rankings, internal security (22 per cent) and disaster relief (13 per cent).[29] This trend toward public acceptance of the military role of the Self-Defense Forces provides the government with some latitude for a policy of gradual rearmament, but it hardly suggests a popular revival of militarism.

Until there is far more evidence of a dramatically intensified concern for defense questions among the masses, careful scrutiny of opinion polls is premature. Now, it is far more important to concentrate attention at the top of the opinion pyramid, on those who regularly express opinions on the nation's security policy.

Articulate Opinion. Party debate of defense policy has been supplemented by extensive press coverage and by articles and commentaries of publicists and academicians in journals and intellectual magazines. Even more than the shifts in the amorphous mass mood, these expressions of articulate opinion suggest changes in the political climate in Japan that affect decision-making and are not fully visible by examining official policy. Western commentators have given exaggerated attention to these opinions because of their visibility, and because the defense analysts deal in a direct way with the security questions that a major power like Japan *ought* to be confronting. To understand fully the significance of these views, however, it is necessary to elaborate not only on the substance of the opinions expressed but on the ways by which these elements of articulate opinion affect the foreign policy formulation process.

Greatly intensified concern for defense has been evident in the press from the mid-1960's, prompted by China's first nuclear test, the escalation of the Vietnam war, and the impending decision regarding extension of the Mutual Security Treaty in 1970. With a few exceptions (notably the respected, business-oriented *Nihon Keizai Shimbun*), both the play given to this subject and the thrust of editorials and articles followed the well-worn, critical, and left-leaning paths the papers have trod throughout the post-war era. China's decision to "go nuclear" was lamented, but, even after repeatedly successful tests and the launching of a Chinese satellite, the press saw the main implications of these developments as political and psychological, not military. China, withal, was not considered a threat. The horrors of the Vietnam war have been lucidly portrayed on television and described and condemned in ways that lay almost all responsibility at the feet of the United States. Indeed, at one point the slant reached such proportions that the U.S. Ambassador was provoked to issue a public request for more balanced coverage. Similarly, a position highly critical of both the government and America was manifested in the play given to political actions related to extension of the Security Treaty and in the views expressed in the special series of publications on defense policy that were brought out at this time by the three national newspapers.[30] In the news media, defense issues took on definition in the rather curious image of international reality held by the opposition parties, especially the socialists, a perspective broadly representative of the trends of opinion among the intellectuals and the Japanese left.

Although the press treatment of security matters continued to have a moral cast and to reflect to an unusual degree the peculiar temper of the defense debate within the domestic Japanese political world, the pressure of external events in East Asia did force an emphasis on specific foreign-policy issues in ways that led to a concern for international realities absent in the past. For example, the fact of Chinese nuclear weapons and Japanese acceptance of the Treaty on the Non-Proliferation of Nuclear Weapons presented a dilemma not easily compatible with the rhetoric of peace and anti-Americanism, as did the Soviet crackdown on Czechoslovakia.* Mirroring the international conditions to which it referred, the dialogue became more complex and confused.

An appraisal of the impact of the press on foreign policy is made difficult, because the views expressed there have been so blatantly and consistently at variance with the government's stand. It is beyond dispute that there is some impact, if only because the news media serve as the main source of facts about which the policy debate is structured. Moreover, the government cannot totally ignore all overt expressions of criticism, and the press is a vehicle for displaying and reinforcing the opinions of the minority parties and other opposition groups. Certainly, the newspapers have done much to create and sustain the pacifist, antimilitary mood with which the government must reckon on specific decisions. It is singularly doubtful that many Japanese were remotely concerned when a minister for agriculture let slip in a press conference at the time of the Pueblo incident that "cannons and battleships" and perhaps nuclear weapons might be needed to protect Japanese interests in the future. Yet, the press and the opposition seized on this "militarist" pronouncement and forced his resignation from the cabinet. At the same time, the press has undoubtedly lost much of its potential influence because of its predictably shrill and critical mien and proposals that are tediously devoid of positive or original ideas. Conservative decision-makers heavily discount the press and self-consciously seek bal-

* On the second day of this stunning event in 1968, the editorials in all the national dailies focused not on the developments in Europe but on the dilemma Japan now faced regarding the Non-Proliferation Treaty, since the Russians had demonstrated (like the Americans in Vietnam) that they would exercise force when they chose to do so.

ancing opinion on critical foreign-policy issues. On the whole, the newspapers are more followers than they are leaders of opinion and are properly viewed as part of the left-wing political subculture of Japan. Consequently, their influence on foreign policy, although potentially great, will remain closely tied to the impact of the political opposition groups.

As defense problems drew increased attention, a group of academicians and publicists surfaced who seemed destined to occupy a place in Japan analogous to that of the foreign-policy and security experts who have left such a strong mark on American diplomacy over the past two decades. What was distinctive about these analysts was the "realism" of their approach to international affairs, an approach that acknowledged the importance of military force and a "balance of power" to maintain peace.[31] This alone marked a definite break from the mainstream of Japanese academic writing on foreign policy, in which pacifism and socialism are the cardinal principles of an intellectual orthodoxy that has seen few heretics.[32] Because the analysts addressed themselves in a pertinent way to the nation's defense problems and made evident their interest in shaping policy, it also appeared as if the chasm between the government and the intellectual world might finally be spanned in a significant way. At first glance, the new pressures of international politics appeared to be responsible for a more realistic debate about national security and a new dimension in the foreign-policy-making process.

A close look at the analysts' arguments, however, reveals some curiously distorted features that are idealistic in the extreme. Although the uniqueness of their approach lies in an acceptance of the orthodox notion that international affairs rest on relations of power, they invariably conclude that Japan can and must avoid active participation in *Realpolitik*. Beginning from the premise that security policy involves a "rational" calculation of national interests (and explicitly acknowledging their debt to Hans Morgenthau), and recognizing that their country is deeply engaged in East Asian international affairs, they nevertheless conclude that Japan can and ought to maintain a nonmilitary posture while playing an expanded role in the region! How, specifically, this is to be done is never elaborated, but special recognition is accorded to the implications for Japanese strategy of relations with the United States and China. Although some concern is expressed over the possibility of American disengagement from Asia, the critical assumption in all their writings is that the United States will remain engaged and credible regarding all of Japan's security needs to a degree that makes unnecessary any basic change from the client relationship of the past. The military threat from China is seen as negligible because of the nuclear umbrella provided by the American alliance, and because the Chinese are not able to mount a conventional attack on the Japanese homeland. Throughout, the scope of the country's security interests is limited to national territorial defense, and nowhere is there explanation of how Japan is to participate effectively in region-wide international politics from an exclusively nonmilitary posture. *Realpolitik* has been discovered intellectually, but systematic discussion of its full implications for Japan's security policy has been scrupulously avoided. The "realistic" defense debate of recent years is remarkable really more for what it fails to say than for what it says, and it is most appropriately seen as a footnote to the postwar intellectual tradition, not as a fresh and important departure.

Thus far, the intensified dialogue regarding security has failed to broaden the pattern of foreign-policy formulation. Instead of operating on fully parallel planes, common points of interest have developed between one sector of the intellectuals and the government, and a few individuals have become consultants to some Liberal-Democratic leaders.* On the whole, however, the links between the intellectual world and that of conservative politics are singularly limited and tenuous. This stands in striking contrast to the ready interchange between the American academic establishment and the government, and to the Bundys, Rostows, and Kissingers who move in and out of both worlds. In Japan, the intellectual orientation of the defense analysts combines with their restricted contact with government leaders

---

* Among those conservative politicians who have had contact with the analysts are Yasuhirō Nakasone, former head of the Defense Agency, Kosaka Zentarō, former Foreign Minister and Chairman of the Liberal-Democratic Party Foreign Affairs Research Committee, and Toshio Kimura, former Secretariat of the Prime Minister's Office.

to inhibit further the development of long-term strategic policy-planning that is needed in Japan during this period of transition in international affairs.

The dynamics of decision-making and the pacifist and trading-company mood that has been nurtured throughout Japanese politics during the entire postwar era serve as major inhibitions to any change toward a radically expanded security policy. Despite the forces inhibiting a decision to go beyond the low-profile *māmā seisaku,* there are no absolute barriers either from public opinion or from within the party system to a defense policy broadened to meet the exigencies of external conditions. Thus, the key to the timing and content of a new Japanese defense posture lies not within the country but without, in the changes in international politics in Asia and the ways in which they affect Tokyo.

8 The Security Problem: External Environment

When and how Japan's security policy will change is essentially a function of international developments in East Asia. If the volatile and violent twentieth-century history of domestic and international politics in this region suddenly reverses course and the area is engulfed by peace, then the passive, nonmilitary posture of Japan will continue to flourish. However, the prospects for the sudden outbreak of harmony over an extended period are singularly remote, and resolution of existing problems through peaceful means presents formidable obstacles.

In the short term, there are four major issues that directly bear on an expanded military role for Japan: the final act of the Vietnam drama, the two-China problem, growing Japanese entanglement in the problems of a divided Korea, and relations with the Soviet Union. The difficult and highly complex local conditions that surround these questions banish to the realm of fantasy any easy assumptions that all will be readily solved in ways that avoid military conflict. Furthermore, it is highly improbable that the superpowers, with their demonstrated incapacities to manage conflict in the region, will succeed in doing so under circumstances that can hardly be considered intrinsically more manageable than those of the recent past. Indeed, the all too evident uncertainties of the United States and the Soviet Union regarding strategic priorities appropriate to the new Asian setting, the unpredictability of Chinese foreign policies, if only because of continuing fluid domestic political conditions, and the difficulties for Japan even to confront international power politics add a dimension of inconstancy that is conducive more to the breakdown of stable international relations than to their creation. To argue that post-Vietnam Asia provides good opportunities for these nations to establish a stable power balance[1] underestimates not only the intractability of local problems (e.g., the division of Korea), but the instability inherent in an international situation in which the major actors are proceeding toward ambiguous ends in stumbling fashion. War and conflict will continue to be part of the East Asian scene, and Japan has been drawn deeply into regional international politics in ways that ultimately will require a new and expanded security policy. Some indication of the basic direction of this policy is provided by considering the major foreign-policy problems in East Asia that currently confront Tokyo and the most important single choice the Japanese face regarding national security—whether to become an independent nuclear power.

SOUTHEAST ASIA AND THE WAR IN INDOCHINA

The circumstances attendant on the settlement of the Indochina war will provide the most immediate pressures for altering Japanese security policy toward Southeast Asia. As the American military presence in the area diminishes, efforts have been made to implicate Japan at least as a partial surrogate for the United States. For example, as an addendum to President Nixon's proposal in mid-1970 for an immediate cease-fire throughout Indochina to be overseen by an international team, Secretary of State Rogers publicly stated that Japan, as well as Malaysia and Indonesia, had "positively expressed interest in joining such a team." Whatever private initiatives were undertaken by Japan on the matter, it was clearly in the interest of the United States to promote this line of action involving responsibilities that would almost inevitably carry some sort of military "peace-keeping" dimension. Similarly, in the meetings between the President and Prime Minister Sato in late October, 1970, the United States secured a pledge from Japan for a "forward-looking posture" regarding greatly augmented aid to the Saigon government, and this was followed by a concrete proposal by the Sato government extending $140 million in assistance to the non-Communist regimes of South Vietnam, Cambodia, and Laos.[2] Because aid of this magnitude obviously carries with it political implications, no matter what the expressed motivations of the donor,[3] and because of mounting private initiatives to participate in the economic reconstruction of the Saigon regime, Japan is being drawn further into the fluid and militarily explosive Vietnam situation. It clearly will be increasingly difficult for Japan to remain totally aloof from the politics of the situation even if a successful formula is found for implementing U.S. disengagement with Japan fully on the sidelines.

Japan has shunned any actions regarding Vietnam that even indirectly suggest military support and has carefully avoided political commitments to Saigon that are unambiguous and absolute. Through 1970, aid to South Vietnam was token and almost entirely on the "humanitarian" level. Although formally supporting the American position, the Japanese Government was at best lukewarm regarding the bombing of the North and has made evident in various ways (e.g., through a report by a quasi-official inspection mission headed by an ex-career diplomat) that the United States has given disproportionate emphasis to a clearly intractable and essentially nationalist and internal war. Past policies have been sufficiently ambiguous to allow future flexibility regarding the Hanoi government should the war be resolved in the Communists' favor. Excepting Russia and China, Japan has become the number-one trading partner of the Democratic Republic of Vietnam. In these ways, the Japanese have sought to insulate themselves from the international pressures that will immediately flow from resolution of the current conflict.

Nevertheless, who wins the war and how will have a direct bearing on Japanese security policy. Should the South Vietnamese stabilize territorial control over large sectors of their nation, Japan will become progressively implicated, especially economically, thereby strengthening the pattern of intercourse with non-Communist Asian nations previously noted. Whatever this leads to in the long run, in the short term there is virtually no likelihood of direct military intervention by Japan. In fact, a Communist triumph throughout Indochina would not *alone* be viewed as critical to Japan's security. A major shift in the Japanese security role in the region would ensue only if a Communist victory presented a clear and present threat to Southeast Asia generally or resulted in fresh and stronger doubts about U.S. military commitments to East Asia as a whole and to Japan in particular. Even contingencies of this sort, implying a full realignment of the East Asian power balance, are not likely to precipitate a dramatic shift in Japanese security policy before 1975 and will of necessity be integrally tied to the China problem.

Strong incentives for further Japanese involvement in the *Realpolitik* of Southeast Asia grow out of the expanding web of regional political and economic interconnections. In the probable event that the Indochina conflict becomes "de-Americanized," with a cloud of doubt still hanging over the security of the nations in the area, the substantial Japanese trade and investment throughout this region would be jeopardized in a way that would at least make a decision not to act an agonizing one. Even more important are the cumulative effects of intensified political contacts of recent years. These were clearly displayed in the Jakarta conference convened after the American intervention in Cambodia in May, 1970. Japan could not avoid playing a major role in this meeting as a "leading Asian nation," and any future conference convened to deal with regional security will require Japanese participation. What would happen if such a group were to agree on positive multilateral military action is far from clear. To "opt out" of all such actions will cause the Japanese very substantial embarrassment and problems in their relations with Asian nations. But to abide by a decision of this sort would lead to military involvement in Asia at a time and place not chosen by the Japanese Government. In any event, the persistence of conflict in and around Indochina will lead the neighboring non-Communist states actively to seek new security arrangements, thereby raising pressures for Japan's military involvement in an area in which policy-makers in Tokyo would not *choose* to be involved.

The Japanese, needless to say, will seek to avoid any choice on behalf of military involvement in such a demonstrably risky and intractable situation, and they will doubtless be aided in procrastinating by a predictable outpouring of international schemes to control or banish conflict in the area immediately touched by the war. Two proposals, simply the first of an inevitable parade, illustrate the generic types. In late 1971, five Southeast Asian nations (Malaysia, Indonesia, Thailand, Singapore, and the Philippines), squirrels of the region, indicated they would attempt to create a zone of "peace and stability" by neutralizing the area and obtaining the necessary guarantees from the United States, the Soviet Union, and China.[4] At the initiative of those nations most affected by the *post bellum* uncertainties, peace is to be created by suspending power politics. A formula suggested by Mike Mansfield, the U.S. Senate Majority Leader, sought the same end but rested on an international perspective appropriate to a superpower. Noting that the world balance of power was in transition, he proposed a meeting of the four principal powers in the Pacific (the United States, the Soviet Union, China, and Japan) to assume a collective responsibility for peace in the region with "a greatly reduced United States military presence."[5] In this vision, peace would be imposed on East Asia through the collective control of conflict by the great powers. This sort of multilateral planning on behalf of regional stability may combine with the inertia of Japanese policy to postpone that country's military engagement in Southeast Asia for some years. How long it is put off and what form it eventually takes depend as much as anything on the relations that Tokyo develops with the People's Republic of China.

CHINA AND SECURITY

A first look at security relations between Japan and China reveals a topsy-turvy world. The People's Republic is rapidly developing a full-scale nuclear arsenal; has one of the highest defense budgets in the world, measured as a ratio of GNP; gives voice to revolutionary international aims; and has, directly or indirectly, participated in the two major East Asian wars since

1945. Japan has no nuclear weapons and the lowest rate of defense expenditures among major nations of the world; has avoided direct overseas military support; and acts as a *status quo* power *par excellence*. Moreover, the Japanese have repeatedly made conciliatory gestures toward Peking, and the November, 1969, Sato-Nixon communiqué dropped the reference to the "China threat" that had appeared in a similar joint statement two years earlier. Yet, it is China that claims to be threatened by Japanese militarism—which has been elevated to a level of parity with Soviet "revisionism" and American "imperialism"[6]—and American and Japanese experts alike warn against rearmament by Japan, because it might provoke China to a belligerent posture![7] Some sense can be made out of this peculiarly distorted world by recapitulating previous references to security relations between China and Japan and explicitly relating them to Japan's defense dilemmas.

The security problem China poses for Japan can be understood only in the broad framework of regional and global international affairs. This broader perspective permits issues such as Taiwan and rearmament to be seen in terms of the fundamental characteristics of the international system in which both nations participate, and it shifts emphasis away from conjecture about limitless specific scenarios that might lead to military confrontation between the two countries. During the past decade, the global bipolar order has gradually dissipated, and the regional power balance has undergone three upheavals, all directly touching on China. The Sino-Soviet split undercut the cold-war premise of the United States–Japan Mutual Security Treaty and transformed regional power politics largely into a competition among the three great military powers.[8] Chinese development of nuclear weapons in defiance of the superpowers added another dimension to East Asian politics. Finally, the war in Vietnam, which overshadowed East Asian international politics from 1965 to 1971, culminated in a radical reduction of U.S. forces and military commitments in the region and in the sudden initiatives to normalize Sino-American relations, and led to severe strain in Japanese-American economic and political relations at the very moment when the regional power balance became very fluid. As a result, the globalism of the bipolar era has been supplemented by a regional pattern of interaction within which the critical participants, the two global superpowers, the pre-eminent regional powers, China and Japan, will respond to security problems in an increasingly independent fashion. It is in this context that Peking's doubts about the military potential of a major international competitor make sense and the meaning of the China threat to Tokyo must be understood.

Within the regional subsystem, China presents the greatest security threat to Japan, in that both nations are engaged in Asia on several levels and place special priority on relations with nations in this area. The Japanese, although markedly more concerned about China's military power since a nuclear component was added, have downplayed the threat from Peking for obvious reasons. American commitments during the Vietnam war provided little room or incentive for gearing national security policy to issues beyond defense of the home islands. Moreover, the credibility of the United States was never seriously questioned until the dramatic economic and diplomatic moves by President Nixon in the summer of 1971. Most importantly, the Japanese have sought to avoid openly confronting China as a full-scale competitor because of the repercussions this would have throughout Asia, and because a decision on rearmament would be forced. In view of the overwhelming pressures generated by American initiatives toward Peking and the seating of China in the United Nations, Japan must move toward full normalization of relations with the Communist Government. Therefore, it is necessary to evaluate the effects of closer bilateral ties on the military threat from Peking.

Few changes are likely to flow from diplomatic normalization that will basically affect the two nations' relations with each other. A dramatic spurt in the already high level of economic intercourse is unlikely because of the limitations of the Chinese market, especially in goods desired by Japan. The very idea that Japanese diplomacy, with its record of equivocation and stolidity, will provide a unique bridge for communication and/or influence over the committed and strong-willed leaders of the greatest revolution in modern history beggars the imagination.

Instead, China will have a better opportunity to fish in Japanese domestic politics and to try to wean Tokyo away from the United States. At the same time, it is difficult to identify ways in which the security relationship will be altered, even though some capacity to communicate is clearly better than none. Nevertheless, the key to international stability and peace in Asia extends far beyond bilateral political interchange and encompasses a complicated set of forces, fundamental to which is some sort of new regional military and political "power balance." It is gratuitous to assume that, following the reduction of the American military presence in East Asia, the Chinese will withdraw from all efforts to employ *Realpolitik* to expand their international influence because of "logistical weaknesses," the enormity of internal problems, or the like.[9] China is still in the throes of revolution under a leadership militantly nationalist, holding universalist and radical ideological commitments, and cultivating sympathetic or allied revolutionary Communist groups in every underdeveloped Asian nation. Whatever the short-term effects of recognition might be, it seems possible, indeed likely, that the Chinese will ultimately stand as international competitors of the *status quo*–oriented Japanese, quite independently of the level of diplomatic intercourse that is established.

Taiwan is the biggest stumbling block to the normalization of bilateral relations and also provides the single issue over which there is seemingly a direct clash between Peking and Tokyo on a security question. Chinese conditions for establishing diplomatic ties with Japan involve (1) recognition of the People's Republic as the only legitimate government of China, (2) acknowledgment that Taiwan is an integral part of China, and (3) the termination of the peace treaty between Japan and the Republic of China. These conditions not only totally repudiate past Japanese policy and run counter to the special and extensive economic and political bonds on which this policy rests, but flatly contradict the 1969 Nixon-Sato communiqué stating that Japan has a special security interest regarding Taiwan. The latter statement, however, must be seen in the context of its time and juxtaposed with the international realities involved. Since it is singularly improbable that the Prime Minister would abruptly expand the scope of Japanese security responsibilities through a vague joint statement with another nation, it is more properly seen as part of the price for the American agreement to return Okinawa, not a carefully considered major policy change. At best, this commitment to Taiwan's security is tenuous and indefinite, with its primary import a symbolic gesture of an impending broader role for Japan in Asia. Currently, the Japanese are totally lacking in the military capabilities to participate effectively in any defense operation, and it is the United States that holds the responsibility and capacity to provide for Taiwan's security. Furthermore, even if the island came under Communist control, only in the remotest sense could this be construed as a serious and immediate military threat to Japan. Internationally, any basic change in the status of Taiwan is currently beyond the reach of Japan's direct influence, and such a development would take on meaning for Japanese security in terms of its implications for American credibility and the general political-military role of Peking in East Asia. If forced to choose, Japanese priorities would have to be on relations with Peking rather than Taipei, but a *volte-face* of this magnitude would profoundly shake the attitudes of the conservatives toward international politics. Thus, resolution of the Taiwan question depends essentially on external events, but the implications of the question cannot but fundamentally shape Japanese security policy.

China's impact on Japanese security policy will grow out of a generally competitive international rivalry in East Asia and not from a direct bilateral military threat. The only direct military threat that China will pose to Japan over the next decade is nuclear, and, as noted above, this would almost inevitably be linked to an external issue related to Japanese engagement in the region. However, for Japan to become a full-fledged competitor in international politics in East Asia would demand a security policy that involved conventional military capacities. Consequently, together with the status of the American alliance, relations with the People's Republic of China will be the critical influence on the timing and nature of Japanese rearmament. How this pressure will develop may be illustrated by considering the security question on the Asian mainland to which Japan accords highest priority—the problem of Korea.

THE KOREAN PROBLEM

For almost a century, Korea has been either the cockpit of international conflict in Northeast Asia or a colony of Japan, and today the tragically divided country stands as a weather vane for the most critical issues of Japanese security policy. A number of problems find clear definition in the Korean context: the specific limits on American military commitments in post-Vietnam Asia, the capacity of Japan to remain aloof from the political-security aspects of international relations with nations that have effectively become economic satellites, and the nature of the rivalry with the Chinese in separate Asian states to which Peking and Tokyo assign high priority. Although similar in some respects, the international circumstances surrounding a divided Korea are notably different from those regarding the two Chinas. Most importantly, for both Japan and the United States, it is not possible to separate the problem of relations with Taipei from that of relations with Peking, and the latter stands as a security matter of the highest order. Because direct relations between Tokyo and Peking and between Washington and Peking are not integral to the Korean case, there is a latitude for maneuver by the powers that is absent from the Taiwan situation and that makes Korea a qualitatively different international issue. At the same time, the commitments to Korea of the superpowers as well as of China and Japan are currently all ambiguous. The previously noted uncertainties introduced by the Nixon Doctrine and the absence of any firm, independent strategic policies by Japan have forced South Korea into a major reassessment of its position. It is to be expected that an element of ambiguity will continue to color relations between the Communist powers and North Korea as the Chinese and the Russians vie for influence in Pyongyang. The extreme uncertainties of this complex situation have led the North and South Koreans to open their first quasiofficial contacts since the end of the war. However, the basic tensions and bitter differences between the North and the South have not eroded, and there is no real hope in the immediate future either for reunification or for neutralization of the peninsula through an international agreement. Consequently, through the rapidly proliferating web of ties with South Korea, Japan is being ever more deeply drawn into what is likely to remain indefinitely a precariously balanced confrontation.

Even during the past two decades of trading-company diplomacy, Japan has displayed an interest in, and undertaken commitments regarding, power politics in Korea. This was formally acknowledged in an exchange of notes in 1951 at the time of the signing of the Mutual Security Treaty[10] and was supplemented by the declaration in the 1969 Nixon-Sato communiqué that asserted that the security of South Korea was "essential" to the security of Japan. Moreover, it has been understood from the outset that the primary purpose of the American bases in Japan was to support the operations of the U.N. forces in Korea. In view of this, Japan would almost surely respond affirmatively to an American request (required under the "prior consultation" clause of the Security Treaty) for full use of the bases to support the conduct of any U.N. military activities in South Korea. However, active collaboration of this sort would at once precipitate stormy domestic dissent and raise pressures for a broader level of military cooperation in the war. Open conflict in Korea during the first half of the 1970's would force into the open a basic dilemma of the past "stand-pat" security policy and require the Japanese Government to decide to what extent Korean security is really identical with Japanese security.

How the South Koreans view their former colonizer as a military ally will have an important influence on the kind of arrangement that emerges. No direct security cooperation between Seoul and Tokyo is likely to develop unless American commitments and credibility toward Korea greatly diminish—a development that would simultaneously spur Japanese defense expenditures and offer incentive to Seoul for an augmented collective security agreement. For understandable reasons, Korea would be a reluctant ally, motivated solely by expediential considerations. Beyond the undifferentiated enmity and disdain in which the Japanese are held, the Koreans would at best be junior partners in any alliance and at worst pawns in international power politics. Already, there is evidence that they would be less than equals in such an arrangement; for the 1969 Nixon-Sato communiqué, which declared Japan's special interest in Korea's security, was issued without consultation with Seoul and was implicitly cast in terms of paternalistic condescension. Because the Koreans have so little real choice in the matter, there is little doubt that some accommodation would be made with Tokyo if it were required by international conditions. Indeed, if the country remains permanently partitioned, it will almost inevitably fall under Japanese control of another sort—economic domination. Short of reunification, the South Koreans will more and more see their security tied to Japanese policy.

Korean security has long been a matter of substantial intrinsic importance to Japan, not just for military reasons but for a full range of political, economic, and psychological considerations. It is an issue involving *Realpolitik*, from which Japan cannot remain aloof; and the instability inherent in the situation graphically exemplifies the mixture of local conflict, Communist–non-Communist confrontation, and great-power politics that makes peace such an improbable condition throughout East Asia. At least in the years immediately ahead, it is most improbable that Japan will "go nuclear" or rearm simply to defend its interests in Korea. However, Tokyo cannot approach this issue in such a narrow and frontal manner. Korea holds a central place in the regional security picture, and a military conflict there would compel China, the Soviet Union, and the United States to lay their strategic cards on the table in ways that directly touch Japan. Whatever the specific scenario might be, Korea, more than any single issue, has the potential to provoke a major change in the direction of Japanese defense policy—to be the proximate cause for a full Japanese plunge into international politics.

THE SOVIET UNION

For Japan, Russia presents a uniquely important security problem, one that cannot be separated from the issues centering on East Asia and that is rooted in the peculiar nature of their economic and political relations throughout modern times. Following the normalization of diplomatic ties in 1956, bilateral relations with the Soviet Union have undergone a substantial transformation, especially in economic terms. Trade has risen from almost nothing to a total of more than $800 million, and tentative agreements have been reached for extensive Japanese participation in joint development projects in Siberia and the Soviet Far East. Moreover, the potential for future growth is great. Russia could easily become an even more important source of raw materials (e.g., oil, lumber, and natural gas) needed by Japan, and there are strong incentives for broadened Japanese economic activities in accelerating the development of Soviet eastern territories. Noneconomic ties have also markedly improved as reciprocal visits by government leaders and frequent trips by Japanese businessmen have brought into being a level of communication and interaction exceeding all past expectations. Despite these positive achievements, however, Soviet-Japanese relations still are essentially coldly formal, beset by unsolved bilateral problems and by mutual uncertainty regarding their future respective roles in East Asia.

Two factors in Japanese domestic politics are particularly important for Soviet relations: the long-standing negative attitude of the Japanese toward Russia, and the still-outstanding territorial dispute regarding ownership of the Southern Kurile Islands. Throughout Japan's modern history, Russia has been seen as a menacing neighbor, a challenge to the nation's security if not an enemy in war. Soviet actions since 1945 have done little to improve this image. Moscow unilaterally broke a nonaggression treaty to participate in the last days of the Pacific War and incarcerated for several years thousands of Japanese civilian and military personnel captured in Manchuria and North Korea. Subsequently, Japanese fishing in the northern seas near the Soviet coast has been restricted and harassed, and all territorial claims have been rejected. From the time of the Korean war, the Russians have also loomed as a protagonist of the cold war and a threat to the peace and security of the country. Understandably, the Soviet Union has consistently ranked as the "most disliked" country in opinion polls throughout the postwar period. Such widespread and intense feelings cannot but inhibit the establishment of truly close relations and augment the opportunities for conflict.

The territorial issue is, and is likely to remain, a major stumbling block in bilateral relations. Japan's historical claim to the disputed territory is strong. Its legal case is not. Under the terms of the Yalta Agreement, the San Francisco Peace Treaty (Article II, Section 3), and the Diet testimony of Prime Minister Yoshida, head of the delegation to the peace conference, Japan renounced all claims to these islands.[11] Since August, 1955, however, Japan (then in the midst of negotiations for normalization of relations) has adamantly claimed the Southern Kuriles, and failure to settle this issue has prevented the conclusion of a formal treaty to end the war. After fifteen years, the campaign of the Japanese Government to regain these lands, with its nationalist and irredentist appeal, has gained a momentum of its own that makes very unlikely any early or compromise settlement.

From the onset of the cold war until the mid-1960's, the Soviet Union was seen as the only possible security threat to Japan. This assumption underlay both the 1952 Security Treaty with the United States and its revision in 1960, as well as most of the planning embodied in the five-year plans under which Japanese military forces have been expanded. However defensible in terms of cold-war logic, the issue is now much more complex, primarily because the People's Republic of China has undertaken an independent and nuclear foreign policy in the shadow of the continuing global standoff of the superpowers and the emergence of Japan as a major regional power. A conventional invasion of Japan by Soviet troops—a basic consideration in initially expanding the Self-Defense Forces—was never really a plausible assumption and today is utterly unthinkable.[12] In addition to the difficulties Moscow would have in reversing its long-standing commitment to the policy of peaceful coexistence, the Soviet Union would inevitably risk full-scale retaliation by the United States in any direct military assault on Japan. The constraints of bipolar strategic confrontation will apply with or without the United States–Japan Mutual Security Treaty.

Basic to understanding the changing nature of the Soviet threat to Japan are the altered strategic and political goals of Moscow in Asia. In the words of the 1950 Sino-Soviet Treaty of Friendship and Alliance, "Japan and any nations allied with it" were the main obstacles to peace in East Asia. Now it is China, not Japan, that the Soviets seek to contain in Asia—an aim shared by the Americans and the Japanese. The tolerant attitude taken by the Russians toward the extension of the Mutual Security Treaty in 1970, contrasting sharply with their position in 1960, reflects this change in goals. The problem of how to "contain" China in the international quicksands of Asia has confounded the Russians as well as the Americans.[13] The Soviet Union has already begun maneuvering to strengthen its now limited and tenuous contacts with non-Communist nations on the periphery of China. But its latitude for maneuver regarding these nations and the Communist buffer states immediately adjacent to China is very limited. Will the Russians, after Vietnam, risk direct military involvement should it be required? How can they cope with initiatives of revolutionary, Chinese-oriented, Communist movements? Like the United States and Japan, Russia in the immediate future will be acting essentially as a *status quo* power in a period of profound upheaval in Asia. In one sense, as the United States reduces its involvement, the Soviet presence will increase; and, to the extent that the Russians are caught up in the swiftly changing circumstances within the East Asian region, they will become directly involved in the external pressures conducing to change Japan's security policy.

NUCLEAR WEAPONS

Will Japan develop nuclear weapons? No single strategic question generates more political controversy within the country or is more important to the future role of the Japanese in East Asian international affairs. Conjecture about the answer to this question has tended to polarize around two positions. Strategic analysts concerned with the problem of proliferation, whose view of reality centers mainly on external relations among states, see Japan, the economic superpower, as inevitably a member of the nuclear club.[14] In contrast, specialists looking mainly at the Japanese domestic political situation tend to view the development of nuclear armaments as singularly improbable for at least a decade. A balanced appraisal requires consideration of the issue from both the internal and the external perspective, but, as was stated in various places in the preceding discussion, it is the external environment that must ultimately determine when and how Japan confronts the issue. Antecedent to any Japanese decision on behalf of nuclear armaments is the more basic decision regarding acceptance of an active role in regional power politics. The two cannot be separated. Once Japan becomes militarily engaged in Asia, the moral opprobrium that now colors the nuclear issue (domestically and internationally) will necessarily be juxtaposed with national political and strategic considerations that have yet to be directly faced. In the turbulent world of East Asia during the latter part of the twentieth century, the possession of nuclear capabilities seems destined to be a necessary component for full and independent participation in international politics. Correspondingly, the strategic questions at stake must be viewed in the broad context of Japanese foreign policy toward the region.

Scope and Permanence of Internal Constraints

A casual inspection of the postwar domestic political scene reveals formidable impediments to even the consideration of the nuclear option. Far more than any other country with real nuclear potential, Japan has consistently disavowed all intentions to move positively in this direction. The government has forsworn any desire not only to develop independent nuclear capabilities but even to allow the permanent deployment of U.S. weapons in the country. Although the international situation has made a position of this sort prudent, if not necessary, it is widely believed that domestic political constraints have made any alternative virtually impossible. In no other society has antinuclear sentiment achieved such strong and continuous political articulation: through the support of parties and pressure groups, through repeated, often violent, protest demonstrations (e.g., against the visits of American nuclear-powered submarines), and in public-opinion polls. For the last two decades, a nonnuclear posture has been one of the few foreign-policy issues on which there seemed to be a national consensus. However, doubts are now increasingly expressed regarding the depth and permanence of the internal political limits that will be imposed on future policies in the face of radically altered international circumstances, and the nature of the domestic constraints on nuclear armament must be re-examined with care.

The bedrock of the Japanese "nuclear allergy" is commonly seen as a profoundly idealistic national mood originating in the experiences of World War II and with roots running deeply and broadly throughout the popular conscience. The physical lesions left by Hiroshima and Nagasaki have been reopened again and again by the press, by reformist pressure groups, and by left-wing politicians, who have sought to transform the atomic tragedies of 1945 into a kind of national moral identification badge. Although the horrors of nuclear war have special and vivid meaning to the Japanese, there is also evidence that future development of nuclear weapons by the country is now seen as more or less inevitable. A *Mainichi Shimbun* poll in mid-1969 indicated that 45 per cent of the people agreed that, "sooner or later," Japan should possess nuclear armaments, while 46 per cent stated that the nation should not do so.[15] Another poll, limited to Japanese college students, showed that 60 per cent believed Japan would "go nuclear" within the next twenty years, while only 30 per cent felt the nation "has no reason whatsoever to develop nuclear weapons."[16] Taken at face value, there would seem to be an erosion of the moral and emotional aversion to the nuclear phenomenon. In fact, these results are all the more surprising because Japanese opinion polls dealing directly and simply with the question, "Do you favor nuclear weapons?" should not be taken at face value. Virtually all people in all societies, and especially those in postwar Japan, when confronted with the choice between "nuclear weapons" and "no nuclear weapons" will take a negative position on the question. The issue cannot be meaningfully raised alone and totally outside any international context, and Japanese opinion polls that are so structured have badly distorted reality. Whether the mass foundation of the "nuclear allergy" was ever very strong is an open question, but, under the current conditions, the burden of proof is definitely on those who maintain that the Japanese public has developed a moral consciousness that is a permanent bar to nuclear capabilities.

Within the context of the current political system, it would not be feasible for a government to choose, *à la* De Gaulle, to "go nuclear." Such a decision would split the country as no other single issue has and would provide a unifying cause for the minority parties, various supporting pressure groups, and the press, in a way that would jeopardize the political life of the Prime Minister and his party. However, no Japanese Prime Minister would or could simply make a dramatic choice to "go nuclear" in the way, for example, a decision was reached on the terms for the reversion of Okinawa. The immobilist character of the foreign-policy-making process, and the reluctance of government leaders to accept *in principle* the need for an independent strategic policy, assures that a decision on behalf of nuclear weapons would almost necessarily be in the context of a major international crisis with a scope of such significance as to affect basically the domestic political milieu. A direct nuclear threat from China related to another Asian conflict or a full breakdown of American credibility would provide circumstances that would seriously undermine the constraints now available to the opposition groups. Additionally, confronted with the imperatives of international events, conservative and many left-wing politicians now opposed to nuclear weapons have made clear that they would bow quickly to the realities of the situation.[17] Not only are there few permanent constraints among the political elite, but, because Japanese foreign policy proceeds incrementally from one crisis to another, the decision to exercise the nuclear option may well be shaped by the exigencies of the moment, with minimal concern for broader and long-term strategic considerations. Finally, because the issue has had such strong moral and political definition, a reversal of course may assume a similarly moral cast on behalf of nationalist and perhaps even militarist principles. Thus, not only are the domestic political constraints likely to be transient, but they seriously impede the easy integration of Japan into an international system in which an independent nuclear capability may well be viewed as a necessary component for participation in power politics—rather than as a desperate, apocalyptic gambit.

Once the political decision has been made, there are no real technical or financial obstacles to Japan's development of nuclear warheads and a delivery system that can operate effectively on a regional level. With an anticipated GNP of $350 million to $400 million by 1975, the costs of development could easily be absorbed without serious impact on the rate of economic growth or a radical disruption of national budgetary priorities. Furthermore, the sizable increase in defense expenditures could be reduced by redirecting some of the technology and resources of the separate but related programs in nuclear power and space research. Any project to develop nuclear weapons would inevitably have highest national priority, and this, *ipso facto,* assures that the necessary adjustments would be made in the world's third largest economy.

Although the technological requirements for a weapons development program are also within reach, the route to their achievement is considerably more complex and difficult. In order to tap the national reservoir of scientific knowledge and personnel, the Diet would have to amend the 1955 Basic Atomic Energy Act, which provides that "research, development, and application of atomic energy are limited to peaceful uses," and the government would have to redefine the basic goal of the space program, which also has been conducted for "exclusively peaceful purposes." Both of these actions would allow opportunities for obstruction by domestic political opponents. Japan has undertaken one of the largest nuclear-power programs in the world, and this contributes in important ways to the potential for weapons development.[18] A pool of scientific personnel and the special facilities required for research are being created, and this program is geared to attain national self-sufficiency at the earliest possible time (e.g., 90 per cent of the equipment for the power stations scheduled for completion in 1974 will be made in Japan). Despite a heavy dependence on foreign sources for enriched as well as natural uranium and U.S. restrictions on use of the former for military purposes, the Japanese should, in the near future, be able to obtain the material necessary to make weapons. Indeed, the reactors employed in power production by 1975 will have the capability to produce enough plutonium—a material applicable for the fabrication of atomic explosives—to build several thousand small nuclear weapons each year without seriously affecting the production of electricity.[19] Although unforeseen problems could produce delays, it is generally estimated that Japan could produce a nuclear warhead no more than a year or two after a decision to proceed.

Japan was the fifth nation to orbit a satellite, and the fifteen-year-old space program, now to be heavily supplemented by U.S. missile technology, has laid the basis for the rapid development of a weapons-delivery system. Indeed, at present, Japan is far more advanced in missile research than in the areas related to atomic explosives, and existing gaps in areas such as that of guidance controls can readily be filled by the advanced technology available in the already large electronic and computer industries. No nation can acquire major peaceful atomic capability and conduct a successful space program without technically moving to the threshold of nuclear-weapons development, and the nuclear option is now clearly within Japan's grasp.

The Treaty on the Non-Proliferation of Nuclear Weapons

From a global perspective, as well as from the viewpoint of Tokyo, the Treaty on the Non-Proliferation of Nuclear Weapons is a curious document.* It represents an attempt by the super-powers to freeze the strategic *status quo* by limiting the number of possessors of nuclear weapons to the current five nations: the United States, the Soviet Union, Great Britain, France, and China. In the current world context, both the goal and the tactics of this strategic maneuver are extraordinary and debatable. It is, first of all, a product of the diplomacy of the bipolar, cold-war era, as is manifested in the treaty's global sweep and the explicit assumption that some nations ought to be recognized as "more equal than others." Yet, it was promulgated at a time when the multipolarity of the international system was universally recognized. The treaty is in one sense a type of disarmament pact, and it was hailed as a "triumph of sanity and man's will to survive"[20] and a "milestone on the road to a more peaceful and secure international order"[21] at the time it was first signed in 1968. However, this was the year when America's conduct of the

* See Appendix D.

Vietnam war and the Soviet quashing of the Czechoslovakian revolt dramatized the continuing role of force in world politics and cast doubt on the purported peaceful intentions of the sponsoring superpowers—trust in which was an essential premise of the treaty. Furthermore, the treaty assumes that the nuclear dimension of international politics can be dealt with separately from other aspects of power politics. Despite the fact that the previous two decades of war and conflict had shown conventional and atomic strategies to be integrally related—a reality vividly illustrated by the nuclearization of China and France— these two newest nuclear powers not only have refused to sign the pact but have stood as painful reminders that it is not possible to control the diffusion of nuclear weapons through the creation of technical, physical, or legal barriers of the sort the treaty seeks to impose. Under current international conditions, proliferation can be controlled only through *political* actions by the great powers, involving, in the first instance, diplomatic maneuver and alliances but extending to joint programs of weapons use or development and, finally, to direct military intervention.[22] Consequently, in appraising the impact on Japan of the Non-Proliferation Treaty, emphasis is here given to the broader political implications of the Japanese response and to the nuclear aspects of the new regional international setting.

Japan hesitated more than eighteen months before signing the Non-Proliferation Treaty, and the reasons behind this delay and the continuing reluctance to ratify indicate some of the varied political forces that bear on the issue. As might be expected, given the character of Japan's foreign policy, commercial interests underlay many of the specific objections cited in the note issued by the Foreign Ministry on the occasion of the signing of the pact in February, 1970.* The proposed inspection procedures were criticized on the grounds that they were too thorough and, therefore, might restrict development of nuclear technology, hamper the efficient operation of the power industry, and possibly lead to leaks of industrial secrets![23] However plausible parts of this somewhat bizarre line of reasoning may be, the expression of these complaints is most notable in displaying how Japan's na-

* See Appendix C.

tional interest receives conspicuous definition in economic terms, even in response to a treaty bearing on the most profound security issue of the time.

The inherent inequities of the international order implicit in the treaty also caused uneasiness in Tokyo. It leaves the superpowers on top as global puppeteers, places on the second level the three lesser nuclear powers, and then consigns the remaining multitude of weak or moral nations into a nonnuclear third class. Although their views were not sharply articulated, the tone as well as the content of the note showed that the Japanese were reluctant to accept permanent status as a third-class global power and a qualitatively inferior posture vis-à-vis China in East Asia. In fact, the government was dismayed at the seemingly discriminatorily harsh inspection criteria of the International Atomic Energy Agency to which Japan would be subjected but which the industrial countries of Western Europe would be spared because of the somewhat easier surveillance of the European Atomic Energy Community. Thus, the Non-Proliferation Treaty at once elicited a reflex nationalist reaction against continued passive dependence on the policies of foreign powers and directly demonstrated the quest for international status that has characterized Japan's foreign policy throughout the modern era.

Basic reservations regarding the security issues raised by the treaty were also included in the government statement and were abundantly manifested in the related domestic political debate. The government was remarkably candid in expressing a desire to keep open the option for nuclear armaments. An analysis of the treaty published by the Foreign Ministry in late 1969 listed the "loss of a free hand for nuclear armaments" as a disadvantage of its acceptance.[24] In the February, 1970, statement, attention was pointedly drawn to Article X of the treaty, which allows any signatory state to withdraw, "in the case of extraordinary events," with only three months' notice. Similarly, this same document made clear that Japan would push ahead without limit on nuclear research and would expect full international cooperation, even though the technology involved may also be applicable for developing weapons.

Although the Non-Proliferation Treaty forced the government

to make public statements leaving the door ajar, there has yet to be any serious move to step through or even to abandon the policy built around the three nonnuclear principles—not to make, not to possess, and not to admit into the country nuclear weapons. The Liberal-Democratic Party is rather closely divided regarding ratification of the treaty. In large part, this is because a substantial sector of the mainstream group wishes to perpetuate the close political-security ties with the United States and the benefits they have brought. However, any serious erosion of American credibility would dissolve this support, and, in view of the uncertainties that have come to cloud regional international affairs since implementation of the Nixon Doctrine, it is virtually certain that the Liberal-Democrats will not move rapidly toward ratification. For a variety of reasons, including anti-Americanism, protonationalism, reflex obstructionism, and short-term political maneuver, the press and all the opposition parties are strongly against the treaty—which makes ratification still more unlikely, unless there is an unexpected outbreak of peace in East Asia. Partly out of choice and partly because of the difficulties of reaching a decision, the nuclear option will be kept available.

No positive decision to develop nuclear weapons is likely to be made in the near future, barring a total collapse of American credibility in the face of major conflicts in East Asia, but the mere existence of the Non-Proliferation Treaty has greatly complicated the international and domestic factors relevant to a decision of this kind. By raising the issue of nuclear armament in a direct, immediate, and politically sensitive way, fuel has been added to an already charged public debate on rearmament. This issue cannot but color the recent tension in the American alliance and the pending resolution of the issue of relations with Communist China to a far greater degree than if the treaty had not been introduced. For good or ill, the nuclear question has been pushed to the fore in Japanese politics, and this has raised the further possibility that the matter will at some point become a domestic political football, caught up in the factional struggle for power within the Liberal-Democratic Party, as has been the case with all past major foreign-policy decisions. If the

Japanese eventually ratify—only to be led by events shortly thereafter to opt for nuclear weapons—the treaty would then bring into being an international situation analogous to that of the 1930's. Then, in pursuit of what was seen as a legitimate national interest in China, Japan embarked on a course of action that *ipso facto* led it to be branded a pariah in world politics, a status that contributed to the fervor with which the nation moved toward a defiantly autonomous security policy. In the fluid and conflict-prone contemporary world of East Asia, the ultimate impact of the Non-Proliferation Treaty on Japan's security policy will remain uncertain.

Asian Security and Nuclear Weapons

The broad features of Japan's foreign policy that have been set forth in this book do not provide specific answers to Tokyo's nuclear conundrum, but a perspective is offered for framing appropriate questions on the subject. When and how Japan may "go nuclear" is, above all, a function of external, not internal, developments, and the strategic *raison d'être* will probably be cast in terms of the regional balance of power, not a challenge to the superpowers. For Japan, acquisition of nuclear arms may well come to be seen as a prerequisite for functioning fully and effectively in East Asian international politics—essentially by other, nonnuclear, means. Although the Japanese will undoubtedly be affected by any moves toward proliferation throughout the world, the two factors most directly bearing on their nuclear policy will be the patterns of relations that develop with the United States on the one hand and with China on the other.

For Tokyo, American nuclear credibility is inextricably involved with America's general strategic credibility throughout the region. Moreover, at a time when Japanese security horizons are being forcibly broadened by mounting material and political interests in East Asia, the United States is trying to distinguish between global and more limited regional strategic priorities. If the credibility of U.S. security commitments to Western Europe proved so troublesome in the 1960's, despite clear and strong strategic commitments in NATO and a unique web of political, economic, and cultural ties, it will require luck as well as skill to prevent the now widening credibility gap between Washing- ton and Tokyo from becoming a chasm. Because of the evident trends within Japan toward a more independent role in the world, and because any nuclear threat to Tokyo would almost inevitably involve another issue in Asia about which American and Japanese priorities may differ, it will prove increasingly difficult politically to maintain the present satellite kind of nu- clear arrangement or even to organize a system of shared control over nuclear weapons similar to the one now operative in NATO countries. In the short term, the United States will certainly be the largest single influence on the direction of Japanese strategic policy, but whether in time Tokyo will choose to develop auton- omous nuclear capabilities will be a function of the international politics of East Asia and the domestic politics of Japan—worlds beyond the control of American statesmen.

The major impetus for nuclear armament by Japan will be the perceived threat from Peking. This is a matter of dispute. Because of the relatively muted Japanese response to China's nuclearization in the 1960's and the formal efforts at conciliation, not competition, with the mainland, and because of the ambig- uous goals and over-all military backwardness of the Chinese, many analysts have concluded that Peking will have little impact on the direction of Japanese security policy.[25] Such a position seems badly wide of the mark at several points. A reserved Japa- nese response to a nuclear China was understandable in the 1960's, when the United States was, if anything, overcommitted in East Asia and security was seen simply as defense of the home islands. Furthermore, it continues to be foolish for the Japanese Government to declare forcefully a concern for, or rivalry with, China on the security level, unless it is prepared to make a deci- sion on rearmament or reopen the whole question of the Ameri- can alliance. Sino-Japanese relations are very special for both countries, and the security problem must be seen as part of the full range of intercourse between the two nations. Permanent peaceful relations between the two regional powers will be an elusive goal, and, if the *status quo*–oriented Japanese and the revolutionary Chinese vie in the context of East Asia, the pres- sures on Tokyo to "go nuclear" will be substantial, except in the improbable event that all concerns of *Realpolitik* are excluded from their rivalry.

Japan is today the sleeping giant of Asia, indeed of the world, with enormous untapped capacities for action. When it will become a major actor in international politics, and whether this will involve nuclear capabilities, ultimately depends on the dynamics of East Asian politics, on variables that are both changing and demonstrably beyond the control of any nation. The situation is thus unpredictable and precarious, but the fate of a bourgeois and *status quo* power in an unstable, transitional setting is, of necessity, insecure.

Appendix A

Security Treaty Between the United States and Japan, September 8, 1951

Japan has this day signed a Treaty of Peace with the Allied Powers. On the coming into force of that Treaty, Japan will not have the effective means to exercise its inherent right of self-defense because it has been disarmed. There is danger to Japan in this situation because irresponsible militarism has not yet been driven from the world. Therefore, Japan desires a Security Treaty with the United States of America to come into force simultaneously with the Treaty of Peace between the United States of America and Japan. The Treaty of Peace recognizes that Japan as a sovereign nation has the right to enter into collective security arrangements, and further, the Charter of the United Nations recognizes that all nations possess an inherent right of individual and collective self-defense.

In exercise of these rights, Japan desires, as a provisional arrangement for its defense, that the United States of America should maintain armed forces of its own in and about Japan so as to deter armed attack upon Japan.

The United States of America, in the interest of peace and security, is presently willing to maintain certain of its armed forces in and about Japan, in the expectation, however, that Japan will itself increasingly assume responsibility for its own defense against direct and indirect aggression, always avoiding any armament which could be an offensive threat or serve other than to promote peace and security in accordance with the purposes and principles of the United Nations Charter.

Accordingly, the two countries have agreed as follows:

Article I. Japan grants, and the United States of America accepts, the right, upon the coming into force of the Treaty of

Peace and of this Treaty, to dispose United States land, air, and sea forces in and about Japan. Such forces may be utilized to contribute to the maintenance of the international peace and security in the Far East and to the security of Japan against armed attack from without, including assistance given at the express request of the Japanese Government to put down large-scale internal riots and disturbances in Japan, caused through instigation or intervention by an outside Power or Powers.

Article II. During the exercise of the right referred to in Article I, Japan will not grant, without the prior consent of the United States of America, any bases or any rights, power, or authority whatsoever, in or relating to bases or the right of garrison or of maneuver, or transit of ground, air, or naval forces to any third Power.

Article III. The conditions which shall govern the disposition of armed forces of the United States of America in and about Japan shall be determined by administrative agreements between the two Governments.

Article IV. This Treaty shall expire whenever in the opinion of the Governments of the United States of America and of Japan there shall have come into force such United Nations arrangements or such alternative individual or collective security dispositions as will satisfactorily provide for the maintenance by the United Nations or otherwise of international peace and security in the Japan area.

Article V. This Treaty shall be ratified by the United States of America and Japan and will come into force when instruments of ratification thereof have been exchanged by them at Washington.

Appendix B

Treaty of Mutual Cooperation and Security Between the United States and Japan, Signed at Washington, D.C., January 19, 1960

The United States of America and Japan,

Desiring to strengthen the bonds of peace and friendship traditionally existing between them, and to uphold the principles of democracy, individual liberty, and the rule of law,

Desiring further to encourage closer economic cooperation between them and to promote conditions of economic stability and well-being in their countries,

Reaffirming their faith in the purposes and principles of the Charter of the United Nations, and their desire to live in peace with all peoples and all governments,

Recognizing that they have the inherent right of individual or collective self-defense as affirmed in the Charter of the United Nations,

Considering that they have a common concern in the maintenance of international peace and security in the Far East,

Having resolved to conclude a treaty of mutual cooperation and security,

Therefore agree as follows:

Article I. The Parties undertake, as set forth in the Charter of the United Nations, to settle any international disputes in which they may be involved by peaceful means in such a manner that international peace and security and justice are not endangered and to refrain in their international relations from the threat or use of force against the territorial integrity or political independence of any state, or in any other manner inconsistent with the purposes of the United Nations.

The Parties will endeavor in concert with other peace-loving countries to strengthen the United Nations so that its mission of maintaining international peace and security may be discharged more effectively.

Article II. The Parties will contribute toward the further development of peaceful and friendly international relations by strengthening their free institutions, by bringing about a better understanding of the principles upon which these institutions are founded, and by promoting conditions of stability and well-being. They will seek to eliminate conflict in their international economic policies and will encourage economic collaboration between them.

Article III. The Parties, individually and in cooperation with each other, by means of continuous and effective self-help and mutual aid will maintain and develop, subject to their constitutional provisions, their capacities to resist armed attack.

Article IV. The Parties will consult together from time to time regarding the implementation of this Treaty and, at the request of either Party, whenever the security of Japan or international peace and security in the Far East is threatened.

Article V. Each Party recognizes that an armed attack against either Party in the territories under the administration of Japan would be dangerous to its own peace and safety and declares that it would act to meet the common danger in accordance with its constitutional provisions and processes.

Any such armed attack and all measures taken as a result thereof shall be immediately reported to the Security Council of the United Nations in accordance with the provisions of Article 51 of the Charter. Such measures shall be terminated when the Security Council has taken the measures necessary to restore and maintain international peace and security.

Article VI. For the purpose of contributing to the security of Japan and the maintenance of international peace and security in the Far East, the United States of America is granted the use by its land, air, and naval forces of facilities and areas in Japan.

The use of these facilities and areas as well as the status of the United States armed forces in Japan shall be governed by a separate agreement, replacing the Administrative Agreement under Article III of the Security Treaty between the United States of America and Japan, signed at Tokyo on February 28, 1952, as amended, and by such other arrangements as may be agreed upon.

Article VII. This Treaty does not affect and shall not be interpreted as affecting in any way the rights and obligations of the Parties under the Charter of the United Nations or the responsibility of the United Nations for the maintenance of international peace and security.

Article VIII. This Treaty shall be ratified by the United States of America and Japan in accordance with their respective constitutional processes and will enter into force on the date on which the instruments of ratification thereof have been exchanged by them in Tokyo.

Article IX. The Security Treaty between the United States of America and Japan signed at the city of San Francisco on September 8, 1951, shall expire upon the entering into force of this Treaty.

Article X. This Treaty shall remain in force until in the opinion of the Governments of the United States of America and Japan there shall have come into force such United Nations arrangements as will satisfactorily provide for the maintenance of international peace and security in the Japan area.

However, after the Treaty has been in force for ten years, either Party may give notice to the other Party of its intention to terminate the Treaty, in which case the Treaty shall terminate one year after such notice has been given.

Exchange of Notes Incorporating Agreed Consultation Formula
(Japanese Note)*

Washington, January 19, 1960

Excellency: I have the honour to refer to the Treaty of Mutual Cooperation and Security between Japan and the United States of America signed today, and to inform Your Excellency that the following is the understanding of the Government of Japan concerning the implementation of Article VI thereof:

* The key sentence of Secretary of State Christian Herter's reply of the same day is: "I have the honor to confirm on behalf of my Government that the foregoing is also the understanding of the United States of America."

Major changes in the deployment into Japan of United States armed forces, major changes in their equipment, and the use of facilities and areas in Japan as bases for military combat operations to be undertaken from Japan other than those conducted under Article V of said Treaty, shall be the subjects of prior consultation with the Government of Japan.

I should be appreciative if Your Excellency would confirm on behalf of your Government that this is also the understanding of the Government of the United States of America.

I avail myself of this opportunity to renew to Your Excellency the assurance of my highest consideration.

Appendix C

Statement of the Government of Japan on the Occasion of the Signing of the Treaty on the Non-Proliferation of Nuclear Weapons, February 3, 1970

The Government of Japan, believing that the proliferation of nuclear weapons would increase the danger of nuclear war, has always been in favor of the spirit underlying this treaty, since the prevention of the proliferation of nuclear weapons is in accord with its policy with regard to the maintenance of world peace.

The Government of Japan is signing this treaty on the basis of its fundamental position which is stated below.

The Government of Japan is convinced that this treaty will serve as a first step toward nuclear disarmament and hopes that as many states as possible will adhere to this treaty to make it effective. The Government of Japan hopes, especially, that the governments of the Republic of France and the People's Republic of China which possess nuclear weapons but have yet to express their intention of adhering to this treaty will become parties thereto at an early date and pursue negotiations in good faith on nuclear disarmament and that they will refrain, even before that, from taking such actions as are contrary to the purposes of this treaty.

This treaty permits only the present nuclear-weapon states to possess nuclear weapons. This discrimination should ultimately be made to disappear through the elimination of nuclear weapons by all the nuclear-weapon states from their national arsenals. Until such time the nuclear-weapon states should be conscious of the fact that they have special responsibilities as a consequence of this special status.

The prohibition under this treaty applies solely to the acquisition of nuclear weapons and other nuclear explosive devices and of control over them. Therefore, this treaty must in no way restrict nonnuclear-weapon states in their research, development, or implementation of the peaceful use of nuclear energy, or in their international cooperation in these fields, nor must it subject them to discriminatory treatment in any aspect of such activities.

The Government of Japan wishes to state that it has a deep interest in the following matters in the light of its basic position stated above.

This Government stresses that it will also concern itself most vigorously with these matters when it decides to ratify the treaty as well as when it participates in the review of its operation in the future as a party to the treaty.

I: DISARMAMENT AND SECURITY

1. Under Article VI of the Treaty each state party "undertakes to pursue negotiations in good faith on effective measures relating to cessation of the nuclear arms race at an early date and to nuclear disarmament, and on a treaty on general and complete disarmament under strict and effective international control." The Government of Japan believes it essential for the attainment of the purposes of this treaty that, above all, the nuclear-weapon states should take concrete nuclear disarmament measures in pursuance of this undertaking. As a member of the Committee on Disarmament, Japan is also prepared to cooperate in the furtherance of disarmament.

2. The Government of Japan deems it important that in the preamble to the treaty there is a provision stating that "in accordance with the Charter of the United Nations, states must refrain in their international relations from the threat or use of force against the territorial integrity or political independence of any state, or in any other manner inconsistent with the purposes of the United Nations." It also wishes to emphasize that the nuclear-weapon states must not have recourse to the use of nuclear weapons or threaten to use such weapons against nonnuclear-weapon states.

3. The Government of Japan also attaches great importance to the declarations of the United States, the United Kingdom, and the Soviet Union affirming their intention to seek immediate Se-

curity Council action to provide assistance, in accordance with the Charter of the United Nations, to any nonnuclear-weapon state, party to the treaty, that is a victim of an act of aggression in which nuclear weapons are used, and hopes that the nuclear-weapon states will continue their studies with regard to effective measures to ensure the security of nonnuclear-weapon states.

4. The Government of Japan, pending its ratification of this treaty, will pay particular attention to developments in disarmament negotiations and progress in the implementation of the Security Council resolution on the security of nonnuclear-weapon states and continue to make a close study of other problems which require consideration for the safeguarding of her national interests.

5. The Government of Japan takes note of the fact that Article X of the Treaty provides that: "Each party shall in exercising its national sovereignty have the right to withdraw from the treaty if it decides that extraordinary events, related to the subject matter of this treaty, have jeopardized the supreme interests of its country."

II. PEACEFUL USES OF NUCLEAR ENERGY

1. The safeguards agreement to be concluded by Japan with the International Atomic Energy Agency in accordance with Article III of the Treaty must not be such as would subject her to disadvantageous treatment as compared with the safeguards agreements which other states parties conclude with the same agency, either individually or together with other states. The Government of Japan intends to give full consideration to this matter before taking steps to ratify the treaty.

2. The Government of Japan greatly appreciates, as a measure supplementing this treaty, the declarations of the governments of the United States and the United Kingdom, which are both nuclear-weapon states, that they will accept the application of safeguards of the International Atomic Energy Agency to all their nuclear activities, excluding only those directly related to their national security, and earnestly hopes that these assurances will be faithfully implemented. It also hopes most earnestly that the other nuclear-weapon states will take similar action.

3. Safeguards should be subject to the principle that they should be applied at certain strategic points of the nuclear fuel

cycle, and the procedure for their application must be rational when considered from the point of view of cost-effectiveness and made as simple as possible by making the maximum use of material control systems of the respective countries. Furthermore, adequate measures must be taken to ensure that the application of safeguards does not cause the leakage of industrial secrets or otherwise hinder industrial activities. The Government of Japan hopes that the International Atomic Energy Agency will make constant efforts to improve safeguards in the light of technological developments with the above aims in mind. This Government is prepared to cooperate in such efforts and hopes that the states concerned will also cooperate to achieve this end.

4. The Government of Japan understands that no unfair burden in connection with the cost of applying safeguards will be imposed on the nonnuclear-weapon states to which such safeguards are to be applied.

5. The Government of Japan considers that, when safeguards are applied in accordance with the safeguards agreement to be concluded by Japan with the International Atomic Energy Agency under Article III of this treaty, steps should be taken to arrange that such safeguards supersede the existing safeguards which are being applied in connection with Japan's cooperation with the United States, the United Kingdom, and Canada in the peaceful use of nuclear energy.

6. Concrete measures should be taken to promote the implementation of the provisions of Articles IV and V of the treaty relating to international cooperation for the peaceful use of nuclear energy and for the peaceful application of nuclear explosions. In particular, no peaceful nuclear activities in nonnuclear-weapon states shall be prohibited or restricted, nor shall the transfer of information, nuclear materials, equipment, or other material relating to the peaceful use of nuclear energy be denied to nonnuclear-weapon states, merely on the grounds that such activities or transfers could be used also for the manufacture of nuclear weapons or other nuclear explosive devices.

Appendix D

Treaty on the Non-Proliferation of Nuclear Weapons, July 1, 1968

The States concluding this Treaty, hereinafter referred to as the "Parties to the Treaty,"

Considering the devastation that would be visited upon all mankind by a nuclear war and the consequent need to make every effort to avert the danger of such a war and to take measures to safeguard the security of peoples,

Believing that the proliferation of nuclear weapons would seriously enhance the danger of nuclear war,

In conformity with resolutions of the United Nations General Assembly calling for the conclusion of an agreement on the prevention of wider dissemination of nuclear weapons,

Undertaking to cooperate in facilitating the application of International Atomic Energy Agency safeguards on peaceful nuclear activities,

Expressing their support for research, development and other efforts to further the application, within the framework of the International Atomic Energy Agency safeguards system, of the principle of safeguarding effectively the flow of source and special fissionable materials by use of instruments and other techniques at certain strategic points,

Affirming the principle that the benefits of peaceful applications of nuclear technology, including any technological by-products which may be derived by nuclear-weapon States from the development of nuclear explosive devices, should be available for peaceful purposes to all Parties to the Treaty, whether nuclear-weapon or non-nuclear-weapon States,

Convinced that, in furtherance of this principle, all Parties to the Treaty are entitled to participate in the fullest possible exchange of scientific information for, and to contribute alone or in cooperation with other States to, the further development of the applications of atomic energy for peaceful purposes,

Declaring their intention to achieve at the earliest possible date the cessation of the nuclear arms race and to undertake effective measures in the direction of nuclear disarmament,

Urging the cooperation of all States in the attainment of this objective,

Recalling the determination expressed by the Parties to the 1963 Treaty banning nuclear weapon tests in the atmosphere in outer space and under water in its Preamble to seek to achieve the discontinuance of all test explosions of nuclear weapons for all time and to continue negotiations to this end,

Desiring to further the easing of international tension and the strengthening of trust between States in order to facilitate the cessation of the manufacture of nuclear weapons, the liquidation of all their existing stockpiles, and the elimination from national arsenals of nuclear weapons and the means of their delivery pursuant to a treaty on general and complete disarmament under strict and effective international control,

Recalling that, in accordance with the Charter of the United Nations, States must refrain in their international relations from the threat or use of force against the territorial integrity or political independence of any State, or in any other manner inconsistent with the Purposes of the United Nations, and that the establishment and maintenance of international peace and security are to be promoted with the least diversion for armaments of the world's human and economic resources,

Have agreed as follows:

ARTICLE I

Each nuclear-weapon State Party to the Treaty undertakes not to transfer to any recipient whatsoever nuclear weapons or other nuclear explosive devices or control over such weapons or explosive devices directly, or indirectly; and not in any way to assist, encourage, or induce any non-nuclear-weapon State to manufacture or otherwise acquire weapons or other nuclear explosive devices.

ARTICLE II

Each non-nuclear-weapon State Party to the Treaty undertakes not to receive the transfer from any transferor whatsoever of nuclear weapons or other nuclear explosive devices or of control over such weapons or explosive devices directly, or indirectly; not to manufacture or otherwise acquire nuclear weapons or other explosive devices; and not to seek or receive any assistance in the manufacture of nuclear weapons or other nuclear explosive devices.

ARTICLE III

1. Each non-nuclear-weapon State Party to the Treaty undertakes to accept safeguards, as set forth in an agreement to be negotiated and concluded with the International Atomic Energy Agency in accordance with the Statute of the International Atomic Energy Agency and the Agency's safeguards system, for the exclusive purpose of verification of the fulfillment of its obligations assumed under this Treaty with a view to preventing diversion of nuclear energy from peaceful uses to nuclear weapons or other nuclear explosive devices. Procedures for the safeguards required by this article shall be followed with respect to source or special fissionable material whether it is being produced, processed or used in any principal nuclear facility or is outside any such facility. The safeguards required by this article shall be applied on all source or special fissionable material in all peaceful nuclear activities within the territory of such State, under its jurisdiction, or carried out under its control anywhere.

2. Each State Party to the Treaty undertakes not to provide: (a) source or special fissionable material, or (b) equipment or material especially designed or prepared for the processing, use or production of special fissionable material, to any non-nuclear-weapon State for peaceful purposes, unless the source or special fissionable material shall be subject to the safeguards required by this article.

3. The safeguards required by this article shall be implemented in a manner designed to comply with article IV of this Treaty, and to avoid hampering the economic or technological development of the Parties or international cooperation in the field of peaceful nuclear activities, including the international exchange of nuclear material and equipment for the processing, use or production of nuclear material for peaceful purposes in accordance with the provisions of this article and the principle of safeguarding set forth in the Preamble of the Treaty.

4. Non-nuclear-weapon States Party to the Treaty shall conclude agreements with the International Atomic Energy Agency to meet the requirements of this article either individually or together with other States in accordance with the Statute of the International Atomic Energy Agency. Negotiation of such agreements shall commence within 180 days from the original entry into force of this Treaty. For States depositing their instruments of ratification or accession after the 180-day period, negotiation of such agreements shall commence not later than the date of such deposit. Such agreements shall enter into force not later than eighteen months after the date of initiation of negotiations.

ARTICLE IV

1. Nothing in this Treaty shall be interpreted as affecting the inalienable right of all the Parties to the Treaty to develop research, production and use of nuclear energy for peaceful purposes without discrimination and in conformity with articles I and II of this Treaty.

2. All the Parties to the Treaty undertake to facilitate and have the right to participate in, the fullest possible exchange of equipment, materials and scientific and technological information for the peaceful uses of nuclear energy. Parties to the Treaty in a position to do so shall also cooperate in contributing alone or together with other States or international organizations to the further development of the applications of nuclear energy for peaceful purposes, especially in the territories of non-nuclear-weapon States Party to the Treaty, with due consideration for the needs of the developing areas of the world.

ARTICLE V

Each Party to the Treaty undertakes to take appropriate measures to ensure that, in accordance with this Treaty, under appropriate international observation and through appropriate international procedures, potential benefits from any peaceful applications of nuclear explosions will be made available to non-nuclear-weapon States Party to the Treaty on a non-discriminatory basis and that the charge to such Parties for the explosive devices used will be as low as possible and exclude any charge for research and development. Non-nuclear-weapon States Party to the Treaty shall be able to obtain such benefits, pursuant to a special international agreement or agreements, through an appropriate international body with adequate representation of non-nuclear-weapon States. Negotiations on this subject shall commence as soon as possible after the Treaty enters into force. Non-nuclear-weapon States Party to the Treaty so desiring may also obtain such benefits pursuant to bilateral agreements.

ARTICLE VI

Each of the Parties to the Treaty undertakes to pursue negotiations in good faith on effective measures relating to cessation of the nuclear arms race at an early date and to nuclear disarmament, and on a treaty on general and complete disarmament under strict and effective international control.

ARTICLE VII

Nothing in this Treaty affects the right of any group of States to conclude regional treaties in order to assure the total absence of nuclear weapons in their respective territories.

ARTICLE VIII

1. Any Party to the Treaty may propose amendments to this Treaty. The text of any proposed amendment shall be submitted to the Depositary Governments which shall circulate it to all Parties to the Treaty. Thereupon, if requested to do so by one-third or more of the Parties to the Treaty, the Depositary Governments shall convene a conference, to which they shall invite all the Parties to the Treaty, to consider such an amendment.

2. Any amendment to this Treaty must be approved by a majority of the votes of all the Parties to the Treaty, including the votes of all nuclear-weapon States Party to the Treaty and all other Parties which, on the date the amendment is circulated, are members of the Board of Governors of the International Atomic Energy Agency. The amendment shall enter into force for each Party that deposits its instrument of ratification of the amendment upon the deposit of such instruments of ratification by a majority of all the Parties, including the instruments of ratification of all nuclear-weapon States Party to the Treaty and all other

Parties which, on the date the amendment is circulated, are members of the Board of Governors of the International Atomic Energy Agency. Thereafter, it shall enter into force for any other Party upon the deposit of its instrument of ratification of the amendment.

3. Five years after the entry into force of this Treaty, a conference of Parties to the Treaty shall be held in Geneva, Switzerland, in order to review the operation of this Treaty with a view to assuring that the purposes of the Preamble and the provisions of the Treaty are being realized. At intervals of five years thereafter, a majority of the Parties to the Treaty may obtain, by submitting a proposal to this effect to the Depositary Governments, the convening of further conferences with the same objective of reviewing the operation of the Treaty.

ARTICLE IX

1. This Treaty shall be open to all States for signature. Any State which does not sign the Treaty before its entry into force in accordance with paragraph 3 of this article may accede to it at any time.

2. This Treaty shall be subject to ratification by signatory States. Instruments of ratification and instruments of accession shall be deposited with the governments of the United States of America, the United Kingdom of Great Britain and Northern Ireland and the Union of Soviet Socialist Republics, which are hereby designated the Depositary Governments.

3. This Treaty shall enter into force after its ratification by the States, the Governments of which are designated Depositaries of the Treaty, and forty other States signatory to this Treaty and the deposit of their instruments of ratification. For the purposes of this Treaty, a nuclear-weapon State is one which has manufactured and exploded a nuclear weapon or other nuclear explosive device prior to January 1, 1967.

4. For States whose instruments of ratification or accession are deposited subsequent to the entry into force of this Treaty, it shall enter into force on the date of the deposit of their instruments of ratification or accession.

5. The Depositary Governments shall promptly inform all signatory and acceding States of the date of each signature, the date of deposit of each instrument of ratification or of accession, the

date of the entry into force of this Treaty, and the date of receipt of any requests for convening a conference or other notices.

6. This Treaty shall be registered by the Depositary Governments pursuant to article 102 of the Charter of the United Nations.

ARTICLE X

1. Each Party shall in exercising its national sovereignty have the right to withdraw from the Treaty if it decides that extraordinary events, related to the subject matter of this Treaty, have jeopardized the supreme interests of its country. It shall give notice of such withdrawal to all other Parties to the Treaty and to the United Nations Security Council three months in advance. Such notice shall include a statement of the extraordinary events it regards as having jeopardized its supreme interests.

2. Twenty-five years after the entry into force of the Treaty, a conference shall be convened to decide whether the Treaty shall continue in force indefinitely, or shall be extended for an additional fixed period or periods. This decision shall be taken by a majority of the Parties to the Treaty.

.   .   .   .

Notes

CHAPTER 1

1. See *Japan Times Weekly* (International Edition), June 27, 1970, p. 3, for the text of the government statement on the occasion of the extension of the Japan–United States Mutual Security Treaty.
2. *Ibid.*
3. For elaboration, see Chapter 4 and Donald C. Hellmann, *Japanese Domestic Politics and Foreign Policy* (Berkeley: University of California Press, 1969), esp. Chapters 1 and 9.
4. For a good critical review of the main arguments for retrenchment, see Charles Gati, "Another Grand Debate? The Limitationist Critique of American Foreign Policy," *World Politics*, XXI, 1 (October, 1968), 133–51.
5. Richard M. Nixon, "Asia After Vietnam," *Foreign Affairs*, XLVI, 1 (October, 1967), 111–25. See also his statement in an interview in the *Washington Post*, December 8, 1968.
6. *Asahi Shimbun*, May 16, 1970.
7. Harold Isaacs, *No Peace for Asia* (Cambridge, Mass.: MIT Press, 1965), *passim*.

CHAPTER 2

1. In President Nixon's words, "If we are thinking down the long road—not just four years or five years, but ten, fifteen, or twenty—the greatest threat to peace will be in the Pacific [East Asia]." *New York Times*, July 26, 1969.
2. A similar view is elaborated in Alastair Buchan, "An Asian Balance of Power," *Encounter*, XXVII (December, 1966), 62–71.
3. Among the best general works on regionalism are Joseph R. Nye, Jr., ed., *International Regionalism: Readings* (Boston: Little, Brown, 1968); Louis J. Cantori and Steven L. Spiegel, *The International Politics of Regions* (Englewood Cliffs, N.J.: Prentice-Hall, 1970); Bruce M. Russett,

International Regions and the International System: A Study in Political Ecology (Chicago: Rand McNally, 1968); and the December, 1969, issue of the *International Studies Quarterly XIII,* 4, ed. by Peter Berton. For a stimulating critique of the theoretical basis of Russett's book, see Oran R. Young, "Professor Russett: Industrious Tailor to a Naked Emperor," *World Politics,* XXI, 486–511.

4. Such theoretical freedom has occasionally become license. To include, in an East Asian regional trade group, South Korea, Taiwan, Japan, the Philippines, and *Saudi Arabia* (Bruce M. Russett, "Delineating International Regions," in J. David Singer, ed., *Quantitative International Politics* [New York: The Free Press, 1968], p. 345) may make statistical sense but is nonsense by any other standard.

5. This is a modification of a definition offered by Karl Kaiser, "The Interaction of Regional Subsystems," *World Politics,* XXI, 1 (October, 1968), 86.

6. For an interesting discussion of the differences in these approaches, see Roger D. Hansen, "Regional Integration: Reflection on a Decade of Theoretical Effort," *World Politics,* XXI, 2 (January, 1969), 242–71.

7. See, for example, Michael Brecher, "International Relations and Area Studies: The Subordinate State System of Southern Asia," *World Politics,* XV, 2 (January, 1963), 213–35; Werner Levi, *The Challenge of World Politics in South and Southeast Asia* (Englewood Cliffs, N.J.: Prentice-Hall, Inc., 1968), esp. pp. 49–73; Bernard K. Gordon, *The Dimensions of Conflict in Southeast Asia* (Englewood Cliffs, N.J.: Prentice-Hall, Inc., 1968), *passim;* and Louis J. Cantori and Steven L. Spiegel, *op. cit., passim.*

8. Cantori and Spiegel, *op. cit.,* p. 25.

9. This is well elaborated in Bruce Grant, "Toward a New Balance in Asia: An Australian View," *Foreign Affairs,* XLVII, 4 (July, 1969), 711–20.

10. Stanley Hoffmann, *Gulliver's Troubles* (New York: McGraw-Hill, 1968), pp. 26–33.

11. This general change has heightened interest in the relationships between the global system and the regional subsystems, as well as among the subsystems themselves—a peripheral subject when regionalism was largely the concern of the area specialist. See, for example, Oran R. Young, "Political Discontinuities in the International System," *World Politics,* XX, 3 (April, 1968), 369–92.

12. For all the factors encouraging persistence of the bipolar order and the limitations on the actions of the middle powers, see Kenneth N. Waltz, "The Stability of a Bipolar World," *Daedalus,* LXIV, 3 (Summer, 1964), 887–99.

13. Oran R. Young, *op. cit.,* p. 389. For similar opinions, see Michio Royama, "The Asian Balance of Power: A Japanese View," *Adelphi Papers,* 42 (London: Institute for Strategic Studies, 1967), 14, and John T. McAlister, Jr., "The Possibilities for Diplomacy in Southeast Asia," *World Politics* XIX, 2 (January, 1967), 258–305.

14. Stanley Hoffmann, *op. cit.,* pp. 30–31.

15. For the initial and most revealing official statement of this policy, see

President Nixon's press conference in Guam in July, 1969, published in the *New York Times,* July 26, 1969. An interesting and benign summary of this policy one year after it was announced is provided by former Assistant Secretary of State William Bundy in "The Policies in Asia and the Pacific," *Pacific Community,* II, 1 (October, 1970), 77–86.

16. Fred Greene, *U.S. Policy and the Security of Asia* (New York: McGraw-Hill, 1968) pp. 71–83 and 102–24.

17. For a summary of the recent positions of the two countries regarding East Asian Communist countries and movements, see the *New York Times,* May 11, 1970.

18. For an interesting interpretation of the entrance of East Asia into global international politics, see Maruyama Masao, *Thought and Behavior in Japanese Politics* (London: Oxford University Press, 1963), pp. 138–39.

19. Raymond Aron, *Peace and War* (New York: Praeger, 1968), p. 391.

20. See Marius B. Jansen, *The Japanese and Sun Yat-sen* (Cambridge, Mass.: Harvard University Press, 1954), pp. 2–5, 160–61, 210–12, and 217–18.

21. Willard Elsbree, *Japan's Role in Southeast Asian Nationalist Movements* (Cambridge, Mass.: Harvard University Press, 1953), *passim.*

22. For the use of GNP as an international power index, see Charles Hitch and Dayton McKean, *The Economics of Defense in the Nuclear Age* (Cambridge, Mass.: Harvard University Press, 1961), Chapter 1, and Bruce M. Russett, *Trends in World Politics* (New York: Macmillan, 1965), pp. 4–8.

23. See, for example, Waltz, *op. cit.,* pp. 892–93, and A. F. K. Organski, *World Politics* (New York: Alfred A. Knopf, 1964), Chapters 5–8.

24. See Bruce Russett, *Trends in World Politics,* pp. 4–8.

25. The complexities of the roles of small states in international politics are clearly and carefully elaborated in Robert O. Keohane, "Lilliputians' Dilemmas: Small States in International Politics," *International Organization,* XXIII, 2 (Spring, 1969), 291–310.

26. Japan Economic Research Center, "Preliminary Report of Medium-Term Projection of Japanese Economy for 1975" (Tokyo: July 15, 1969), cited in Saburo Okita, "Japanese Economic Cooperation in Asia in the 1970's," in Gerald L. Curtis, ed., *Japanese-American Relations in the 1970's* (Washington, D.C.: Columbia Books, Inc.), pp. 110–11.

27. Oran R. Young, *op. cit.,* pp. 383–84.

28. This broadened definition of security was accepted by the United States at the height of its efforts in Vietnam. See, for example, President Lyndon Johnson's speech at Johns Hopkins University in April, 1965, and his statement to the American Alumni Council in July, 1966, in the *New York Times,* April 8, 1965, and July 13, 1966, respectively.

29. See, for example, Hans J. Morgenthau, *A New Foreign Policy for the United States* (New York: Praeger, 1969), pp. 201–3. Professor Morgenthau sees as inevitable the "political and cultural predominance" of China on the Asian mainland.

30. Bernard K. Gordon, *Toward Disengagement in Asia* (Englewood Cliffs, N.J.: Prentice-Hall, Inc., 1969), pp. 62–67.

CHAPTER 3

1. The Japan Socialist Party emerged as a major political force immediately after the war but split into left- and right-wing groups for four years after a dispute over the acceptability of the San Francisco Peace Treaty of 1951. After reunification in 1955, another split occurred three years later, with the non-Marxist right wing establishing the still operative Democratic-Socialist Party. This latter group draws its main monetary and organizational support from the moderate labor federation *Domei Kaigi*, just as the larger Social-Democrats rely on *Sōhyo*, the largest Japanese labor organization. For an excellent history of the socialist movement in the postwar period, with special emphasis on foreign policy, see J. A. A. Stockwin, *The Japanese Socialist Party and Neutralism* (Carlton, Australia: Melbourne University Press, 1968), *passim*.

2. See, for example, Edwin O. Reischauer, *Beyond Vietnam: The United States and Asia* (Tokyo: Charles E. Tuttle, 1967), pp. 122–24; and James W. Morley, *Japan and Korea: America's Allies in the Pacific* (New York: Walker and Co., 1965), pp. 32–36.

3. It has also been persuasively argued that the Socialists are not predominantly an urban party and have, in fact, been steadily losing electoral support in the urban areas for the last decade. Gerald L. Curtis, "The 1969 General Election in Japan," *Asian Survey*, X, 10 (October, 1970), 866.

4. The disparity between the popular vote and the proportion of Diet seats is largely explained by the nature of the electoral system. Under the present arrangement, the country is divided into multiple-member constituencies, each having three, four, or five representatives, with every voter casting a single ballot. Members of the same party are thus placed in competition with each other, and over-all success falls to the party that can best predict the division of votes among the candidates in each district—and not simply to the party obtaining the largest absolute total of votes. A good general description of the operation of the electoral system is provided in Nathaniel B. Thayer, *How the Conservatives Rule Japan* (Princeton: Princeton University Press, 1969), Chapter 5.

5. J. A. A. Stockwin, "Foreign Policy Perspectives of the Japanese Left: Confrontation or Consensus," *Pacific Affairs*, XLII, 4 (Winter, 1969–70), 438–39.

6. Good general discussions of conservative factions are found in: Robert A. Scalapino and Junnosuke Masumi, *Parties and Politics in Contemporary Japan* (Berkeley and Los Angeles: University of California Press, 1962), Chapter 3; Haruhiro Fukui, *Party in Power: The Japanese Liberal Democrats and Policy-Making* (Berkeley and Los Angeles: University of California Press, 1970), Chapter 5; and Nathaniel P. Thayer, *op. cit.*, Chapter 2. Of the numerous Japanese works on the subject, two of the best are Tsuneo Watanabe, *Habatsu (Factions)*, 2d ed. (Tokyo: Kobundo, 1964), and Asahi Shimbun, *Jimintō: Hōshu Kenryōku no Kōzō (The Liberal*

Democratic Party: Structure of Conservative Power) (Tokyo: Asahi Shimbunsha, 1970), esp. pp. 287–326.

7. For elaboration, see Donald C. Hellmann, *Japanese Domestic Politics and Foreign Policy: The Peace Agreement with the Soviet Union* (Berkeley and Los Angeles: University of California Press, 1969), Chapters 3 and 9.

8. For elaboration, see George R. Packard, *Protest in Tokyo: The Security Treaty Crisis of 1960* (Princeton: Princeton University Press, 1966), Chapter 3.

9. For a fuller discussion, see Donald C. Hellmann, "Basic Problems of Japanese–South Korean Relations," *Asian Survey*, II, 5 (May, 1962), 19–24.

10. The formation of these groups and the multifaction nature of their membership received extensive attention from Japanese political commentators. See, for example, *Yomiuri Shimbun*, March 10 and 20, 1966; "Chugoku Seisaku wo Mukawareru Hōshu Kakushin" ("Changes Within the Conservatives Caused by the Issue of China Policy"), *Ekonomisuto*, XLIII, 8 (February 23, 1965), 14–23; and Yomiuri Shimbun Seiji-bu, *Seitō* (*Political Parties*) (Tokyo: Yomiuri Shimbunsha, 1966), pp. 86–89.

11. Regarding the connections between these groups and the factions, see *Yomiuri Shimbun*, March 22, 1966.

12. See, for example, *ibid.* and Fukui, *op cit.*, pp. 141–42.

13. *Asahi Shimbun*, November 14 and December 8, 1970.

14. For a good general summary of conservative party organization and the impact on policy-making, see Junnosuke Masumi, "Jiyuminshutō no Soshiki to Kinō" ("The Liberal-Democratic Party: Organization and Function"), in *1967 Seijigaku Nenpō: Gendai Nihon no Seitō to Kanryō* (*1967 Political Science Yearbook: The Parties and Bureaucracy in Contemporary Japan*), pp. 66–77.

15. For an outspoken statement of this position, see Richard Barnet's contribution to Richard M. Pfeffer, ed., *No More Vietnams? The War and the Future of American Foreign Policy* (New York: Harper & Row, 1968), pp. 50–74. See also the discussion of this paper, pp. 74 ff.

16. See James W. Morley, "Growth for What? The Issue of the Seventies," in Gerald L. Curtis, ed., *Japanese-American Relations in the 1970's* (Washington, D.C.: Columbia Books, Inc., 1970), pp. 48–93, esp. pp. 81–88.

17. See Masumi, "Jiyuminshutō no Soshiki. . . ," p. 64.

18. A review of these actions is provided in Nobuo Nakayama, "Japan–Republic of Korea Economic Cooperation Underway," *Asahi Journal*, May 15, 1966, trans. in *Selected Summaries of Japanese Magazines* (Tokyo: U.S. Embassy, June 20, 1966), pp. 9–16.

19. The main points of the extensive literature on the relationship between public opinion and foreign policy in the United States are concisely summarized in Ernst B. Haas, *Tangle of Hopes: American Commitments and World Order* (Englewood Cliffs, N.J.: Prentice-Hall, Inc., 1969), Chapter 3, esp. pp. 33–37 and 56–59.

20. For an elaboration of this distinction, see Bernard C. Cohen, *The Political Process and Foreign Policy: The Making of the Japanese Peace Settlement*

(Princeton: Princeton University Press, 1957), p. 29 and Chapters 3–6, 10.

21. Regarding Prime Minister Yoshida Shigeru and the U.S. Peace Treaty, see Kōsaka Masataka, "Saishō Yoshida Shigeru Ron" ("Prime Minister Yoshida Shigeru"), *Chūō Kōron*, LXXIX, 2 (February, 1964), 80–85 and 105; regarding Prime Minister Kishi and the 1960 Security Treaty, see Packard, *op. cit.*, Chapter 8; regarding Prime Minister Hatoyama and the Soviet Peace Agreement, see Hellmann, *Japanese Domestic Politics. . .*, pp. 10–13 and Chapter 5.

22. Council on Foreign Relations, *The American Public's View of U.S. Policy Toward China* (a report prepared for the Council on Foreign Relations by the Survey Research Center, University of Michigan) (New York: Council on Foreign Relations, 1964), Table 1, p. 5, and Table 6, p. 11.

23. *Japan Times Weekly* (International Edition), July 22, 1967 (a report of the Kyōdo News Agency poll of June, 1967).

CHAPTER 4

1. Cobden's main opinions on international affairs appear in his writings included in Arnold Wolfers and Laurence W. Martin, eds., *The Anglo-American Tradition in Foreign Affairs* (New Haven: Yale University Press, 1956), pp. 192–205. See also Kenneth N. Waltz, *Man, the State and War* (New York: Columbia University Press, 1959), esp. pp. 103–14 and 160–64, for an elaboration of Cobden's place in theories of international politics.

2. Arnold Wolfers and Laurence W. Martin, *The Anglo-American Tradition . . .*, p. 194. Author's additions in brackets.

3. *Ibid.*, pp. ix–xxvii.

4. See James B. Crowley, *Japan's Quest for Autonomy* (Princeton: Princeton University Press, 1966), p. 187–96, for a discussion of the premises of Japanese foreign policy in the immediate prewar period.

5. Speech before the U.N. General Assembly, October 21, 1970. *Japan Times*, October 22, 1970.

6. This point is well illustrated in a statement by Albert Wohlsetter, which moves ethnocentrism a bit further by laying basic responsibility for any current Japanese interest in Asia to American policy:

> We [the United States] keep pushing Japan into assuming a role in regard to any number of Asian nations in which it has only the faintest interest, simply because they are all in Asia. It should be obvious that Japan's interests will be linked increasingly with such distant places as the United States and Europe.

Pfeffer, ed., *No More Vietnams? . . .*, p. 287. It is instructive to contrast this statement with the views expressed by Takeo Miki, a leader of the "progressive" wing of the Liberal-Democratic Party, on the place of Asia in American and Japanese policy in *Nihon Kogyō*, June 12, 1966.

7. The persistence of prewar concepts of Japanese leadership in Asia is explored in James F. McGarry, *A Study of Decision-Making in Japan's Post-*

war Economic Policy (unpublished Ph.D. dissertation, University of Pennsylvania, 1964), *passim.*

8. For a provocative, but highly conjectural, discussion of the potential of a new Shōwa (1926–) generation of political leadership with distinct and "rational" predispositions toward foreign affairs coming to power in the late 1970's, see Kei Wakaizumi, "Japan Beyond 1970," *Foreign Affairs* XLVII, 3 (April, 1969), 509–14.

9. The basic features of Japan's policy toward East Asia during this period are well summarized in James W. Morley, "Japan's Position in Asia," *Journal of International Affairs,* XVII, 2 (1963), 146–51.

10. "Kishi Shushō Tonan Ajiya Rekiho no Seika" ("The Results of Prime Minister Kishi's Visit to Southeast Asia"), *Ekonomisuto,* XXXV, 23 (June 8, 1957), 9–10, and *Sankei Jiji,* June 15, 1958.

11. Hayato Ikeda, "Rekishitaki Kodai ni Tachimaku Nihon Kokumin" ("The Historical Tasks Confronting the Japanese People"), *Seisaku Geppō,* 85 (February, 1963), pp. 268–73. Not only did Ikeda assert a kind of parity with Western powers, but Japan was at this time accepted into the OECD, an international organization widely considered to be a "rich man's club" and tangible proof of international respectability. These developments tended to overshadow the positive commitments regarding Asia that were simultaneously cultivated.

12. Hayato Ikeda, "Jiyū to Seiji ni Tatsu Sekai Heiwa" ("World Peace Built on Freedom and Justice"), *Seisaku Geppō,* 66 (July, 1961), pp. 57–63.

13. The most interesting elaboration of the concept of the "Asia-Pacific zone" is provided in an interview with Miki in mid-1967 by Shizuo Maruyama, " 'Ajia-Taiheiyō Ken' Kōsō to Miki Gaikō," ("Asia-Pacific Zone and Miki Diplomacy"), *Asahi Jānaru,* IX, 29 (July 9, 1967), 18–22.

14. *New York Times,* August 25, 1965.

15. A good summary of the factions in the Foreign Ministry is provided in Yasuyuki Suzuki, "Gaimu Kanryō to Nihon no Gaikō" ("Foreign Ministry Bureaucrats and Japan's Diplomacy"), *Jiyū,* XVII, 6 (June, 1965), 58–63.

16. R. P. Dore, "Japan's Place in the World," *World Today* (July, 1966), p. 295 and Robert A. Scalapino, "In Search of a Role: Japan and the Uncertainties of Power," *Encounter,* XXVII, 6 (December, 1966), 24.

17. See, for example, editorial in *Asahi Shimbun,* September 12, 1971.

18. *Japan Times Weekly* (International Edition), August 1, 1970.

19. As testimony to the strength of nationalist sentiments on the left, the campaign posters of the Japanese Communist Party in the 1969 general election involved a motif with the national flag.

CHAPTER 5

1. Unless otherwise indicated, the trade statistics cited throughout this section are from various issues of *The Direction of Trade Annual* and *International Financial Statistics,* published by the International Monetary Fund.

2. This point is made with specific regard to Japan and other East Asian economies in Robert S. Ozaki, "Japan's Role in Asian Economic Development," *Asian Survey*, VII, 4 (April, 1967), 238.

3. One estimate holds that American military expenditures in the 1965–68 period are indirectly responsible for half of the increase in Japanese exports to these countries. Morgan Guaranty Trust Company, *Japan's International Economy* (New York, 1970), p. 15.

4. A complete breakdown of trade by commodity and country is provided in the annual *White Paper (Tsūshō Hakushō)* of the Ministry of International Trade and Industry (Tsūshō-sangyōshō).

5. The Chase Manhattan Bank, "Japan," *World Business*, 18 (1st Quarter, 1970), p. 55.

6. Shigeharu Matsumoto, "Japan and China," in A. M. Halpern, ed., *Policies Toward China: Views from Six Continents* (New York: McGraw-Hill, 1965), pp. 133–34.

7. See, for example, *Asahi Shimbun*, July 11, 1966.

8. See, for example, the translation of the communiqué signed in 1971, in the *Japan Times*, March 3, 1971.

9. Kaoru Murakami, "The Korean Peninsula and Japan's Munitions Industry," *Gendai no Me* (October, 1970), trans. in *Selected Translations of Japanese Magazines* (Tokyo: U.S. Embassy, January, 1971).

10. The data for this paragraph are from a report published by the Government of Indonesia, "Foreign Investments in Indonesia, 1967–70" (Jakarta, January, 1971) (mimeo.).

11. A good summary treatment of the role of foreign (especially Japanese) capital in South Korea in the years immediately after normalization is provided in Kakutake Hora, *Kankoku Keizai no Kiseki (The Korean Economic Miracle)* (Tokyo: Nihon Kokusai Mondai Kenkyujo, 1970), pp. 40–53. The figures in this paragraph were obtained from two 1970 publications of the Economic Planning Board, Government of the Republic of Korea, *Major Economic Indicators* and *Economic Survey*.

12. A brief summary of foreign investment in Thailand during the 1960's is provided in Hiroshi Komai, *Tai no Gendaika (Conditions of Modern Thailand)* (Tokyo: Nihon Kokusai Mondai Kenkyujo, 1971), pp. 91–97.

13. On the limits on interdependence among nations with highly unequal capabilities, see Kenneth N. Waltz, "The Myth of National Interdependence," in Charles P. Kindleberger, ed., *The International Corporation* (Cambridge, Mass.: MIT Press, 1970), pp. 207–14.

14. See, for example, *Yomiuri Shimbun*, September 22, 1969.

15. The facts in this paragraph are drawn mainly from the pamphlet *Overseas Technical Cooperation Agency, 1970–71* (Tokyo, 1971), published by the Agency.

16. *Asahi Shimbun*, May 1, 1971.

17. *Japan Times*, December 10, 1970.

18. *The Overseas Economic Cooperation Fund: Its Role and Activities* (Tokyo,

1970), p. 3. This pamphlet provides an excellent summary of the Fund's activities through 1970.

19. See, for example, Masao Sawaki, "Idea and Moot Points of Economic Aid," *Kokusai Jihyō* (October, 1970), trans. in *Selected Summaries of Japanese Magazines* (Tokyo: U.S. Embassy, January, 1971), pp. 47–49.

20. See the statement of Foreign Minister Aichi at a meeting of the Development Assistance Committee of the OECD, September 15, 1970: *Asahi Shimbun*, September 16, 1970.

21. Ministry of Foreign Affairs, *Highlights of Japan's Foreign Aid* (Tokyo, 1969).

22. U.S. Embassy (Tokyo), "Japanese Economic Assistance to Developing Countries," 1971 (mimeo.).

23. These developments are well summarized in Nagao Kato, "Kyutenkai suru Nihon no Tonan Ajiya Enjo" ("A Sudden Turn in Japan's Aid to Southeast Asia"), *Ekonomisuto*, XLIV, 47 (November 15, 1966), 56–61.

24. On the concept of "inverse Marxism," see Ernst Haas, *Tangle of Hopes* (Englewood Cliffs, N.J.: Prentice-Hall, Inc., 1969), pp. 144–46.

25. *Yomiuri Shimbun*, November 29, 1969.

26. Two excellent articles on this point are Mancur Olsen's "Rapid Growth as a De-stabilizing Force," *Journal of Economic History*, XXIII (March, 1963), 529–58, and Ronald G. Riker's "Discontent and Economic Growth," *Economic Development and Cultural Change*, XI (October, 1962), 1–15.

CHAPTER 6

1. Supreme Command for the Allied Powers, Report of the Government Section, *Political Orientation of Japan: September, 1945–September, 1948* (Washington, D.C.: G.P.O., 1959), p. 765.

2. John M. Maki, ed., *Conflict and Tension in the Far East: Key Documents, 1894–1960* (Seattle: University of Washington Press, 1961), p. 129.

3. These assumptions underlie the famous article by Edwin O. Reischauer, "The Broken Dialogue with Japan," *Foreign Affairs*, XXXIX, 1 (October, 1960), 11–26.

4. U.S. Embassy (Tokyo), "U.S.-Japan Bilateral Trade, 1970" (mimeo.).

5. Frederick S. Dunn, *Peace-Making and the Settlement with Japan* (Princeton: Princeton University Press, 1963), pp. 45–52.

6. In the Presidential Report to Congress, *United States Foreign Policy for the 1970's* (Washington, D.C.: 1971), Japan is listed as one of the "major powers" of Asia (together with the United States, the Soviet Union, and the People's Republic of China), all of whose future decisions will "centrally affect the international situation in the region"; pp. 77–78 and 86–89.

7. *New York Times*, November 29, 1969.

8. *Asahi Evening News*, March 11, 1971.

9. Robert S. McNamara, *The Essence of Security* (New York: Harper & Row, 1968), pp. 149 ff.

10. See the statement of President Nixon accompanying his request to Congress for a new aid appropriation and a proposed reorganization of the aid program: *New York Times,* April 12, 1971.

11. Robert E. Osgood *et al., Japan and the United States in Asia* (Baltimore: The Johns Hopkins Press, 1968), pp. 14–15.

12. Thomas C. Schelling, "Peace and Security in Asia and the Roles of Japan and the United States" (paper presented at the Japan–United States Kyoto Conference, January, 1969), p. 1.

13. Although the purpose was clearly propagandistic, it is notable that Japan was the first country against which such threats were directed by Peking. Morton H. Halperin, "Chinese Nuclear Strategy: The Early Post-Detonation Period," *Adelphi Paper,* 18 (London: Institute for Strategic Studies, May, 1965), pp. 12–13.

CHAPTER 7

1. Martin E. Weinstein, *Japan's Postwar Defense Policy, 1947–68* (New York: Columbia University Press, 1971), pp. 106–7.

2. Bōeichō (Defense Agency, Japan), *Nihon no Bōei* (Japan's Defense) (Tokyo: 1970), p. 3.

3. See Haruhiro Fukui, "Twenty Years of Revisionism," in D. F. Henderson, ed., *The Constitution of Japan: Its First Twenty Years, 1947–67* (Seattle: University of Washington Press, 1968), pp. 45–58.

4. Toshitaka Shiomi, "Jieitai to Kokumin Seron" ("The Self-Defense Forces and Popular Opinion"), *Sekai* (June, 1967), pp. 100–103.

5. Kenzō Tokayanagi, "Some Reminiscences of Japan's Commission on the Constitution," in Henderson, *op. cit.,* pp. 83–88.

6. Bōeichō, *op. cit.,* pp. 36–37.

7. See, for example, Yasumasa Tanaka and Yoko Iwamatsu, "An Exploratory Semantic Differential Study of the Affective and Cognitive Components of the Attitudes Held by Japanese College SS Toward Nuclear Testings and Proliferation," *Peace Research in Japan* (1968), pp. 28–30.

8. Bōeichō, *op. cit.,* p. 29.

9. For a summary of the draft of the Fourth Defense Plan, see *Asahi Shimbun,* April 28, 1971.

10. Bōeichō, *op. cit.,* pp. 74–75.

11. See Tomohisa Sakanaka *et al., Nihon no Jiei Ryoku (Japan's Self-Defense Power)* (Tokyo: Asahi Shimbunsha, 1967), pp. 225–62, for an account of the intragovernmental debate over the budget for the Third Defense Plan. See also Weinstein, *op. cit.,* pp. 125–26.

12. For a contrary view, see Weinstein, *ibid., passim.,* esp. pp. 104–35.

13. Bōeichō, *op. cit.,* p. 29.

14. *Japan Times,* April 28, 1971.

Notes

15. See *Asahi Shimbun,* March 19 and 20, 1970, and Kobun Ito, "Japan's Security in the 1970's," *Asian Survey,* X, 12 (December, 1970), 1032–34.

16. The phrase "nonnuclear middle-class nation" was used by Nakasone in his personal statement introducing the White Paper (*Asahi Shimbun,* October 21, 1970); the Prime Minister made clear his disagreement in testimony before the Budget Committee of the House of Councillors (*Yomiuri Shimbun,* March 28, 1971).

17. These views are embodied in the 1966 report by the party's Security Problem Research Committee, whose members are heavily drawn from conservatives with a special interest in defense. Jiyu Minshutō Anzen Hoshō ni Kan Suru Chōsakai, "Waga Kuni no Anzen Hoshō ni Kan Suru Chūkan Hōkoku" ("Interim Report Concerning the Defense of Our Country") (Tokyo: 1966), esp. pp. 24–30 and 34–38.

18. A remarkable collection of equivocal statements by conservative party leaders on the question of nuclear weapons is found in the *Mainichi Shimbun,* December 31, 1967. See also Kaoru Murakami, "Liberal-Democratic Party Factions' Sense of Defense," *Jiyū,* July, 1966, trans. in *Summaries of Selected Japanese Magazines* (Tokyo: U.S. Embassy, June 27, 1966).

19. The policy of the JSP is "unarmed positive neutrality"; that of the JCP is "peace and neutrality"; while the Kōmeitō favors "complete neutrality." For a good review of the foreign policy of the socialists, see J. A. A. Stockwin, *The Japanese Socialist Party and Neutralism* (London: Cambridge University Press, 1968).

20. See, for example, the statement by the then chairman of the Socialist Party's Foreign and Defense Policy Committee, Masashi Ishibashi, "Security in a Nuclear Age," *Economisuto,* May 24, 1966, trans. in *Selected Summaries of Japanese Magazines* (Tokyo: U.S. Embassy, June, 1966). For the Democratic-Socialist position, see the statement by the chairman of the party's foreign policy committee, Eiichi Nagasue, "Boei Hakushō Hihan to Senshu Bōgyo" ("Criticism of the Defense White Paper and the Concept of Solely 'Defensive' Defense"), *Kokubō* (January, 1971), pp. 60–73.

21. For statements of the Japanese Socialist Party, the Japanese Communist Party, and the Kōmeitō, see *Mainichi Shimbun,* November 6, 1969, and *Asahi Shimbun,* February 3, 1970. As on most other defense issues, the Democratic-Socialists adopted a different posture, closer to that of the conservatives.

22. See, for example, *Tokyo Shimbun,* September 12, 1969; and Keidanren, Bōei Seisan Iinkai, *Bōei Seisan Iinkai Tokuhō* (*Defense Production Committee Special Report*) (Tokyo: 1970), esp. pp. 1–14, and *Bōei Kiki Kenkyū Kaihatsu Jittai Chōsa* (*A Survey of the Real Conditions of Research and Development of Defense Equipment*) (Tokyo: 1970), esp. pp. 1–46.

23. The most notable statement of this sort was made by Takeshi Sakurada, the Standing Director of *Nikkeiren,* one of the four national business federations. He called for revision of the constitution and expansion of ar-

maments, and his organization openly opposed ratification of the non-proliferation treaty. See *Tokyo Shimbun,* September 12, 1969, *Nihon Keizai Shimbun,* September 4, 1969, and *Asahi Shimbun,* October 19, 1969.

24. Naikaku Sōri Daijin Kambō Kōhōshitsu, *Seron   Chōsa Nenkan, 1967 (Public Opinion Research Yearbook, 1967)* (Tokyo: Naikaku Sōri Daijin Kambō Kōhōshitsu, 1967), pp. 217–18.

25. Shigeki Nishihara, "Sato Naikaku to Ryōdo—Bōei Seron" ("The Sato Cabinet and Public Opinion on Territory and Defense"), *Jiyū,* X, 4 (April, 1968), 92–95.

26. See, for example, Douglas H. Mendel, Jr., "Japanese Views of Sato's Foreign Policy: The Credibility Gap," *Asian Survey,* VII, 7 (July, 1967), 444–56; and John Welfield, *Japan and Nuclear China* (Canberra: Australian National University Press, 1970), pp. 37–44.

27. Naikaku Sōri Daijin Kambō Kōhōshitsu, *Kempō ni Kansura Seron Chōsa: Sōgō Hōkoku (Summary Report of Public Opinion Polls Regarding the Constitution)* (Tokyo: 1967), pp. 36–37.

28. Minoru Tada, "Nihon no Anzen Hoshō to Kokumin Kanjō" ("National Sentiment Regarding Japan's Security"), *Gunji Kenkyū* (January, 1967), p. 34.

29. Sōrufi Kōhoshitsu, ed., *Seron Chōsa (Public Opinion Research)* (April, 1970), p. 33.

30. The *Asahi Shimbun,* the *Mainichi Shimbun,* and the *Yomiuri Shimbun* all established special research groups on security problems and undertook to publish collections of documents and histories of postwar defense policy. The *Asahi* published a fifteen-volume series that provided interpretative appraisals of many facets of the security problem.

31. This group includes many younger scholars who have studied international relations in the West, among whom the most senior and perhaps best known is Kiichi Saeki, currently President of Nomura Research Institute and former head of the Japanese Defense College. The term "analysts" is borrowed from Robert Osgood's study of this group several years ago, "Japan and the United States in Asia," in Robert Osgood *et al., Japan and the United States in Asia* (Baltimore: The Johns Hopkins Press, 1968), pp. 1–28. A useful general survey of the security debate among Japanese intellectuals is provided in Lawrence Olsen, *Japan in Postwar Asia* (New York: Praeger, 1970), pp. 118–37.

32. Some of the analysts are within the academic establishment, and almost all share in some degree the orthodox predilections of the postwar intellectual world. A perceptible difference in emphasis, however, distinguishes their works from the writings on foreign affairs of such persons as Professors Takeshi Ishida and Yoshikazu Sakamoto.

CHAPTER 8

1. See, for example, William P. Bundy, "New Tides in Southeast Asia," *Foreign Affairs,* XLIX, 2 (January, 1971), 187–200.

2. *Asahi Shimbun,* October 26, 1970, and *Yomiuri Shimbun,* January 12, 1971.

3. On the political implications of economic aid, see David A. Baldwin, "Foreign Aid Intervention and Influence," *World Politics,* XXI, 3 (April, 1969), 425–37.

4. *New York Times,* November 26, 1971.

5. *New York Times,* November 19, 1971.

6. See, for example, James Reston's interview with Chou En-lai, *New York Times,* August 21, 1971.

7. See, for example, the article by Edwin O. Reischauer, *Mainichi Daily News,* May 25, 1971.

8. Hedley Bull, "The New Balance of Power in Asia and the Pacific," *Foreign Affairs,* XLIX, 4 (July, 1971), pp. 669–81.

9. For elaboration of a contrary position, see "The Aggressive People's Republic of China: Menace or Myth" (colloquy among Edwin O. Reischauer, J. W. Fulbright, Mark O. Hatfield, and Ezaki Masumi), in Alaine H. Burnell, ed., *Asian Dilemma: United States, Japan and China* (Tokyo: Charles E. Tuttle, 1969), pp. 81–90.

10. Martin E. Weinstein, *Japan's Postwar Defense Policy, 1947–1968* (New York: Columbia University Press, 1971), pp. 50–53.

11. See Japan, Shugiin (House of Representatives), *Heiwa Jōyaku oyobi Nichi-Bei anzen hōsho jōyaku tokubetsu iinkai giroku (Proceedings of the Special Committee on the Peace Treaty and the Japan–United States Security Treaty),* No. 4, 12th Diet, pp. 18–19; and Donald C. Hellmann, *Japanese Domestic Politics and Foreign Policy,* pp. 34–35 and 59–60.

12. For a discussion of the assumptions underlying Japanese-American strategy, see George F. Kennan, "Japan's Security and American Policy," *Foreign Affairs,* XLIII, 1 (October, 1964), 14–18.

13. This is drolly illustrated by the tentative proposal for a "collective security system along the frontiers of China," introduced fifteen years after John Foster Dulles created SEATO! *New York Times,* June 14, 1969.

14. See, for example, Herman Kahn, *The Emerging Japanese Superstate: Challenge and Response* (Englewood Cliffs, N.J.: Prentice-Hall, 1970), esp. pp. 12–13 and 166–67.

15. *Mainichi Shimbun,* May 12 and 29, 1969.

16. *Mainichi Shimbun,* November 21, 1969.

17. For conservative opinions on this question, see *Mainichi Shimbun,* December 31, 1967; and, for samples of socialist opinion, see Masashi Ishibashi, "Security in a Nuclear Age," *Ekonomisuto* (May 24, 1966), trans. in *Selected Summaries of Japanese Magazines* (Tokyo: U.S. Embassy), and Eiichi Nagasue, "Bōei Hakushō Hihan to Senshu Bōgyo" ("Criticism of the Defense White Paper and the Concept of Solely 'Defensive' Defense"), *Kokubō* (January, 1971), pp. 60–73.

18. A good, brief description of the nuclear-power program and other technological aspects of Japan's capacity to develop nuclear weapons is provided in John K. Emmerson, *Arms, Yen and Power: The Japanese Di-*

lemma (New York: Dunellen, 1971), pp. 316–34. Another good overview in English of Japan's past nuclear program is provided in Victor Gilinsky and Paul Langer, *The Japanese Civilian Nuclear Program* (The RAND Corporation, 1967), *passim*.

19. Kahn, *op. cit.*, p. 165.

20. President Lyndon Johnson, in his message transmitting the treaty to the United States Senate. United States, Department of State, *Bulletin*, LIX, 1518 (July 29, 1968), 126.

21. Ambassador Arthur Goldberg, in an address to the United Nations on June 10, 1968. Cited in Walter B. Wentz, *Nuclear Proliferation* (Washington, D.C.: Public Affairs Press, 1968), p. 1.

22. This general line of argument is developed more fully in *Ibid., passim,* and esp. pp. 11 ff.

23. For elaboration of this point, see George E. Questor, "Japan and the Nuclear Non-Proliferation Treaty," *Asian Survey*, X, 9 (September, 1970), 766–70.

24. *Asahi Shimbun,* October 13, 1969.

25. See, for example, John Welfield, *Japan and Nuclear China* (Canberra: Australian National University Press, 1970), *passim*.

Bibliography

ENGLISH SOURCES

Books and Monographs

ARON, RAYMOND. *Peace and War.* New York: Praeger, 1968.

BERTON, PETER, ed. "International Subsystems," a Special Issue of *The International Studies Quarterly,* XIII, 4 (December, 1969).

BURNELL, ALAINE H., ed. *Asian Dilemma: United States, Japan and China.* Tokyo: Charles E. Tuttle, 1969.

CANTORI, LOUIS J., and STEVEN L. SPIEGEL, eds. *The International Politics of Regions.* Englewood Cliffs, N.J.: Prentice-Hall, 1970.

Chase Manhattan Bank. "Japan," a Special Edition of *World Business,* 18 (First Quarter, 1970).

COHEN, BERNARD C. *The Political Process and Foreign Policy: The Making of the Japanese Peace Settlement.* Princeton, N.J.: Princeton University Press, 1957.

Council on Foreign Relations. *The American Public's View of U.S. Policy Toward China.* A report prepared for the Council on Foreign Relations by the Survey Research Center, University of Michigan. New York: Council on Foreign Relations, 1964.

CROWLEY, JAMES B. *Japan's Quest for Autonomy.* Princeton, N.J.: Princeton University Press, 1966.

CURTIS, GERALD L., ed. *Japanese-American Relations in the 1970's.* Washington, D.C.: Columbia Books, Inc., 1970.

DUNN, FREDERICK S. *Peace-Making and the Settlement with Japan.* Princeton, N.J.: Princeton University Press, 1963.

ELSBREE, WILLARD. *Japan's Role in Southeast Asian Nationalist Movements.* Cambridge, Mass.: Harvard University Press, 1953.

EMMERSON, JOHN K. *Arms, Yen and Power: The Japanese Dilemma.* New York: Dunellen, 1971.

FUKUI, HIROHARU. *Party in Power: The Japanese Liberal Democrats and Policy Making.* Berkeley and Los Angeles: University of California Press, 1970.

GILINSKY, VICTOR, and PAUL LANGER. *The Japanese Civilian Nuclear Program.* Santa Monica, Calif.: The Rand Corporation, 1967.

GORDON, BERNARD K. *The Dimensions of Conflict in Southeast Asia.* Englewood Cliffs, N.J.: Prentice-Hall, 1966.

———. *Toward Disengagement in Asia: A Strategy for American Foreign Policy.* Englewood Cliffs, N.J.: Prentice-Hall, 1969.

GREENE, FRED. *U.S. Policy and the Security of Asia.* New York: McGraw-Hill, 1968.

HAAS, ERNST B. *Tangle of Hopes: American Commitments and World Order.* Englewood Cliffs, N.J.: Prentice-Hall, 1969.

HELLMANN, DONALD C. *Japanese Domestic Politics and Foreign Policy: The Peace Agreement with the Soviet Union.* Berkeley and Los Angeles: University of California Press, 1969.

HITCH, CHARLES, and DAYTON MCKEAN. *The Economics of Defense in the Nuclear Age.* Cambridge, Mass.: Harvard University Press, 1961.

HOFFMANN, STANLEY. *Gulliver's Troubles, Or the Setting of American Foreign Policy.* New York: McGraw-Hill, 1968.

ISAACS, HAROLD. *No Peace for Asia.* Cambridge, Mass.: MIT Press, 1965.

JANSEN, MARIUS B. *The Japanese and Sun Yat-Sen.* Cambridge, Mass.: Harvard University Press, 1954.

KAHN, HERMAN. *The Emerging Japanese Superstate: Challenge and Response.* Englewood Cliffs, N.J.: Prentice-Hall, 1970.

LEVI, WARNER. *The Challenge of World Politics in South and Southeast Asia.* Englewood Cliffs, N.J.: Prentice-Hall, 1968.

MCGARRY, JAMES F. "A Study of Decision Making in Japan's Postwar Economic Policy." Unpublished Ph.D. dissertation, University of Pennsylvania, 1964.

MCNAMARA, ROBERT S. *The Essence of Security.* New York: Harper & Row, 1968.

MAKI, JOHN M. *Conflict and Tension in the Far East.* Seattle: University of Washington Press, 1961.

MARUYAMA, MASAO. *Thought and Behavior in Japanese Politics.* London: Oxford University Press, 1963.

Morgan Guaranty Trust Company. *Japan's International Economy.* New York, 1970.

MORGENTHAU, HANS J. *A New Foreign Policy for the United States.* New York: Praeger, 1969.

MORLEY, JAMES W. *Japan and Korea: America's Allies in the Pacific.* New York: Walker & Company, 1965.

NYE, JOSEPH S., JR. *International Regionalism: Readings.* Boston: Little, Brown and Company, 1968.

OLSEN, LAWRENCE. *Japan in Postwar Asia.* New York: Praeger, 1970.

ORGANSKI, A. F. K. *World Politics.* New York: Alfred A. Knopf, 1964.

OSGOOD, ROBERT E., GEORGE R. PACKARD, III, and JOHN H. BADGLEY.

Japan and the United States in Asia. Baltimore: The Johns Hopkins Press, 1968.

PACKARD, GEORGE W., III. *Protest in Tokyo: The Security Treaty Crisis of 1960*. Princeton, N.J.: Princeton University Press, 1966.

PFEFFER, RICHARD M., ed. *No More Vietnams? The War and the Future of American Foreign Policy*. New York: Harper & Row, 1968.

REISCHAUER, EDWIN O. *Beyond Vietnam: The United States and Asia*. New York: Alfred A. Knopf, 1967.

RUSSETT, BRUCE M. *International Regions and the International System: A Study in Political Ecology*. Chicago: Rand, McNally, 1968.

————. *Trends in World Politics*. New York: Macmillan, 1965.

————, et al. *World Handbook of Political and Social Indicators*. New Haven, Conn.: Yale University Press, 1964.

SCALAPINO, ROBERT A., and JUNNOSUKE MASUMI. *Parties and Politics in Contemporary Japan*. Berkeley and Los Angeles: University of California Press, 1962.

STOCKWIN, J. A. A. *The Japanese Socialist Party and Neutralism*. Carlton, Australia: Melbourne University Press, 1968.

THAYER, NATHANIEL P. *How the Conservatives Rule Japan*. Princeton, N.J.: Princeton University Press, 1969.

WALTZ, KENNETH N. *Man, the State and War*. New York: Columbia University Press, 1959.

WEINSTEIN, MARTIN E. *Japan's Postwar Defense Policy, 1947–1968*. New York: Columbia University Press, 1971.

WELFIELD, JOHN. *Japan and Nuclear China* (Canberra Papers on Strategy and Defense, No. 9). Canberra: Australian National University Press, 1970.

WENTZ, WALTER B. *Nuclear Proliferation*. Washington, D.C.: Public Affairs Press, 1968.

WOLFERS, ARNOLD, and LAURENCE W. MARTIN, eds. *The Anglo-American Tradition in Foreign Affairs*. New Haven, Conn.: Yale University Press, 1956.

Articles

BALDWIN, DAVID A. "Foreign Aid, Intervention and Influence," *World Politics,* XXI, 3 (April, 1969), 425–47.

BRECHER, MICHAEL. "International Relations and Area Studies: The Subordinate State System of Southern Asia," *World Politics,* XV, 2 (January, 1963), 213–35.

BUCHAN, ALASTAIR. "An Asian Balance of Power?" *Encounter,* XXVII, 6 (December, 1966), 62–71.

BULL, HEDLEY. "The New Balance of Power in Asia and the Pacific," *Foreign Affairs,* XLIX, 4 (July, 1971), 669–81.

BUNDY, WILLIAM P. "New Tides in Southeast Asia," *Foreign Affairs,* XLIX, 2 (January, 1971), 187–200.

————. "The Nixon Policies in Asia and the Pacific," *Pacific Community*, II, 1 (October, 1970), 77–86.

COHN, STANLEY H. "Soviet Growth Retardation: Trends in Resource Availability and Efficiency," in Subcommittee on Foreign Economic Policy of the Joint Economic Committee of the Congress of the United States, *New Directions in the Soviet Economy* (Washington, D.C.: 1966), pp. 99–132.

CURTIS, GERALD L. "The 1969 General Election in Japan," *Asian Survey*, X, 10 (October, 1970), 859–71.

DORE, R. P. "Japan's Place in the World," *World Today* (July, 1966), pp. 293–306.

GATI, CHARLES. "Another Grand Debate? The Limitationist Critique of American Foreign Policy," *World Politics*, XXI, 1 (October, 1968), 133–51.

GRANT, BRUCE. "Toward a New Balance in Asia: An Australian View," *Foreign Affairs*, XLVII, 4 (July, 1969), 711–20.

HALPERIN, MORTON H. "Chinese Nuclear Strategy: The Early Post-Detonation Period," *Adelphi Paper, No. 18* (London: Institute for Strategic Studies, May, 1965), pp. 1–19.

HANSEN, ROGER D. "Regional Integration: Reflections on a Decade of Theoretical Effort," *World Politics*, XXI, 2 (January, 1969), 242–71.

HELLMANN, DONALD C. "Basic Problems of Japanese–South Korean Relations," *Asian Survey*, II, 5 (May, 1962), 19–24.

ISHIBASHI, MASASHI. "Security in a Nuclear Age," *Ekonomisuto*, May 24, 1966. Trans. in *Selected Summaries of Japanese Magazines* (Tokyo: U.S. Embassy, June, 1966).

ITO, KOBUN. "Japan's Security in the 1970's," *Asian Survey*, X, 12 (December, 1970), 1031–36.

KAISER, KARL. "The Interaction of Regional Subsystems," *World Politics*, XXI, 1 (October, 1968), 84–108.

KENNAN, GEORGE F. "Japan's Security and American Policy," *Foreign Affairs*, XLIII, 1 (October, 1964), 14–28.

KEOHANE, ROBERT O. "Lilliputians' Dilemmas: Small States in International Politics," *International Organization*, XXIII, 2 (Spring, 1969), 291–310.

McALISTER, JOHN T., JR. "The Possibilities for Diplomacy in Southeast Asia," *World Politics*, XIX, 2 (January, 1967), 258–305.

MATSUMOTO, SHIGEHARU. "Japan and China," in A. M. Halpern, ed., *Policies Toward China: View from Six Continents* (New York: McGraw-Hill, 1965), pp. 123–64.

MENDEL, DOUGLAS H., JR. "Japanese Views of Sato's Foreign Policy: The Credibility Gap," *Asian Survey*, VII, 7 (July, 1967), 444–56.

MORLEY, JAMES W. "Japan's Position in Asia," *Journal of International Affairs*, XVII, 2 (1963), 142–54.

MURAKAMI, KAORU. "Liberal-Democratic Party Factions' Sense of Defense," *Jiyū,* July, 1966. Trans. in *Summaries of Selected Japanese Magazines* (Tokyo: U.S. Embassy, June 27, 1966).

————. "The Korean Peninsula and Japan's Munitions Industry," *Gendai no Me,* October, 1970. Trans. in *Selected Translations of Japanese Magazines* (Tokyo: U.S. Embassy, January, 1971).

NAKAYAMA, NOBUO. "Japan–Republic of Korea Economic Cooperation Underway," *Asahi Journal,* May 15, 1966. Trans. in *Selected Summaries of Japanese Magazines* (Tokyo: U.S. Embassy, June 20, 1966).

NIXON, RICHARD M. "Asia After Vietnam," *Foreign Affairs,* XLVI (September, 1967), 111–25.

OLSEN, MANCUR. "Rapid Growth as a De-stabilizing Force," *Journal of Economic History,* XXIII (March, 1963), 529–58.

OZAKI, ROBERT S. "Japan's Role in Asian Economic Development," *Asian Survey,* April, 1967, pp. 237–44.

PERKINS, DWIGHT. "The Chinese Economy and Its International Impact," *SAIS Review,* Winter, 1968, pp. 30–42.

QUESTOR, GEORGE E. "Japan and the Nuclear Non-Proliferation Treaty," *Asian Survey,* X, 9 (September, 1970), 765–78.

REISCHAUER, EDWIN O. "The Broken Dialogue with Japan," *Foreign Affairs,* XXXIX, 1 (October, 1960), 11–26.

RIKER, RONALD G. "Discontent and Economic Growth," *Economic Development and Cultural Change,* XI (October, 1962), 1–15.

RŌYAMA, MICHIO. "The Asian Balance of Power: A Japanese View," *Adelphi Paper, No. 42* (November, 1967), pp. 1–16.

RUSSETT, BRUCE M. "Delineating International Regions," in J. David Singer, ed., *Quantitative International Politics* (New York: The Free Press, 1968), pp. 317–52.

SAWAKI, MASAO. "Idea and Moot Points of Economic Aid," *Kokusai Jihyō,* October, 1970. Trans. in *Selected Summaries of Japanese Magazines* (Tokyo: U.S. Embassy, January, 1971).

SCALAPINO, ROBERT A. "In Search of a Role: Japan and the Uncertainties of Power," *Encounter,* XXVII, 6 (December, 1966), 21–27.

SCHELLING, THOMAS C. "Peace and Security in Asia and the Roles of Japan and the United States." Paper presented at the Japan–United States Kyōto Conference, January, 1969, pp. 1–8.

STOCKWIN, J. A. A. "Foreign Policy Perspectives of the Japanese Left: Confrontation or Consensus," *Pacific Affairs,* XLII, 4 (Winter, 1969–70), 435–45.

TAKAYANAGI, KENZŌ. "Some Reminiscences of Japan's Commission of the Constitution," in D. F. Henderson, ed., *The Constitution of Japan: Its First Twenty Years, 1947–67,* pp. 71–88.

TANAKA, YASUMASA, and YŌKO, IWAMATSU. "An Exploratory Semantic Differential Study of the Affective and Cognitive Components of the Attitude Held by Japanese College SS Toward Nuclear Testings and Proliferation," *Peace Research in Japan, 1968,* pp. 25–70.

WAKAIZUMI, KEI. "Japan Beyond 1970," *Foreign Affairs*, XLVII, 3 (April, 1969), 509–20.

WALTZ, KENNETH N. "The Myth of National Interdependence," in Charles P. Kindleberger, ed., *The International Corporation* (Cambridge, Mass.: MIT Press, 1970), pp. 205–23.

———. "The Stability of a Bipolar World," *Daedalus*, LXIV, 3 (Summer, 1964), 881–909.

WILSON, DICK. "China's Economic Prospects," in Ruth Adams, ed., *Contemporary China* (New York: Vintage Press, 1966), pp. 179–93.

YOUNG, ORAN R. "Political Discontinuities in the International System," *World Politics*, XX, 3 (April, 1968), 369–92.

———. "Professor Russett: Industrious Tailor to a Naked Emperor," *World Politics*, XXI, 3 (April, 1969), 486–511.

Government and Quasi-official Documents and Newspapers

Agency for International Development. *Gross National Product: Growth Rates and Trend Data*. Washington, D.C.: February, 1971.

Economic Planning Board, Government of the Republic of Korea. *Economic Survey*. Seoul: 1971.

———. *Major Economic Indicators*. Seoul: 1970.

Far Eastern Economic Review Yearbook, 1969, 1970, 1971. Hongkong.

Foreign Assistance Program: Annual Report of the President to Congress, 1962–1969. Washington, D.C.: 1970.

Government of Indonesia. "Foreign Investments in Indonesia, 1967–70." Mimeo. Jakarta: January, 1971.

International Monetary Fund. *International Financial Statistics, 1958–1970*. Washington, D.C.

International Monetary Fund and International Bank for Reconstruction and Development. *Direction of Trade, Annual 1958–62, Annual 1963–67*. Washington, D.C.

———. *Direction of Trade, 1958–1970*. Washington, D.C.

Japan Times.

Japan Times Weekly.

Ministry of Finance, Government of Japan. *The Summary Report: Trade of Japan*. 12 (1970).

Ministry of Foreign Affairs, Japanese Government. *Highlights of Japan's Foreign Aid*. Tokyo: 1969.

New York Times.

Overseas Economic Cooperation Fund. *The Overseas Economic Cooperation Fund: Its Role and Activities*. Tokyo: 1970.

Overseas Technical Cooperation Agency. *Overseas Technical Cooperation Agency, 1970–71*. Tokyo: 1971.

Presidential Report to Congress. *United States Foreign Policy for the 1970's*. Washington, D.C.: 1971.

Supreme Command for the Allied Powers, Report of the Government

Section. *Political Orientation of Japan: September, 1945–September, 1948*. Washington, D.C.: G.P.O., 1959.

U.S. Bureau of International Commerce. *Foreign Economic Trends and Their Implications for the U.S., 1969, 1970*. Washington, D.C.: 1970, 1971.

U.S. Department of Commerce. *Foreign Trade, FT 455* (Annual, 1969). Washington, D.C.: 1970.

————. *Foreign Trade, FT 990* (May, 1970).

U.S. Embassy. "Japanese Economic Assistance to Developing Countries." Mimeo. Tokyo: 1971.

————. "U.S.-Japan Bilateral Trade, 1970." Mimeo. Tokyo: 1971.

JAPANESE SOURCES

Books and Pamphlets

Asahi Shimbun. *Jimintō: Hoshu Kenryoku no Kōzō (The Liberal Democratic Party: Structure of Conservative Power)*. Tokyo: Asahi Shimbunsha, 1970.

Bōeichō (Defense Agency): *Nihon no Bōei (Japan's Defense)*. Tokyo: 1970.

Gaimushō (Foreign Ministry). *Sekai no Ugoki (Trends of the World)*, No. 2 (1971), pp. 28–29.

HORA, KAKUTAKE. *Kankoku Keizai no Kiseki (The Korean Economic Miracle)*. Tokyo: Nihon Kokusai Mondai Kenkyūjo, 1970.

Jiyūminshutō Anzen Hoshō ni Kan Suru Chōsakai (Liberal-Democratic Party Security and Defense Research Committee). "Waga Kuni no Anzen Hoshō ni Kan Suru Chūkan Hōkaku" ("Interim Report Concerning the Defense of Our Country"). Tokyo: 1966.

Keidanren Bōei Seisan Iinkai. (Federation of Economic Organizations Defense Production Committee). *Bōei Kiki Kenkyū Kaihatsu Jittai Chōsa (A Survey of the Real Conditions of Research and Development of Defense Equipment)*. Tokyo: 1970.

————. *Bōei Seisan Iinkai Tokuhō (Defense Production Committee Special Report)*. Tokyo: 1970.

KOMAI, HIROSHI. *Tai no Gendaika (Conditions of Modern Thailand)*. Tokyo: Nihon Kokusai Mondai Kenkyūjo, 1971.

Naikaku Sōri Daijin Kambō Kōhōshitsu (Prime Minister's Cabinet Secretariat Public Relations Office), ed. *Kempō ni Kansuru Seron Chōsa Sōgō Hōkoku (Summary Report of Public-Opinion Polls Regarding the Constitution)*. Tokyo: 1967.

————. *Seron Chōsa Nenkan, 1967*. Tokyo: Nakaku Sōri Daijin Kambō Kōhōshitsu, 1967.

————. *Seron Chōsa (Public Opinion Research)*, Tokyo, April, 1970.

SAKANAKA, TOMOHISA, et al. *Nihon no Jiei Ryoku (Japan's Self-Defense Power)*. Tokyo: Asahi Shimbunsha, 1967.

Shūgiin (House of Representatives). *Heiwa Jōyaku oyobi Nichi-Bei Anzen Hoshō Jōyaku Tokubetsu Iinkai Giroku (Proceedings of the Special Committee on the Peace Treaty and the Japan–United States Security Treaty)*, No. 4, 12th Diet, House of Representatives Committee Proceedings, V. Tokyo: 1951.

Sōrifu Tōkeikyoku (Statistics Bureau of the Prime Minister's Office). *Nihon Tōkei Nenkan (Japan Statistical Yearbook)*, 1935–37.

TADA, MINORU. "Nihon no Anzen Hoshō to Kokumin Kanjō" ("National Sentiment Regarding Japan's Security"), *Gunji Kenkyū* January, 1967, pp. 32–38.

Tsūshō-Sangyōshō (Ministry of International Trade and Industry). *Tsūshō Hakusho, 1970 (International Trade White Paper, 1970)*. Tokyo: 1971.

WATANABE, TSUNEO. *Habatsu (Factions)*, 2d ed. Tokyo: Kōbundo, 1964.

Yomiuri Shimbun Seiji-bu, *Seitō (Political Parties)*. Tokyo: Yomiuri Shimbunsha, 1966.

Articles

EIMATSU, EŪCHI. "Bōei Hakushi Hihan to Senshu Bōgyo" ("Criticism of the Defense White Paper and the Concept of Solely 'Defensive' Defense"), *Kokubō,* January, 1971, pp. 60–73.

IKEDA, HAYATO. "Jiyū to Seiji ni Tatsu Sekai Heiwa" ("World Peace Built on Freedom and Justice"), *Seisaku Geppō,* 66 (July, 1961), pp. 57–63.

———. "Rekishiteki Kadai ni Tachimukau Nihon Kokumin" ("The Japanese People Confront Historical Tasks"), *Seisaku Geppō,* 85 (February, 1963), pp. 268–73.

KATŌ, NAGAO. "Kyūtenkai suru Nihon no Tōnan Ajiya Enjo" ("A Sudden Turn in Japan's Aid to Southeast Asia"), *Ekonomisuto,* XLIV, 47 (November 15, 1966), pp. 56–61.

"Kishi Shushō Tōnan Ajiya Rekihō no Seika" ("The Results of Prime Minister Kishi's Visit to Southeast Asia"), *Ekonomisuto,* XXXV, 23 (June 8, 1957), pp. 9–12.

KŌSAKA, MASATAKA. "Saishō Yoshida Shigeru Ron" ("Prime Minister Shigeru Yoshida"), *Chūō Kōron,* LXXIX, 2 (February, 1964), pp. 76–111.

MARUYAMA, SHIZUO. " 'Ajia–Taiheiyō Ken' Kōsō to Miki Gaikō" (" 'Asia–Pacific Zone' and Miki Diplomacy"), *Asahi Jānaru,* IX, 29 (July 9, 1967), pp. 18–22.

MASUMI, JUNNOSUKE. "Jiyūminshutō no Soshiki to Kinō" ("The Liberal-Democratic Party: Organization and Function"), in JUNNOSUKE MASUMI, ed., *1967 Seijigaku Nenpō: Gendai Nihon no Seitō to Kan-*

ryō (1967 Political Science Yearbook: The Parties and Bureaucracy in Contemporary Japan), pp. 34–78.

NISHIHARA, SHIGEKI. "Satō Naikaku to Ryōdo-Bōei Seron" ("The Satō Cabinet and Public Opinion on Territory and Defense"), *Jiyū*, X, 4 (April, 1968), pp. 92–95.

SHIOMI, TOSHITAKA. "Jieitai to Kokumin Seron" ("The Self-Defense Forces and Popular Opinion"), *Sekai*, June, 1967, pp. 100–103.

SUZUKI, YASUYUKI. "Gaimu Kanryō to Nihon no Gaikō" ("Foreign Ministry Bureaucrats and Japan's Diplomacy"), *Jiyū*, 17, 6 (June, 1965), pp. 58–63.

Newspapers

Newspapers are the most frequently cited Japanese-language sources, particularly

Asahi Shimbun
Mainichi Shimbun
Nihon Keizai Shimbun
Sankei Jiji
Yomiuri Shimbun

Index

89767

DS
518.45
H44

HELLMANN, DONALD
JAPAN AND EAST ASIA.

DATE DUE